ALSO BY DOUG BOYD

Rolling Thunder
Swami
Mystics, Magicians, and Medicine People

MAD BEAR

Spirit, Healing,
and the Sacred
in the Life of
a Native American
Medicine Man

◐

Doug Boyd

A TOUCHSTONE BOOK
Published by Simon & Schuster
New York   London   Toronto
Sydney   Tokyo   Singapore

TOUCHSTONE
Simon & Schuster Building
Rockefeller Center
1230 Avenue of the Americas
New York, New York 10020

Designed by Deirdre C. Amthor

Manufactured in the United States of America

1   3   5   7   9   10   8   6   4   2

Library of Congress Cataloging-in-Publication Data

Boyd, Doug.
Mad Bear : spirit , healing, and the sacred in the life of a Na-
tive American Medicine man / Doug Boyd.
          p.   cm.
"A Touchstone book."
Includes index.
1. Mad Bear. 2. Tuscarora Indians—Biography. 3.
Shamans—Biography. 4. Spiritual life. I Title.
E99.T9M333   1994
299'.7'092—dc20
[B]   94-28435
                                             CIP

ISBN: 0-671-75945-0

For my coadventurers of the Cross-Cultural Studies Program—those with whom I have long traveled, those who have joined in the journey, and those whom we are about to meet.

Author's Note

I am grateful to all my friends and colleagues and to all the traditional tribal people who were a part of the events told here and who are a part of the ongoing story. My thanks to our founding Cross-Cultural team: Dudley Bush, Jon Cates, and Bill Hale; to Tim and Pamala Ballingham, who were an invaluable support to me personally as well as to our work with traditional peoples; and to all my friends of the International Center for Integrative Studies—Anne Habberton, Helen Robinette, and Ursula Thunberg, to name a few—for their unending help, friendship, and encouragement. My thanks also to the staff of the Cross-Cultural Institute of New York for providing me the time and encouragement to complete this book. For Mad Bear, with whom I worked and traveled on a nearly daily basis for many years, and who continues to be a source of inspiration and instruction, I hope I can offer more than gratitude.

Contents

Prologue

◑ The Story of False Face was among the first of many tales and legends I heard from Mad Bear. The False Face that hung on the dark, paneled wall of his den was the first one I ever saw. It looked like a mask to me—an impossibly distorted and grotesque face whose nose, cheeks, chin, and protruding lips had been pushed horribly off center. I learned it was a living deity. His hair grew.

He was a wooden carving, a hollow face hung high on a peg near the ceiling. The coarse, dried "hair" that draped down past the chin on either side of the face appeared to be glued to the top of the head. But it grew. Over the years of our acquaintance, I often stayed at Mad Bear's Tuscarora cabin; and whenever there was a sufficient gap of time between my visits, I was sure that those dry, yellow thatches hung perceptibly closer to the floor. It was never mentioned by Mad Bear nor by me.

Over time I came to feel grateful that I had never inquired or remarked about that sacred object, or worse yet, pointed at it or even waved a hand in its direction before I knew what it was. Whenever an occasional visitor performed such an in-fraction, I could see Mad Bear's discomfort.

On my first visit to Mad Bear's place, as we ate and drank coffee and started plans for our upcoming adventures, as I listened to his cheerful voice and easy laughter, I believe my eyes remained long fixed upon that False Face. I watched it hanging there, still and breathless and looking very much alive.

Mad Bear noticed. He stopped talking and watched me for a moment. Then he turned in his chair to face the Being on the wall and spoke something in his own language. "This is False Face," he said to me, still facing the wall. "He is in my keeping. I feed him and watch over him. He goes with me to ceremonies, and I take him to the traditional rites that are for him and his people. I belong to the False Face Society. To me this is a big responsibility and a big, big honor."

He paused and turned to look at me. I had no questions. They weren't necessary. He would tell me what he wished, and nothing more.

"I will tell you his story—who he is and how he came to look like that. But he is gone on now, evolved beyond this. These Beings have graduated and gone to a higher world—and they are high, high, high, beyond us. Yet we keep the False Face in this form and we pay honor and respect to it. It reminds us of a lesson far ahead of us—a hard lesson that we have yet to learn.

"I call him False Face even though that wasn't his name at his time. That was never the name of him or his people but that is how we refer to it. False Face had studied and learned all the basic things in the universe. Then he had prepared and developed himself in all the medicine ways. It took centuries of hard work, but eventually he developed all the spiritual powers known on this Earth. He knew all the ways of the Creator.

"One day False Face stood out in a large field looking at the skies and at the mountains in the distance. And he thought to himself: Knowing as I do all the ways of the Creator, all things in this world are possible for me. I now understand how all things are done. Why, if it should be my will, those mountains should have to move.

"And then he heard the voice of the Creator whom he knew as the Great Lord of the Universe. The voice said, 'Yes, I am the Lord and the mountains are there by my will.'

"False Face paused for a moment. Many times he had heard the voice of the Creator; but now he was thinking only of himself. Speaking aloud, he announced in a powerful voice: 'I have come to know the ways of the Lord and I can duplicate them all! I can move these mountains if I wish!'

"And the Creator repeated: 'Yes, I am the Lord and I can move mountains.'

" 'Not you!' shouted False Face. 'I am referring to myself. I am talking about me. Have I developed all this for nothing? Can I do nothing myself? I have learned all the rules of power and creation! Do you still think I am useless without you?'

" 'You are never without me,' the Great Spirit answered in a gentle voice, 'for I am always with you.'

" 'But I know all your secrets now,' False Face protested. 'I know how you do all these things.'

" 'It is because you have come to me,' said the Great Spirit.

"In spite of all that he had learned, in spite of all his training and wisdom, False Face experienced a rush of great pride and anger, and he shouted at the Creator. 'Go away. Leave me alone. I don't need you anymore. I am now powerful and you want to think of me as your little child. I am not your little child anymore. I can do anything that you can do. So just leave me alone.'

" 'Alone?' said the Great Spirit. 'There is no alone. How can I leave you? We are one and cannot be apart.'

"These gentle, loving words only made False Face more angry. It seemed to him, in his anger, that the Lord was discrediting him in spite of all his long efforts and the remarkable knowledge and power that he had attained. It seemed to him that the Great Spirit was still claiming all power for himself. In his angry state, False Face determined to have a contest with the Lord of the Universe and he challenged Him:

" 'I know you don't want these mountains moved, Lord. But I am going to move them against your will. Then you will see that I am something in my own right. You can pit your power against me if you wish, Lord!'

" 'I do not pit anything against anything,' answered the Lord. 'This idea of a contest is a temporary dream. Wake up and come to me now and you will see that nothing is anything in its own right apart from all that is.'

"But False Face repeated his challenge: 'You are trying to take everything away from me, Lord. You cannot take this chance away. Do what you like. Oppose me if you like, but I am going to move these mountains anyway, knowing that you want them where they are, so that it will be clear that it is done by my will alone.'

"False Face waited there in the field, grim and determined, and there was nothing but silence. So he went about the contest. Though he strained with all his might, trying everything that he had learned and developed over the centuries, nothing happened. Nothing at all. There was only a soft breeze, and the mountains stood in the distance as always. He flew into a rage, cursing in a way that cannot be repeated and, when there was only silence, daring the Lord to respond. He called the Great Spirit a fake and a liar, claiming the Creator had pitted his Great Will against him in spite of promising he would not.

"Then an idea occurred to him. He would have his contest yet. He shouted at the Lord, daring the Lord to move the mountain while he tried to block Him with his own will as the Lord had done to him. He believed that if the Lord had neutralized his power then he could do the same to Him. But he also believed that the Lord might well want the mountains where they were and would be unwilling to move them. In either case, nothing would happen. He craved to claim victory over the Lord and he felt sure he would win his dare. He shouted his challenge again. He clenched his fists and squinted his eyes and screamed into the sky; and before he could finish his sentence, he heard a trembling and a rumbling. He spun around to look just as the mountain was coming to his side. That was a mistake, for that caused the mountain to strike his face and break his nose.

"And at that the gentle voice of the Great Spirit was heard again: 'Now look what we have done to our beloved self. No matter. It is very temporary. We shall now set it right with our collective will, shall we?'

"False Face felt a moment of great pain, and then he had a sudden awareness. There was no contest. There had never been any contest. This was another of his countless lessons. But this was the ultimate lesson and he had arranged it—he and His Own Self—so that he could be free from the desire to be a separate, independent something in its own right. So that he could be free from being apart and alone."

Mad Bear leaned back in his chair and picked up his coffee. "But this is not one person," he went on, "this is a whole people. And this kind of look represents their humility and their awareness of their incompleteness." He turned away from me again, and now both of us stared at the face on the wall. "Just think what we have to look forward to. After all our learning and development, we are still going to come to that last great contest—that last big hurdle for the powerful ego. Isn't that something? But once you have made that last hurdle, that's it. Then you graduate and go on to a higher level."

I looked at the back of Mad Bear's head. I tried to imagine him at this "last big hurdle." I tried to picture him standing in such a field, engaged in such a contest—and coming out looking like False Face. He turned around and grinned at me as though he'd sensed my thoughts. "Looks like we're outa coffee," he said, holding his cup upside down. "This darn pot's too small. Whatya say we crank 'er up again and then get down to business? We gotta lot to talk about!"

CHAPTER ONE

The End of the World

"There's no such thing as doomsday—only the end of one era and the beginning of another."

◖ I sat staring at the False Face on the wall. I could hear Mad Bear rustling around in his kitchen putting together yet another snack, and I could hear the coffeepot perking.

"We'll have something ready here in a minute," he called out from the other room. "I can throw a meal together in no time! And delicious too!"

False Face was only one of many strange objects and ancient relics that Mad Bear had collected or acquired. There were medicine objects and other ceremonial paraphernalia related to his calling; there were trade beads and old medals from the days of the first settlers, and there were sacred artifacts that had been given him on his journeys to other lands. Along one wall stood a glass display case filled with traditional jewelry and ornaments from many tribes, and on the top shelf in this case was a small sign that read MUSEUM.

Hanging on the wall in the entranceway, there was another small sign with the words: MAD BEAR'S TRADING POST, and I wondered whether that sign ever hung outside for passersby to see. Because it was too small to attract attention, one would really have to be looking for it to see it. Mad Bear did have some items for sale if anyone were interested—authentic traditional jewelry that was very expensive. The jewelry was turquoise and silver, mostly, but there were items made of bone and some had teeth or claws. There were also oil paintings, carvings, old coins, and other items that held enchanting histories.

Mad Bear's home was not a very public place, however, and much of the time he remained here in total seclusion. The little house on Mount Hope Road on the Tuscarora Indian Reservation near Niagara Falls, New York, had been built to Mad Bear's specifications. It was made of cinder block and had high windows with one-way glass so that no one could see in, and the windows were protected with iron grating. His bright red Toyota Land Cruiser usually stood on the gravel drive in front of the house; but when he wanted to be alone, he simply parked it in the garage and people assumed he was away. It was a known fact among his acquaintances and neighbors that Mad Bear simply "disappeared" for days or weeks at a time. There were times when he was locked up in his house, times when he was on the road, and times, some said, when he was nowhere at all.

The first time I saw Mad Bear, when I was with Rolling Thunder in the Berkeley Hills in California in 1972, I thought he looked like a comic strip character I remembered from my childhood. With his Hawaiian-print shirt; his big, round belly; wide, smiling face; and that Tiparillo cigar clamped in his teeth, he looked like Smilin' Jack in the flesh. But once I got to know him, I thought he looked like a bear. It was much more than a simple name association: He seemed to walk like a bear, and he had the face and hands and manner of a bear. There were those who knew him, I discovered, who found it

possible during his mysterious disappearances to imagine that
he might be wandering in the woods and fields in the actual
form of a bear.

• • •

"Come on in here and try some of these sandwiches I put together!" Mad Bear called to me.

I sat down on my folding chair at the little metal table in the
kitchen. This table, like everything else in the house, was covered with books, magazines, papers, herbs, and trinkets. But
these were easily pushed aside or stacked up against the wall
to make room for the plates.

"I tried a new idea with these things," he said, "and I think
you're gonna hafta admit they're pretty doggone delicious!"

"What's your new idea?" I asked.

"All these ingredients in here, the tomato slices, cheese,
and everything, I soaked it all in pickle juice, and then I even
sprinkled just a few drops on the bread. —Here, let's pour
this coffee while it's piping hot." He yanked the plug from the
wall. "This little pot's not automatic, you know. —And then I
put these sandwiches in that little grill thing, heated 'em up
just enough so they wouldn't be damp with the pickle juice.
It's not just the liquid from the jar, either. I actually squeezed
a bit outa some pickles."

From where I sat, I could see into the garage where I slept,
and I looked at my bed in the middle of the cement floor. This
bed, when it was down, used up Mad Bear's garage space,
making it necessary for him to park his Land Cruiser out in
the yard. But he—or some helpful neighbor, no doubt—had
rigged this bed with pulleys so that, by drawing the ropes on
both ends, it could be hoisted clear up to the casters that were
screwed into the ceiling, making space for the car to come in
underneath. It was a clever idea—one Mad Bear had claimed
to his own credit—and one of the first things he had shown me
when I arrived.

"Dig in!" Mad Bear said, snapping his fingers. "These

◐

things were made for eating!" And he took a big chomp out of one of the sandwiches. "Delicious!" he exclaimed through his mouthful of food, "What'd I tell you?"

"They are delicious," I admitted, as soon as I had chewed enough to comment.

"Not only that," Mad Bear chuckled, "but they taste good too!"

Mad Bear took great delight in food—preparing it, eating it, discussing it—too much delight, I supposed, for he was constantly overeating and was very overweight.

"It just makes you wonder," Mad Bear went on, speaking and chewing at the same time, "how's come nobody ever thought about this idea before. But then someone could have, and we would not even know it. I never found this in any restaurant, though. We could get some kind of exclusive sandwich line going. Our own secret recipe. People would be pretty taken by it—no pickles on here, and yet it's got this flavor! Kind of a subtle thing, you know? Well, we got too much to think about, we can't bother about that kind of stuff."

It occurred to me that Mad Bear had no mealtime rites that he performed before eating—nothing, at any rate, that I had ever seen. He simply said "Dig in!" There was no saying of prayers or grace, no offering made, no "moment of silence," no singing or chanting such as I had experienced with so many monks and swamis. There was, nonetheless, something very warm and meaningful in the way he said "Dig in!"

"Well, you're right," Mad Bear said. I looked up at him. He was smiling. He paused, as though waiting for me to make some gesture of surprise.

I simply smiled back and asked, "Why not?"

"I have nothing against it, nothing whatsoever. But I'm praying all the time—if you want to call it that. All our traditional people are always praying. For others it may be good to pray every time they eat, because that's when they manage to get around to it. We look at it like this: There's only two reasons to pray about your food. One is to ask, and the other is to give thanks—and we always give thanks, but we never,

never ask. Now, the Christians, some of them, they see it different. They say, 'Give us this day our daily bread,' and we don't believe in that. But I have nothing at all against those people, each have their own way.

"In our way, we consider we're the very hands and fingers of the creator. All the living creatures are extensions of the Great Spirit. All the living creatures are hunting and gathering, and that's all part of the experience of the Great Spirit. That's our job. That's what we do for the Great Spirit. So I have no criticism about Christianity or any of these religions, at least in their original form. But there's this one thing where I think they've gotten way off the track from their original teachings. Because we do not ask of the Great Spirit. The Great Spirit asks of us.

"Now on the other hand, the thanks are always given, that's never left out. But the time to do that is as soon as we finish eating. Or anything else, whatever, we give thanks for everything. But you'll never see me push back my plate or get up from the table—here at home, or the restaurant, or anyone else's home, without saying '*nyawe*!' That means 'thank-you.' That's our Indian word for giving thanks, and I say it all the time. Everything acknowledging everything else. Even our struggles and our duties, we give thanks for that."

"That does make sense," I agreed. I appreciated his explanation, and I had not had to ask for that either. "*Nyawe*," I said, and I hoped I'd pronounced it satisfactorily.

"Now this brings to my mind—we might just interrupt ourselves here for a minute and take care of a little important business. Well, you can just sit there." He got up and took some pinches of leaves from one of the baskets of dry herbs that were hanging over his old log-burning stove, and placed a dark black metal pan over the fire.

I put down my sandwich. With his back to me, Mad Bear bent over the fire and spoke in Tuscarora as he sprinkled his offering into the pan. Soon there was smoke. It smelled beautiful. I closed my eyes and listened to the sing-song tones of the ancient language that Mad Bear only used for prayer and ritual. The sound was familiar to me now, from those several ceremonies I had observed that Mad Bear had conducted in the Berkeley Hills.

"I just made a little offering," Mad Bear said, removing the pan from the fire and returning to his chair. "I gave thanks for your visit, for your being here, and for your interest, and I asked for a good, clear feeling in this house and for protection for you and me and our work that we're about to do. I should have already done that. I should have taken care of that yesterday, when you first got here. But we got right off on our conversation, and I kind of let it go. Maybe that's just as well. That way we kinda made our agreement on this level first. Well, now it's done. Later I'll give you some smoke, medicine smoke. It's a peace smoke, you could say, that might come in handy for you to use for yourself in certain situations. I might even show you some of what I prepare to put in there."

I tried a sip of coffee, but it was still too hot and it burned my upper lip slightly. I picked up my sandwich and continued eating. There was a small pyramid of sandwiches on the plate between us.

"Now, what were we just talking about?" Mad Bear scratched his head. "Oh, yeah, giving thanks. The prayers are always for giving thanks. Then, at times, there are things we can ask, like I just did. But not for ourselves. We ask when it's related to what we're supposed to be doing, that we may be guided in the right manner."

He looked at me and grinned, and then glanced suddenly at the ceiling. His eyes moved along the ceiling toward the cupboard above the sink. "Did you see that? Little spirits! You didn't see it? Right up there, just like little lights, dancing around. By golly, look at that! Maybe it's for you, for our prayers. I think you ought to see it."

I wished I could. I stared at the ceiling. I blinked my eyes and stared again. I tried to convince myself that I could see some faint little sparkles, but I knew I could not. They just weren't there for me. I was tempted to pretend because I

wanted to please Mad Bear. But I shook my head. Perhaps
some day . . .

"By golly, these are delicious!" Mad Bear exclaimed, attending, once more, to his ingenious sandwiches. "Now! I
picked up something else—right out of your thoughts! You
want me to tell you? When I picked up your thoughts before,
you knew that, right? I said 'dig in' and you started thinkin'
about that. I just thought I'd mention it, in case you were
wondering. Just now you were thinking about something cold
to drink. You were thinking about that orange juice we left in
the icebox this morning. But you don't want to ask. That's
why I mention these things. That's why I pick up your
thoughts, I think. Because you don't ask much. Me, I'm a little more pushy. Well, you just help yourself. But get some of
that Coke, though, not the orange juice. That Coke'll go one
heck of a lot better with this pickle juice. It's just a suggestion."

Mad Bear and I stayed up late that evening. We sat at a
card table in the front room, making notes. He had pens and
paper so that we could make outlines for what he called the
upcoming books. I could not think of what to outline. This
was only my second day with Mad Bear, and what was ahead,
I thought, was some travel, some sitting, and a great deal of
listening on my part. I had thought I needed nothing more
than to be available and attentive.

"Well, we just have to make the bare bones outline," Mad
Bear declared, "and then that'll put us right on the beam.
See, we just plan our books, just the bare sketch, then everything comes along our way to fill that up. It's like if you think
it's going to rain, you put out a container. So you put that out
first, and then along comes the rain."

He jumped up again to unplug the coffeepot in the kitchen.
"You gotta watch that thing, it'll get too strong. We'll just let
'er settle a bit, and cool off." That little coffeepot was forever
perking, it seemed, but it was a comforting and homey sound.

Mad Bear returned to his notes, and I watched him with
amusement. He had brought from the kitchen a big, fat grease

pencil and he began to write. He wrote the words "Earth Mother Crying," and it took up nearly a whole page. He looked up at me and grinned. "Well, this's for the title and the main headings—so it'll come out good and strong. See, this is the name of my book, *Earth Mother Crying*. Pretty good, huh? Maybe you didn't know I was writing a book myself. People say 'Mother Earth, Mother Earth' all the time now, but here I've got it 'Earth Mother.' There's a difference. When you refer to the Earth you say 'Mother Earth,' and when you refer to the Mother, you say 'Earth Mother.' That's the being herself, the spirit that's behind this Earth. It's a female creation, it's a child of the Great Spirit too. We look at her as our mother."

We sat in silence for a while. Mad Bear made several notes with his grease pencil and filled up several sheets of paper. I jotted down a couple of tentative subheadings from my recollections of Mad Bear's explanations, but I had fewer than a dozen words.

"Well, you've got a different situation than me," Mad Bear said. "See, I'm writing about the past, so mine's already in my head. Just how to get it down. I'm starting out telling the vision I had years back in the sweat lodge. That sweat, that's not traditional with the Iroquois, so this story is my first sweat. I'm not writing it out, just making the outline. This outline business, this is all new to me because this is my first book. Hope I didn't waste any paper—you can't erase this marker. Take a look. See what you think."

He handed me his several pages with their big, bold markings. I was not sure how to comment. I could not easily understand his lists of phrases because I was not aware of what thoughts were behind them.

"Oh!" he exclaimed. "We're forgetting something here. What are we forgetting?"

I looked at his pages spread out before me. If he had forgotten something, I had no way of knowing.

"The coffee," he said, "the coffee. Good thing I thought of it. Maybe it'll still be warm."

◗

"I'll get it," I said, starting up from my chair. Just then, there was a sharp, insistent rap on the window above our heads. I looked up. Several spontaneous images flashed through my mind. I pictured some kid reaching up with a stick, tapping on the window, and scampering to hide. At the same time I realized that it would be hard to reach a stick through the metal grating from below and that the sound seemed to have been produced on the inside.

I turned to look at Mad Bear. He was staring at me and grinning. He appeared to be pleased. "You heard that, right? You actually heard it! That's good. But you don't know what it was?"

"No."

"Messengers! Messengers for me. The same ones that we saw there in the kitchen. Well, you can't see them, but I guess you can hear them. Can you pick up any meaning?"

"No, I just heard a tapping on the window—'tak, tak, tak!'—like that."

"Well, that was a message for me. They're wanting to get in touch. Not the ones who tapped, these are just go-betweens, little elementals. They're physical, in a way, so they're not so hard to see and hear, once you get the hang of it. They have their own thing going, so we don't look for them. They mind their own business and we mind ours. But then, when the elders send them, they come as messengers. They don't really understand our work and our objectives, but they don't have to. They're just useful for getting our attention."

Mad Bear gathered his papers, arranged them in a stack, and walked into the kitchen. "I'm gonna hafta pass on this coffee here, but you come get some. It's all yours. I'll take a little dream medicine and hit the hay, so they can get to me. That's what the message is, just like you heard it, it's telling me to hit the hay. It's like, 'We're callin' you right now, and we're gonna have a little meeting.' So, Doug, you go ahead and stay up, whatever you like. G'night!"

Within minutes he was snoring loudly. I might have thought that such snoring meant that he had fallen fast asleep—that

●

he had blown it by dozing off when something was trying to reach him. But I had learned from Rolling Thunder and others that only the body sleeps—and when the body sleeps, conscious attention is not lost at all, but simply directed elsewhere.

•   •   •

I realized there was no need for me to sit alone at the card table and ponder over an outline. I turned off the light in the front room and carried my coffee into the garage. I sat on my bed and sipped from my cup and watched a little spider making a web between the rope and the pulley wheel. For a long time I lay awake, listening to Mad Bear's snoring, which came loud and clear through the wall between us, and watching the little spider.

I thought of the spider that Mad Bear had once told me about—the spider that had led the people through an underground passage from the old world to the new. I recalled our conversation of the day before, and I recalled the circumstances that led to my being here.

When the book *Rolling Thunder* was completed, in 1973, I had set out for New York to rendezvous with Alyce and Elmer Green and their team from the research department at The Menninger Foundation and then to depart with them for India. I had arrived early and taken a side trip to Niagara Falls in an attempt to contact Mad Bear. It was largely due to his subtle urging that I had left The Menninger Foundation months earlier in order to develop the Rolling Thunder story from a field report into a book, and I wanted to apprise him of what I had done. I had the phone number of a relative who lived nearby, and that number led me to another number and then to yet another number until, at last, I reached him somewhere on the Ute Reservation near Salt Lake City, Utah. Standing at a pay phone within view of Niagara Falls and only a few miles from his home, I told him about the book and thanked him for helping to invoke it. I told him that I was going to India and that I should have liked to have met with him prior to this adventure, as I knew he had traveled much in India. "But we'll talk when you get back," he had responded. "We'll have a lot to talk about when you get back."

But when I returned from India, I became preoccupied with my new manuscript about my travels and meetings in India. For months I could think of nothing else. During that period Mad Bear had phoned me again and again. He told me about his new indoor toilet and his water heater, and about this bed that he had rigged up. I knew he was suggesting that I come, especially when at last he said, "You'll be comfortable here for as long as you'd like to stay."

About the time that I finished the Swami book, Mad Bear's calls became insistent. "We have to get together," he would say. "We have to talk. There are things we can communicate about present and future events that might be important to share at this time. I think it might be our work to do this, something we're s'posed to do. We can maybe offer some ideas that might help people make it over the bridge from this world to the next—and make it in a balanced way. That's the main thing, in a balanced way. So when can you make it up here?"

I had phoned Mad Bear from California only a few weeks before, suggesting that since I had at last completed my manuscript and was considering being in New York to deliver it in person, it might give us a chance to get together. We made arrangements for my arrival. I was to phone him when I was ready to head up his way from New York City, and then again when I reached Buffalo. "You could just get that bus out to La Guardia and hop a plane up to Buffalo," he had told me. "Meanwhile, I'll be waiting up here, knowin' you're on your way. Then, when you land in Buffalo, you inquire about that bus that takes you up to Niagara Falls and what time it leaves, and give me a ring back, 'cause I'll be all set to head out for the rendezvous. Just tell the driver to let you out on the corner of Second and Fall streets and I'll be right there, sittin' in the car."

◑

When I arrived in New York City, I delivered my manuscript and met some friends. It was early evening when I
phoned to let Mad Bear know I was on my way. There was no
answer. I allowed the phone to ring. At last I gave up. I ought
not to board the airport bus, I decided, until I was sure he
was home. It had been a few weeks since we had last spoken.
In all the previous times I had been with him, he had always
found a chance to mention how he liked to "move as the wind
blows." I could recall him saying, "You just can't pin me
down." I knew I shouldn't start out for his place without talking to him first.

I waited for a long time in the station, and I tried the telephone again and again. There was no problem postponing my
arrival at Mad Bear's. Mad Bear could easily have been
called away on some important matter. For all I knew, he
could have simply gotten up and headed out—like a free
spirit—like a gust of wind. Or for that matter, he might be
walking about as a bear in the wilderness up north. Still, I felt
that something was wrong; and it was for that reason that I
tried him, again and again, every few minutes, and let the
phone ring and ring.

It was late at night when I left the station. I spent a couple
of days with friends in Manhattan. Then I took the train to
Connecticut to stay with other friends. Every few minutes,
day after day, I had dialed Mad Bear's number and had let
the phone ring.

When at last he answered, with a muffled "Hullo?" it surprised me. "Mad Bear!" I shouted into the phone.

"Doug!" he shouted back. "Hey, you're lucky you got me.
By golly, your timing's right on the button."

Lucky? I thought to myself. "Mad Bear, I've been trying to
call you practically every few minutes for the past four days!"

"Well, you couldn'ta got me, 'cause I was in the hospital. I
just now got out. I just this minute walked in the door to get
some of my medicine and things and Beeman and I are heading into the hills for a few days. We've gotta do some pretty serious medicine on me, pretty quick like, so I can't talk now.
You coming up here?"

"Well, I was going to. I mean, if it's still okay."

"Yeah, look, call me Tuesday. I'll be home on Tuesday, and I'll be all straightened out. Just get on up to Buffalo, and call me from there. I'll be ready and waitin'."

So on Tuesday, I returned to New York City, flew up to Buffalo, phoned Mad Bear, took the little bus up to Niagara Falls, and got out on the corner of Second and Fall streets, just as he had instructed me. There he was, sitting in his car on the corner, with a big smile on his face.

It was turning autumn in Iroquois country. This was all Iroquois country—everywhere I'd been during all these days—during my stay in New York City and in Connecticut, my flight up to Buffalo, and my bus ride to Niagara Falls—it was all Iroquois country. I supposed that every acre of this entire land was now totally changed and much damaged by the "progress" of civilization. I was not part of that lineage or that heritage, and I did not belong to those who inherited the vast oral histories of this land; but I could recall the images from my coloring books and from the stories and poems my mother used to read to me. Here, long ago, must have lived the Indians of those childhood conceptions. They were the Indians who lived out of doors, whose neighborhoods were big and wild and full of adventure, who were friends with the birds and the animals and even the wind and the moon. The Indians in my childhood storybooks lived long before the made-up and misrepresented Indians of my school-day textbooks.

"Now you can't really see it," Mad Bear said, pointing out the window as we drove along, "but that's the reservoir up there atop that hill. To this side of us, this hill we're driving alongside of here, this's all the reservation—the Tuscarora Reservation—what's left of it. This's my tribe, you know. I'm full-blood Tuscarora. My people migrated up from North Carolina and we joined the five nations—the Onondaga, Oneida, Seneca, Mohawk, and Cayuga—and we became the last of the Six Nations, the so-called Little Brothers of the Iroquois Confederacy.

"Of course, this is not our reservoir, this is just our land. This was all taken over by the New York Water Authority. All this land here was at one time intended to be reservoir. They were going to flood all this area out here, and there wouldn't have been hardly any Tuscarora land left at all. Some people were prepared to give their lives to try and stop it. They would have sat right here and let themselves be flooded and drowned if necessary. The reservoir turned out only half as big as planned. This is Tuscarora land, and these big companies and local governments haven't got a deed or a legal claim to it, but they just take it."

•   •   •

Mad Bear had just been in the hospital, and he had to sign himself out on his own recognizance, he explained, against the doctors' protests. On the day I had reached him, he had been about to set out to accomplish his own "medicine" in his own way. He had had a very serious heart attack. Fortunately, he had seen it coming. So clearly did he see it before it reached him, he told me, that he could even be certain who had "sent" it. I got the sense, as he told his story, that some group who had been working in opposition to his cause of intertribal and intercultural dialogue had been performing some steady ritual to send him, in etheric form, some harmful potential. Apparently, there were individuals and groups in many realms who were opposed to unity and harmony. He did not identify the opponents, and I did not ask about them.

"I was out mowin' the lawn," Mad Bear explained. "I don't usually do it. I'm not s'posed to be doing it, especially in the heat—and with my weight and all. Though I don't have a bad heart, actually. The kid that usually comes around—I don't know what happened to him. I couldn't stand to let it go anymore. Well, I was kind of miffed, I guess, and, against my better judgment, I wore myself out. I went on without rest or water, and I provided the perfect opportunity. As soon as I saw it coming—I mean, I just looked up and I could actually see it coming—I knew I'd left myself wide open. And I knew it was going to be a heart attack, though I had no symptoms at the moment. I tried to call Beeman and them, and some of the medicine people, and it just happened they were all out. I mean, it was like everything was made to order for those particular ones' medicine to succeed against me.

"I got in the car and tried to outrun it, and a motorcycle cop stopped me on the highway for speeding. He asked me if I had any idea how fast I was going, and I asked him if he realized I was about to die of a heart attack right there while he was writin' up a ticket. So he actually escorted me to the hospital, and I got rushed into the emergency room. Well, it hit me that very moment, and it was a real doozy. So then came the heavy medications, and those things cause fatigue and dull your energy systems. You can even lose contact with your spirit helpers that way. I knew, even as I was fading, that I had to bring up my will real strong and get free before I slipped too far and lost all my contacts."

That afternoon, as I was about to arrive at Mad Bear's house for the very first time, he let me in on the little people. I was not told the details of the medicine that he and Beeman Logan had performed in the mountains; but I was told that the little people had come to the ceremonial fireside and had made their presence known by tugging on their pant legs. The little people, I learned, are a parallel evolution of human beings whose physical forms reach less than one foot in height. The most highly developed of them come and go from this Earthly realm and are seldom seen by our own people in contemporary times. Those without long cultural histories and records, in fact, know nothing of them; but they join the traditional Iroquois and others frequently and regularly in ceremonies that are arranged for those special times, and they appear at other times as serves a purpose.

Mad Bear's street looked like the typical street of a very rural area. There was an occasional small house on one side of the road and an occasional small house on the other. All the residents were Indians. This was the rule on this reservation, I learned. It was the only way to protect what little the Tuscarora had that had not already been taken from them.

◑

It's like a little fortress, I thought to myself, as we pulled up
into the driveway at Mad Bear's house. His was not a wooden
house like all the others. It was built of concrete blocks, and
the windows, so high off the ground that no one could look in,
were covered with wrought-iron grating.

"I live alone, as you know," he explained as we got out of
the car, "and it's a small place. But anyway, it's all my own,
and it's done pretty well for me. It's good and secure, and no
one ever knows whether I'm home or not. I like it that way.
And sometimes I just lock it up and take off. This place is protected. I have medicine on this place that protects it."

The house did look small, but sound and solid indeed.
There was a screened-in front porch, a smaller inside porch,
and then the front room, just big enough for a standard desk,
a file cabinet, a couple of folding chairs, and a photocopy machine.

"You can bring your things right on through and set them
down anywhere back here," Mad Bear said, leading the way.

The crowded back room was a kitchen–dining room–den
combination with a four-burner gas stove, a stainless-steel
double sink, a large wooden cupboard, a metal table with
three kitchen chairs, one stuffed armchair, and a little black-
and-white TV high on a shelf that was nailed to the wall right
over the refrigerator. There was also a large metal cabinet,
which I later learned stored a variety of Mad Bear's own medicines, and a wood-burning space heater over which hung a
couple of baskets for drying herbs. Through this kitchen was
a garage, and in the garage was a bed on which I laid my luggage. The only other room was Mad Bear's bedroom; but with
three multipurpose rooms plus a front porch and a garage
equipped with a bed, toilet, and shower, the house seemed not
so small after all.

In only a moment, we were seated at the little metal table,
and I was struck for the first time by the profound sense of
urgency that lay behind Mad Bear's cheerful and buoyant
manner.

"So what's on your mind?" Mad Bear started. His opening
was direct and somehow surprising and, as I searched for the

right answer, I felt his powerfully engaging energy.

"Well, I was interested in our phone conversations," I offered, after some hesitation, "and I thought we might . . . No, actually, what matters is what's on your mind."

He responded instantly, but with a slow and thoughtful seriousness that I had never yet seen in him. "Everything in this physical dimension," he said softly, "is divided into fours. This physical world is the lowest manifestation, and every aspect of it is measurable. In fact, it is created and defined and maintained by measurement. Dividing and adding, adding and dividing. Every aspect of time and space seems to divide naturally into fours—as if it's all composed of four parts—like, for example, the four quarters of an hour and the four quarters from moon to moon. Then there's the four seasons, and the four directions.

"Then, the next step up the ladder, there's another different level, a little less solid than this so-called physical level, where everything is measurable in a way. But on that next step up from this physical dimension, everything seems to be in threes. The lowest levels come out of the ones above them, and it goes on. So, the next highest level—the second highest level above this material world—how do you suppose things seem to break out—to break up into equal parts? See, it's gettin' closer and closer to the source of creation, where everything is self-contained. Do you think on that second level up things come in fives—or maybe in twos?"

"It seems to me that above the level of threes would be twos," I suggested, "leading more toward wholeness—or oneness."

"Well, this's sort of the right idea. But the truth is, even the level of threes has no exactness like we're used to. I mean, you know, breaking down—separating. And beyond that, there're no parts, no measurements. Really, there's no time and space that can be measured in the way we think of it. But the history of our physical world can be divided into fours—something like four major periods. So that's what I've been wanting to talk about."

We waited for a moment.

◗

"Just as we could speak of four parts of a day, four parts of
a month, four parts of a year, four parts of a human lifetime,
we could speak of four parts of the whole history of this
Earth. I call them worlds—there are four worlds to go
through in the experience of the Earth herself. You could sub-
divide them, you could talk about different kinds of periods
and cycles within these. But they all fit into the four eras.
There are the four major divisions of the life of this planet
just as there are the four elements—earth, water, air, and
fire. Each new era is brought about by the action of one of
these elements in particular—though they are all in motion all
the time. We're coming to the end of the third world and
about to embark upon the fourth. Have you heard of the end
of the world?"

"You mean like the doomsday that various people have
predicted from time to time?"

"Yeah, but there's no such thing as doomsday—only the
end of one era and the beginning of another. And it's not just
arbitrary, like dates on a calendar. It involves a lot of
changes—destruction and re-creation. From the human's
point of view, it's going to be something really heavy. It's like
a purification—a transition from one world to the next. Yet,
it's no doomsday. People should understand it. People should
know what's going on in terms of the larger picture. People
should be involved in it in a conscious way—in a constructive
way. This means waking up out of materialism and connecting
up again with the spirit world—learning to understand and
cooperate with all the living forces of nature. In all the history
of the world, we can find traditional peoples going back thousands of years without destroying or depleting or degrading
the land—living with nature and spoiling absolutely nothing
for thousands of years. In all of history, wherever we find
people turning toward materialism and losing sight of their
true source, they begin to destroy the world. Twice before,
the human's world has been brought right up to the brink of
death by so-called civilization and then thrown into a great
transition and renewal. This time makes the third time."

Mad Bear had gone on for a long time, speaking about the elements and the forces of nature, about spiritual dimensions and angelic beings, about nature sprites and elementals, and about the little people. He had explained to me his view that humans inevitably become destructive when, through their materialistic and technological preoccupations, they lose sight of their own source and begin to imagine that with their physical forms and fashionings they are complete in themselves. He had talked until it was time for our supper (though we had been sipping coffee and nibbling all the while) and then time for an early sleep. Then, in the morning, he had told me the story of False Face.

I thought about the little people and tried to see them in my mind as I lay on that bed in Mad Bear's garage, watching the spider and listening to him snore. I even allowed my imagination to wonder who this little spider might be, persistently ascending and descending above me, its fine threads glistening in the lamplight—and whether, when I turned off the light, it would even still be there.

I had fallen asleep long after Mad Bear's snoring had begun, and I should have awakened long after he did; but he could not wait to talk to me, and he purposefully banged and rattled our breakfast pans as loudly as he could in the kitchen and startled me out of a very sound sleep.

He had been peering through the open door, it seemed, as he stood noisily at the stove, watching for my eyes to pop open. "Boy, did they talk to me last night," he said with a grin. "My people and your people too. I mean, the minute I hit the hay, there they came, and I sure got a earful! I'll hafta tell you about it. You better get up quick like and put on your appetite. I can rustle up one of the speediest breakfasts you've ever seen. I even used to be kinda famous for it at one time."

CHAPTER TWO

Transition and Survival

"The key to survival is to embrace the transition."

◗ Breakfast looked more voluminous than we could handle. Fortunately I felt almost up to the task (it was that Northern autumn air, Mad Bear's exuberant "dig in," and my confidence in his own appetite). I knew Mad Bear was opposed to wasting food.

"Yeah," he boasted as he chewed, "I used to be famous for my cooking. Still am, I s'pose, but I used to feed people when I had my log cabin, way back. You saw pictures of my log cabin where I lived right here on the reservation. That was years ago. But people used to come from all over and I would always rustle up a full breakfast in a matter of minutes—just like magic—just like I did here today. Nothing fancy, like really uptown or anything, just good and plenty—just like we got here today."

What we had here today was scrambled eggs, hash brown potatoes, bacon, sausage, hotcakes, toast and muffins and jelly, fried tomatoes, doughnuts, and, of course, that little percolator. What else could there be, I thought to myself, that one could have for breakfast—except maybe some orange juice.

"Well there is some orange juice," he responded aloud. "It's right there in the icebox, but you'll have to help yourself, 'cause I don't care for any myself, with all this coffee, and I'm not going to jump up again. I guess you already know I pick up your thoughts. It's because of this arrangement."

I found the orange juice and a large glass and poured it half full, trying not to think about any additional foods or drinks. I had only vaguely thought about orange juice, and I didn't think I'd told myself I needed it.

"They call you 'Doug,'" Mad Bear said. "They call you 'Doug,' and that's pretty interesting."

"Who?"

"We had quite a conversation last night, like I said. Well, I didn't do much talking or even questioning, but sure did a lot of listening. Those who always deal with me directly—that is with my own life—they're all female beings. At least, that's the way they look to me. Especially the one—she's always with me, looking over me—she's like a grandmother. She makes me think of my grandmother. She's not really that person, exactly, but I know there's some connection there. Your person is like a male—was when he talked to me—like a grandfather. It's not a person, really, more like a mind. Way beyond a human mind. But we get words from them—whatever we can understand. You do too, pretty much, though you may not remember when you wake up. Of course it's not in your culture—your usual daily life. Yet it's such a natural thing. Well, he talked to me. It's pretty easy to get through to me—and I can hang on to it. Especially when I use my dream medicine. They can get through to me in English or in my own language. Maybe it depends who it is—or what they're talking about. So yours, he's with you. I never had seen him before. But I got a kick out of him calling you 'Doug.' See, they've known us so long—thousands of years—can you believe it?

Our contemporary names are temporary and they don't usually use these names. They know you by some other name from way back—or maybe your true, true name. But 'Doug,' that's what they call you. So it had a kinda good feeling—close like, like a friend."

"What did he tell you?"

"Well, about you. Things about you, not about me, really, except it was good for me to know it. I can understand better from that. These things you'll come to know yourself, anyways—things I don't have to tell you. You could try listening more. But it doesn't matter, it all works out in time. Still, these days we have to speed things up. There's some kind of time limits with events concerning the Earth."

He got up to fill the coffeepot, and went on talking with his back to me and with the water running. His way was to let things come casually. Whether a healing, a teaching, an insight, or a warning, matters of significance were always offered lightly—as if to sneak in past the mechanisms of resistance.

"Well, I could mention a few things you could think about a little bit down the line. You really ought to formalize your work as much as you can—organize it—that's what I picked up. Not just you, I mean a group, like a team. This is a general thing, really. It concerns everybody. But a lot of people won't apply it for maybe decades or generations to come. People are caught up too much in themselves—even the good workers who are so needed. They're still into the Lone Ranger kind of thing. But teams have to be formed—groups of warriors—kind of like spiritual armies. In your case, you need to formalize such a thing. You have to file or register or something. I'm using my own words here, I'm just trying to snatch some specific hints out of the whole picture.

"We'll just plug this thing in," he said, resettling in his chair, "and we'll have more coffee in a jiffy. We probably shouldn't be eating so many doughnuts. At least you'd think we could wait until the coffee's ready." (I had not yet had one doughnut. In fact, I had become quite full, and there was still

a piece of toast on the plate in front of me.) "When you have
an organization, you have to give it a name, right? Yours already exists—the name, I mean. And you may pick it up on
your own, and it'll be the right one. On the other hand you
might dream up a name that suits your own interests, and it'll
be a mistake. It's something to think about because words
have power—especially names. Names can steer an organization, or at least set the whole stage anyway, for the way it may
be received. Most organizations are named after a certain
person or a certain system. They're set up to serve some idea
or even hang on to a certain religion. That might be okay. I
mean, it serves their purpose. But the organizations trying to
come about for the sake of the new world are entirely different. They are not set up to serve any purpose of their own, so
they are not named after any person or system. Actually these
organizations will be much more powerful than any self-
serving systems, because the spiritual forces can work right
through them. This you know. I mean, you've been thinking
about all this right along. But you still have to be careful.
That's what I was told. I could help you out with some hints,
he said. Like I was told you love this word 'international.' It
can be poor strategy to use this word too much and you may
be inclined to overuse it. That's what I was told; I didn't know
that myself, or I never really thought about it."

He was silent and we sipped our coffee. I looked at that
piece of toast. Perhaps I'd better eat it, I thought, though I'd
finished several. But I'd rather have a doughnut before Mad
Bear ate them all, even though I wasn't really hungry. Mad
Bear jumped up and grabbed my toast.

"We never waste any food here, you know. Nothing goes to
waste, so you don't have to worry about that. Eat what you
like and what's left gets shared. There's no lack of mouths in
this world—mouths of all sizes. He opened his back door that
looked out on a patch of bright green lawn and then a large
field of weeds with his now-unnecessary outhouse and then
the woods beyond. He clamped my toast in his hands and
crushed it between his palms. Holding his cupped hands to-

gether, he stepped briefly out of sight, and then he reappeared, briskly brushing his hands. "Even the ants enjoy some toast now and then. They're part of our whole community, so nothing ever goes to waste—you just never throw food in the trash is all—not even the tiniest morsel—unless it's gone bad or something."

Again with his back to me, he busied himself examining the herbs that were drying in the baskets hanging over the old wood stove in the corner. "We just never forget to give thanks. You can say it out loud or just think it in your own mind. Help yourself to some doughnuts—whatever you want—and don't hesitate to let me know when you're hungry for lunch. Anyways, these new organizations have to come around and get prepared to serve some purpose outside of themselves, like a task force with an open agenda—whatever they're called for that needs doing and they're prepared to handle—and they'll be very powerful. But it will take time. Maybe we'll just be able to manage the preparatory ones. Anyway, you're s'posed to come up with a name on your own. It exists, and it was even mentioned to me, but I guess I don't even recall it. But that part about 'international,' I was told to pass that on, and then maybe you'll come up with what the name really is. See, some words, they can raise eyebrows, if you know what I mean, and that we should avoid. The point is to be neutral, really neutral—like we want to help out the whole picture without pushing our own agenda."

He returned to his place at the table and reached for the last doughnut. At his suggestion, I had managed to experience one of them. "If you're thirsty there's some kinda cola in the icebox, I forget which, and I'll be heading out to the Thank-you Store pretty quick here. You been to the Thank-you Store? That's its real name. You can come along if you're up to it. Or we could go to the supermarket, come to think of it, and really stock up on some major supplies."

I wasn't up for thinking about groceries, but certainly up for some fresh air and some movement. "Yeah, I'll go," I said.

"And they had some messages for me too—that is, my ones

●

who talk to me. That was about the kind of places that will be suitable for the upheavals and the Earth changes during the transition—survival places, you could call them. I'm thinking about setting such a place up myself. Someday I'll show you where. That'll come later. We'll get around to thinking about that. Then I did some dreaming too. That's a different kind of thing—just dreaming—but I think it was related to the messages about the survival places. I dreamed I worked on this place like I'd planned, up there in the mountains where I'll show you. And while I was working on that, you were talking about one too. We were writing letters back and forth, and you were talking about setting up a place out in California—behind the second range of mountains—that was the way it was described by the guidance that was given to us—in my dream, you know. But then I didn't hear from you for a long time, and came to find out—I don't know how I found out—you were traveling all over the place—India, Japan, everywhere. Then I finally heard from you that you came back and planned to put your place together in a hurry, just like you were instructed, because there wasn't much time. When I finished my place I decided to come out to yours and give you a hand. So I sent you a letter and headed out West. It took me only a few days, 'cause, you know, I drive pretty steady. I was surprised to find your place was all finished by the time I got there. You had sent me a letter saying it was ready and inviting me out to take a look, and our two letters had crossed in the mail. Boy, was your place ever something. I mean, I was pretty surprised.

"We better head out to the store. Tonight I'll tell you about your place. I can describe it, but it doesn't mean you should try to bring it about just like my dream. I think it was symbolic. It felt pretty real, but now I think maybe it wasn't a physical thing."

Mad Bear pointed to a group of trees standing near the edge of the reservation and told me that they were dying. That fact was somewhat apparent, once it was brought to my attention, but Mad Bear elaborated on the step-by-step dying process as if to instruct me in the technique of confirmation. As we drove along the highway, he caused me to notice a number of trees that were thoroughly dead. Most were still standing, but some were lying on the ground.

I supposed he was about to make some reference, once again, to our contemporary environmental insensitivity. I recalled the time I first met him—in 1972 when he had come out to the Berkeley Hills to assist Rolling Thunder. Then we had observed how the tops of many trees were bending over—bowing down in fear and sadness toward the belly of the Mother, as he had put it. Perhaps these trees along the highway had died of sadness and desperation? Or had there been some epidemic? But many of the trees looked healthy—those that were not dead or dying. "What happened to these trees?" I asked. "What killed them?"

"Killed them? No one killed them, everything dies. Everything dies, it's nature's way. They simply lived and died. It just goes to show that as long as there are plenty of trees, there'll always be plenty of dead ones."

But why, I wondered, were we observing tree mortality this day?

Walking with Mad Bear through the aisles of the supermarket, I began, to my slight embarrassment, to get into the mood for lunch already. Mad Bear scouted out and studied the items on the shelves with the craft and curiosity with which he surveyed the details of the fields and forests. We filled the shopping cart, and we each had a weighty box to carry out to the car—weighty, particularly, because Mad Bear appreciated the handy expedience of canned items.

"Well, we ought to go ahead and pop in the Thank-you Store, just to see what they might have of interest. It's not a big market, you know, not for all that we needed here, but it's a good one—good people—and I do like to stop in whenever I pass."

An elderly woman in a large sedan was driving very slowly down the middle of the road, and Mad Bear became impatient. "Well, she can't help it, maybe, but we've got ice cream in here, and we've got to get home. She could at least move over. Look there on the floor between your feet. That's a speaker there. Just hand it to me." He put it through the window on his side of the car and rolled up the glass to hold it in place. "I use my CB to help out other drivers," he said turning a few knobs in the dash in front of him, "and there'll come a time this sort of thing may save the day. I don't mean like this, though." He picked up the small microphone and held it right against his mouth. A low, wailing sound started deep in his chest, and it became high and piercingly shrill as it reached his lips. Then it dipped down again, and then rose again. It was a quite realistic siren sound that came out of that speaker, and the woman in front steered her car sharply to the side. Mad Bear dropped the mike in his lap and quickly pulled in the speaker. He grinned widely as we went around, and waved politely, but she just stared with an open mouth.

"We were talking about transition and survival," he said, clicking off his CB radio. "Or that's what I was thinking about, anyway. I mean, that's what we're dealing with here, you and me. And those trees are an excellent example." He stopped there as though he supposed he'd made clear to me some case or lesson relevant to dead and dying trees. We pulled into the driveway. I would think about it later.

By the time lunch was on the table and "dig in" came around again, enough time had been spent in riding, shopping, stowing groceries, and cooking food that it seemed quite reasonable to be eating again. Mad Bear was in the mood for reminiscing. I began to think that the cheerful sound of the percolator was as stimulating to him as the coffee itself. He spoke of Peter Mitten, pointing through the wall in the direction of the house across and down the road where the old medicine man had lived for a time in his closing years. I recalled how Rolling Thunder had often mentioned Peter Mitten—often when he was speaking of Mad Bear—and how later, as I came to know Mad Bear, I had come to think of Peter Mitten as one of Mad Bear's principal mentors.

"I remember about the time that you and Peter Mitten

◗

worked on Richard Oakes in that hospital in San Francisco,"
I said.

"Yeah, I remember telling you about that. But you never
saw Peter Mitten. I wish you could have known him."

"I did get to know Richard Oakes. But he had actually
died, right? And you and Peter Mitten brought him back to
life."

"Peter Mitten did that. He did that more than once. I'll tell
you something. Right out here on this road out here, this kid
was hit by a car. You didn't know this one, it was a while
back. He was injured pretty bad and knocked out cold. The
car hit his bike and then he hit the pavement or struck his
head against the car. Anyways, he was lying in the road without a sign of life. I guess the people called the ambulance and
by the time the ambulance got here, some kids had seen him
and called his mom. I was inside here when I heard the ambulance and I got out there just in time to see them put him on a
stretcher and pull the cover up over his head. The mother was
screaming and hanging on to the stretcher, and the medics
were trying to convince her that the boy was gone. Just then
there was a loud shout from just inside that house over there.
'Put him down!' And then Peter Mitten appeared in the doorway. 'I said put him down! You don't take him anywhere. No
need of it.' Well, they did put him down. They laid him right
back down on the road. They knew they were on an Indian
reservation, otherwise they might not have done that. And
Peter Mitten, that old man—he'd been weak, not too well,
and mostly in bed—he walked up and leaned over the boy. He
stared at him for a while—almost nose to nose. Then he blew
in his face, hard and quick and he said, 'Open your eyes.'
Nothing happened and he repeated, 'Come back, I told you!
You come back here and open up those eyes.' That kid's eyes
started to quiver and again he told him. 'Open your eyes.
Open all the way, but don't move until I tell you.' When that
kid opened his eyes and looked around, his mom got all excited and wanted to pick him up, and I kinda had to keep her
away. Peter Mitten put something in the boy's mouth—some-

thing he'd had in his hand all along, maybe, who knows? Pretty soon he got up—tried to stand up but we had him just sit there, and we talked to him for a while to make sure that he'd come back all the way and was planning on staying. Then the ambulance took him."

"Then what became of him?" I asked. "Is he okay?"

"He's okay, as far as I know. He's not around here anymore, but I know he recovered from that. We let the medics take him. I mean, they had been called all the way over here, and the kid was banged up pretty bad—cut and bruised and all—it made sense. But I'll tell you one thing we never discussed with anybody. The medics told the doctors the whole story. Everybody had to accept what had actually happened. And one of those doctors came to us confidentially with his own personal situation for help from Peter Mitten and me. I'm still in touch with that doctor, although his problem is over. Everybody knew that those medics had actually found that kid dead and had confirmed him dead, but nobody ever put that in writing. See, those things, they're never reported, they're just denied. And even when they're observed and admitted, they just can't be officially acknowledged."

Someone knocked at the door. It sounded loud and insistent. Mad Bear stopped abruptly and ducked slightly in his chair squinting his eyes and glancing about. He looked mischievous. We had hoisted up my garage bed on its pulleys and he had driven in under it when we returned from shopping. I knew he enjoyed the option of not being home whenever his vehicle was out of sight. "That might be the neighbors wantin' a ride to the store. I don't too much like running them around after beer and such." Then there was another knock—this time in that rhythmic pattern intended to suggest familiarity—and Mad Bear peeked out through the crack beside the door frame. He yanked open the door with a grin and in came an almost middle-aged Indian man I had not seen before. He was introduced to me as "the medicine man I was telling you about," but I did not converse with him. I sat for what seemed like hours watching as those two hovered over Mad Bear's

chessboard. Mad Bear talked him into another and then another game long after he had mentioned something about having to leave.

Mad Bear sat quietly in his chair musing over the remnants
of the last game. It was nearly dark now, and the air was still.
We could hear the tires on the gravel as the car pulled out of
the driveway. Mad Bear appeared content as he always did after a few games of chess. Perhaps because he always won most
of them.

"Wasn't that something! There we were just thinking about
him and he shows up at the door. And he came all the way
from Rochester. He was one of the ones I was trying to get
hold of when that heart attack was coming at me. Sometimes
we work together in certain ways. His father was a medicine
man too—another one of my teachers—and very, very powerful. His father was one who had mastered invisibility. Is that a
word—'invisibility'? Anyway, he was the one who helped me
to be invisible when I needed that—the one who gave me that
hat. I told you about that hat?"

"No, I don't think so."

"Well, that's a story in itself. And it's related to that
Canada business. I know I told you about that."

We were back to our recollections. The Canada story was
retold. I had heard it from Mad Bear not long after I'd met
him, but now I got more details—including those about the
hat—and we sat there until it was completely dark and Mad
Bear once again began to think of food. Mad Bear was one of
those "troublemaker" activists who was always making an issue out of everything. This "Canada business" had to do with
a provision in an early treaty between the United States and
Great Britain. The treaty was supposed to give Indians both
north and south of the border free and clear passage back
and forth across the border in recognition of the fact that this
newly contrived national boundary was a line drawn through
the middle of the Iroquois Confederacy, slicing apart not only
nations but also tribes and even families. Eventually, this
treaty was violated and ignored, along with all the others, and

this became cause for ongoing objections and protests on the part of the traditional people. At times, people were prohibited from crossing the border to assemble for powwows or even for family gatherings. The Indians claimed that the governments of Canada and the United States contrived to solidify this separation as a sort of divide-and-conquer tactic—and they attempted to defy the prohibition.

In one such incident, Mad Bear crashed his Jeep through a wooden barrier at a border crossing. Later, in a published statement, he offered, as his ongoing policy, to pay for or to repair himself any government property that became damaged during his only available recourse in the exercise of his legal rights. This action and offer for restitution was not met with approval, and he was informed that if he were to appear at an upcoming intertribal rally scheduled to be held in Toronto, he would be arrested in the interest of maintaining the peace. In a subsequent published statement, Mad Bear announced that he would indeed present himself at the rally, not to disturb the peace but in order to carry out his official duties. The press became intrigued, and elaborate preparatory steps were taken to intercept and detain him at the border. His photograph adorned the walls of guardhouses at the likely entry points. Each car was to be carefully checked as the caravans of Indians crossed to the north.

"I was sitting in the backseat," Mad Bear told me, "kinda squinched down between a couple others, and I got through. I don't know whether I was actually invisible or not. I think maybe I could be seen. I just looked different somehow so I couldn't be recognized. It was that hat. Well, we did a couple other things, but it was the hat that did the trick—and that was the first time I used it. We went through in the early evening. Kinda twilight. Our car was right in the middle of the caravan, and there were reporters in the car right behind us. This thing had a lot of press, partly because of me. But it was a constructive thing because the publicity was necessary. Anyway, the guard stuck his head right in through the window. I recognized him and I looked right at him and smiled—

and he looked right at me. But he didn't recognize me.

"This white guy from the newspaper down in Buffalo was hanging out the window in the car right behind us. He thought I'd get nabbed, I guess, and he was going to get the whole story. When we got waved on through, he hollered, 'Hey! That's Mad Bear in that car up there!' That kinda shocked us—I mean he really shouldn't have said anything. I guess he just couldn't believe what happened. Or maybe he just wanted some news. Of course, he got his story. He knew I was in there because he saw me get in when we set up the caravan. But when the guard stopped us to take an even closer look, he waved us on again. I heard him holler back, 'Well, he's not in this car!' And then he checked those guys out real close.

"Later, everyone was asking me how we managed to pull that off, and of course I didn't say much—just that I was supposed to be there. But, I'll tell you, that darn hat, that was something. Every time that guard looked at me, it felt like sand was sprinkling all down over my face. I felt real weird, real different. Of course I didn't speak. I was hoping I wouldn't have to speak. But every time he looked at me, what he saw was someone else. Come here, let me check something here."

We walked into the bedroom. "This is it!" he said, handing me a large black hat. I was not sure whether I should touch it. "Go ahead," he urged, "put it on. Let me just look at you." I put on the hat and he sat down on his bed and grinned at me. He looked amused, and I felt strange. The hat was too large for me for one thing, and I knew I looked funny. But though I felt no sand sprinkling down such as Mad Bear had described, I did feel different. It could have been my imagination. Yet Mad Bear stared so long and so intently.

"Let me look in the mirror," I said, starting for the door.

"No, no! You better not. You better take it off. Here let me take it." He put it back on its hook. I thought about it during supper. I would have liked to have checked it out in the mirror. I also was curious to see Mad Bear in it—especially if he really changed. (But the next time I was in that room, the hat was not on its hook, and I supposed that Mad Bear had put it away. I never saw it again.)

We settled ourselves back in "the living room," as Mad Bear called it. Actually, it was a sort of office-museum combination. Mad Bear felt around in the dark and clicked on a small lamp, and we sat in near darkness so that Mad Bear could maintain his option of not being at home. He went on talking about that medicine man and his invisibility hat and about Peter Mitten, Beeman Logan, and others and as I watched him in the dim light, I could almost see the others there beside him. For a moment I felt as though we were sitting in a cave, Mad Bear and I and a number of his peers. "Oh, yeah, that's right," he interrupted himself. "I was going to tell you about your place—the place you built out West that I saw in my dream."

It would be amazing to see a place such as he described. Earlier he had said that perhaps it was not a physical place. I could hardly imagine myself building—or even causing to be built—such a place. As Mad Bear described, it was cut right into the middle of a mountain: a long tunnel that led into a huge cave at the back of which were carved stairways that led into passageways that led into numerous interior rooms on many levels. "And there was a stone stairway outside—up around the side of the mountain," Mad Bear explained. "And I went inside and out again and then walked up those stairs and came down in from the other side. The place was not empty. There were people in there from all over, and everyone seemed busy preparing for some sort of large gathering. It didn't really feel like a survival kind of thing, though. It felt more to me like when we're getting ready for a powwow or something. I guess when I was dreaming I sort of knew what was going on. I don't remember talking with anyone about it. I remember you were showing me around, and the first thing you showed me was a large stone tablet rising out of the ground with Sanskrit writing on it."

"It's interesting," I said. "I don't believe I've ever thought of anything like that."

◐

"Well, like I said, I think it might be mostly symbolic. You might have thought of what that's supposed to represent—just in a totally different way. But I've been saying 'survival place, survival place' and that might throw it off—the real meaning of it. 'Transition place' might be a better word. Or, if it's not actually a place, maybe 'transition project.' "

He stood up and began pacing back and forth. He looked restless and impatient. His large silhouette in the dim light really did invoke the image of a bear.

"Transition and survival. The way they're related—that's what's so important. See, people get it wrong mostly, though they don't even think about it consciously. We're starting into the transition now, and there'll be no stopping it—no holding it back. It's already begun, and people feel it. Then with their so-called natural survival instinct, people resist it. You can see this kind of survival reaction all around. People panic. They get grabby—snatching at the mountains and the forests and everything else—tearing everything apart. If I could put out the strongest message I could think of—just one powerful statement—I would say: 'The key to survival is to embrace the transition, not to resist it. People should participate in the transition, creatively, like they really want it. The Fourth World. It's a good thing. It means coming back to the Earth—for one thing—back to the Mother in all respects. Those who fight against the Mother—Earth and Nature—there's no winning and no reason to win. It's useless, and yet the cost is so great.

"It's a big issue these days—the destruction of the forests. We're wiping out the rain forests on this planet. We're wiping out the forests right here in our own country—the logging industry—gone berserk, absolutely berserk. Some people say it's out of greed. They say it's just plain, blind selfishness. It's not. It's fear. These loggers, these contemporary industrialists—they're full of fear."

To the American Indian, I thought to myself, the tree is the symbol of life. There is the "Sacred Tree of Life" and the ancient tenet that whoever should be in fear or pain or need may

◑

find refuge and comfort beneath its branches. It was the tree that was painted on the faces of the Indian braves for protection in battle as they struggled to defend their lives and lands. It was the "Sacred Tree of Life" that was mistakenly referred to by the white man as "war paint." I realized that we could construct a very long list of do's and don'ts for survival; but I also realized that there was one main principle, one paramount rule, basic to the continuing survival of humankind—basic even, perhaps, to the continuation of a living planet. Do not be competitive. Do not compete for survival. Compete, combat, and die. Cooperate, cultivate, and live.

"Well, this is the main point to bring out," he said, again following my thoughts. "This is the basic communication. The ones who will survive understand and support the process of survival. Most people think survival is competitive, a me or you sort of thing—or us against the 'wilderness,' whatever that's supposed to mean. I guess it means that some people think nature is against them. That's the real danger we face. They talk about 'survival of the fittest' like it's a competitive thing. It's not. In the process of natural selection, nature picks whoever cooperates best with nature. People don't need to cut down living trees. It's a panic reaction. So-called green trees aren't good for anything, except their own life and growth. The teaching is in the trees. It's so beautifully symbolic. It's the only lesson humanity needs. The trees. The more living trees people kill out of blind anxiety, the more they kill the prospects for a healthy world—prospects for their own survival and for the ever-coming generations. Once people can pick up on the trees as their living relatives and feel for them, then they'll understand the whole picture!"

CHAPTER THREE
Rolling Thunder Hears

"He has his own way of looking into things and working things out."

◑ The long-setting sun produces a spectacular light show across the Arizona sky almost every evening; it was a beautiful introduction to Tucson as we approached the airport. The Sonora Desert looked like gold to my eyes and the mountains turned blood red as we descended below them. By the time the shuttle was on the road into town, the entire sky was a soft, cool violet and the Catalinas to the north looked like cold slate. The atmosphere felt exciting. Of course there was the prospect of the coming event, but this was something about the air itself. It was early autumn, 1975. I had just come from my visit to The Menninger Foundation in Topeka, where the air was already beginning to feel chill.

I had left Mad Bear's reservation home for Topeka only a week earlier. Mad Bear had taken a variety of herbs from his hanging baskets and from the metal cabinet in the corner of the kitchen, crushed them on the top of his table, and stirred them together with his fingers. He had pressed an apple under his palm, rolling it back and forth across the table as he talked. I had no idea when I would be back or how I was to fit into his plans—or even *my* plans as he had forecast them. "This is sort of what you could call peace smoke," he had explained as he sliced his apple and squeezed its juice into the herb mixture. "You can just carry this along and use it once in a while when it seems needed. It's not a chemical thing, you know, it's the medicine behind it." He had given me a clay pipe with a small turtle on the front of the bowl, and that afternoon I had left for Kansas—only one week before the conference in Arizona that I had been committed to attend.

I was arriving in Arizona to rendezvous with Rolling Thunder, and he and his crew were coming by car from the Nevada desert. Here in one of Tucson's large convention-center hotels, the Academy of Parapsychology and Medicine was about to open its First National Congress, and Rolling Thunder was one among an impressive list of speakers. Many months earlier—for this event had been long in planning—officers of the academy had approached me on the phone regarding their request for Rolling Thunder's participation and for my help in bringing it about. So now I was along as the liaison arranger, just as I had been several times in previous years.

The sun bounced off the desert mountains and brightened my hotel room. It seemed I could almost touch the mountain that rose up just outside my window; and I could clearly examine the varieties of bushes and cacti that dotted its sandy hillside. Most of the plants were plump and green. A few were a deep purple and a few still had blossoms. This was a different desert from the ones I had known in southern California when I was in school or in western Nevada when I was staying with Rolling Thunder. When I stepped out to feel the morning, I realized that these mountains that had appeared to be just beyond arm's length were more than a half-day's walk from where I stood. There was nothing inviting to stroll to

near here—only stony sand on three sides of the hotel and a
highway on the other—and the glaring, dry air now felt more
like oppression than like freedom. I went back inside to check
on Rolling Thunder and his party.

There was no need to stop at the desk. I found a young Indian in the lobby, and I asked him. This was a person I had
not seen before, but I assumed he had arrived with Rolling
Thunder. I was correct, and I followed him to Rolling Thunder's room. Rolling Thunder and Spotted Fawn were both up
and about, and so were eight or ten others, all walking in and
out, unpacking, dressing, and grooming and trying to arrange
themselves as they wished to appear to the participants and
public who had gathered for this conference. Though this entourage had taken several rooms, this one was apparently
headquarters. In the familiar spirit of group endeavor that I
had come to know among Indians, they were helping one another pick out and put on chokers, feathers, beaded belts,
and ribbons for braided hair. Rolling Thunder himself was
totally occupied with this process and, though I had not seen
him or Spotted Fawn for some time, this was not a good moment for more than a quick greeting. I could not help here,
and there was no need for me to stand in the way and watch,
so I made my exit and waited in the lobby near the entrance to
the dining room.

Breakfast was buffet-style, and Spotted Fawn and I stood
talking just outside the line while all the others went through
and filled their plates. I realized we were waiting for each
other to step into line. "Go ahead," I motioned.

"You know I can't take my plate in front of a man," she responded. "I'm waiting for you to go ahead."

I recalled the many meals at their home in Nevada in which
Spotted Fawn and all the young women labored in the
kitchen, set out the food, and then disappeared to wait until
the men had had their fill and left the table. "You don't have
to do it that way here," I coaxed. "It's different here. Here, if
we follow any system at all, the men usually let the women go
ahead." She gave me an embarrassed look and glanced about

◗

nervously. With a gentle but insistent push against my arm, she urged me to move. Immediately I could sense her discomfort. She felt out of place here, I knew—embarrassed not to follow present custom but compelled to abide by her own. I wondered how this group would fit in this setting, how they would appear to the others here. The other speakers and participants were professionals, mostly—intellectuals whose reputations were built upon a different set of deeds and credentials. Spotted Fawn, in my view, was never out of place in any setting. She was a matronly woman, gracious and graceful, and her caring, nurturing manner was quickly apparent. The men, on the other hand, especially the younger ones, seemed caught somewhere between trying to fit in and trying not to—defending their identity and its affiliated style with an air of determination that could sometimes be mistaken for defiance.

These observations proved useful throughout the conference as I watched others watch this group of Indians. The conference was for researchers and practitioners who had come to share and to scrutinize so-called alternative methodologies of health and healing—from psychophysiological to psychic to spiritual. They were hoping to know Rolling Thunder's thoughts and techniques but they were unprepared to witness his peculiarities. I had learned that strangers to his ways found Rolling Thunder more difficult to understand in their own milieu than in Rolling Thunder's traditional setting. The group of young "warriors" with Rolling Thunder, thinking to be supportive and aspiring to be impressive, did not make things easier. In a manner that appeared curious at best (though it might have looked quite handsome in a traditional Indian setting), they surrounded him like some sort of tribal honor guard as he made his way about the halls and grounds of the hotel.

Nevertheless, several conference participants—young people, especially—approached Rolling Thunder with genuine interest and respect. Several of them managed to get a bit of his time and attention in spite of his guard troop. The first

group of young people to get to him requested an afternoon
workshop for instruction in the technique of meditation. I
was surprised because that was not a topic, I thought, with
which Rolling Thunder was generally associated. Rolling
Thunder seemed not surprised at all. Given that there was
some available afternoon open time and that I could arrange
a suitable setting, he would be happy to offer a meditation
workshop. He seemed pleased to have been asked. While he
was in an offering mood he suggested that we ought to have a
sunrise ceremony one of these mornings—if we could arrange
a place somewhere on the grounds where we could have a
fire—and everyone at this conference should be invited to attend.

The main program was held in a spacious auditorium with
a large stage and a balcony and hundreds of seats. Rolling
Thunder sat in front with his "warriors" around him, and I
sequestered myself near the back. A rather large woman hurriedly sidled her way between the seats in the row just behind
me. She placed herself just one seat to my left and leaned forward toward my ear. She was panting slightly as though she
had come a bit too quickly up the aisle.

"This man is Rolling Thunder, right? The one you were
with a moment ago. This is the first I've seen this man, an unusual man, very powerful, I thought I'd tell you. This power
is owing to those who are always with him—I don't mean
these other people he's brought here. Spirits! Do you understand what I'm telling you? I see powerful beings around this
man. They're quite visible to me—I just wanted to mention
that."

She was quite right, I supposed, whether or not she could
actually see what she had claimed she could see. But I did not
know this woman and, as the program was about to start and
everyone was now quietly settled, it was not a good time to discuss the "powerful spirits." I had no comment. I only smiled
and nodded and turned back in my seat. The introductions
began and I became engaged with listening; and when next I
glanced behind me, she was gone.

That woman was Olga Worrall, I later learned. She was the widow of the late Ambrose Worrall who was considered by many to be one of humanity's most adept and accomplished spiritual healers and who was certainly one of history's most famous. She had been assistant to Ambrose during his remarkable lifetime and was now admired as a powerful healer in her own right—though she claimed, I was told, that it was Ambrose who was the healer, working from another realm, while she remained the assistant. Now that I had learned who she was, I pointed her out to Rolling Thunder and Spotted Fawn and permitted myself to tell them what she had said. Spotted Fawn looked thoughtful for a moment and then wondered aloud: "Do you think she could help R.T.?" I wanted to ask whether there was some problem, and if so, what it was; but I only responded that I supposed she could.

The next day Spotted Fawn pursued the matter. As soon as she found me alone she asked me to talk to Olga Worrall about Rolling Thunder. "I just have the feeling," Spotted Fawn said, "that she can do something to help Rolling Thunder's ear infections. They're getting worse. He just lets it go, but it worries me. I don't know how she works or what she could do—I just have a feeling about it." I had known about Rolling Thunder's problem with his ears. They had been Rolling Thunder's point of vulnerability. There had even been concern about possible loss of hearing. It had been discussed some years ago when it was feared that an opponent was "making medicine" to worsen the condition, but I had forgotten about it.

Only moments after Spotted Fawn left me, Olga approached. "Where were you yesterday? I don't think you made it over to the lunchroom after the morning session." I explained that I had left the area to have lunch with some people who were wanting to have a workshop with Rolling Thunder. "Oh, you knew!" she said. "You must have known. We had some kind of fake Mexican fare. These people thought they could cook Mexican just by virtue of their geographical proximity. Either that or they thought they could fool us by virtue of our coming from the East. Well, Olga doesn't like to be fooled. Should we try them out today? We could always check on the menu. It couldn't be as bad as yesterday. You should have seen those awful pseudo-Mexican torntillows!" I walked with her to the large convention hall where they had set up tables to handle lunch for our entire conference population. She seemed to know I had been asked to talk with her. I had no idea how she preferred to be approached or preferred to arrange her healing sessions, but she had provided this comfortable opening and the matter was easily handled. We established the hour in which we were to arrive at her room on the following evening. "Now we have only to enjoy our lunch," she said, "or at least to try our best. You can handle having lunch with Olga, can't you? Why I should say so!"

Olga became jaunty, almost frivolous, as she led me to my seat in the center of a long table, and if it had not been for her easy, friendly warmth, I could have been embarrassed. But she was simply being, I later learned, her usual other self— the self she is when she is not being a healer—the light-hearted, humorous self that is needed to sustain stability and to provide relief and recuperation to the healer. "You just sit here and don't move," she said, "and wait for me while I travel around the end of this table." Soon she was sitting directly across from me, smiling into my face. "This way we can see, see? And we can talk and eat and don't have to twist our heads and get a stiff neck." She looked about the room. "Where is everybody?" she shouted as though her volume would bring an answer or bring everyone running.

"They'll be here," answered a waitress, coming up behind her. "You're just a bit ahead of time. We'll be serving in a few minutes."

"Well, we're just trying to look eager and give you some encouragement. And also, by the way, to check the menu. If you stick any more of those silly torntillows in front of me, I may just trot right on out—I don't know about my colleague here. But you're not scheming to push more of those torntillows on us again are you?"

"No," said the waitress simply, as though she were uncertain what sort of question she was answering but hoped she had given the expected response. She poured water in our glasses and made her escape.

"Well, here we have this water in the meantime. I don't s'pose they could do much to this. Still, don't you touch it till I fix it up for you. Water is water, you may say, but you never know. You can't trust it these days. But then you'd better have just a sip first so you can appreciate what I do to it."

I took some swallows of my water.

"No, no, not too much. Wait till I fix it up for you. Isn't that what I just said I'd do? Why have the usual thing when you can have it special. By the way, how did it taste?" She held the glass between her two palms and stared into it. Then she waved one hand over the top of it.

"Well, like water," I answered. "Not too good, but not too bad. Try a taste of yours."

"Oh, I can't do that. I'm already working here. We can't just disturb the process that way. But now it's almost ready, I do believe, in a moment now. And let's let you see the difference." She handed me my glass. "Now you be truthful here and don't you lie to Olga just to make me feel good. I'll know it for sure if you hand me a polite little fib."

I took a small sip and smacked my lips in the manner of a professional wine taster, but she motioned with her hand, urging me to tip my glass. "It does taste different," I exclaimed, "it really does." But then, in regard for the honesty she herself had requested, I added, "It could be my imagination."

"Imagination?" she retorted. "What is that? Taste is taste. It either tastes different or it doesn't. That's like people telling me: 'Maybe I only imagine I feel better.' Well, you either feel better or you don't. So how does it taste?"

"It is better," I told her. "Definitely better." By now I had an aftertaste both rich and fresh. "Yes, it's very pronounced. Strangely, it tastes something like soil to me. That doesn't sound very good, but it is. It's kind of outdoorsy—like green plants or maybe pine trees. Yet it's very subtle."

"Oh, come now!" She shook her head. "Like soil, you say? Give me that! Just let me see." She reached for my glass. "This is not my usual practice. We're just fooling around here, you understand. There can't be any harm in it. But soil indeed!" She raised my glass to her lips and then stopped herself. "Wait! First I'll check my own. Then I'll get the true comparison, just as you experienced it." She took a sip from her own glass and made a face. "Oh! Stinky Davis! That's putrid! I should hope I made it better." Again she picked up my glass and lifted it to her lips, holding out her little finger. She took a sip and imitated my lip-smacking procedure. "Say, this is fun! Aren't we having a wonderful time playing with our water?" She glanced about the room. "But simmer down, Olga, for heaven's sake, and lower your voice."

The dining room was beginning to fill and servers were pouring water into many glasses. Several people were watching us intently. "It's not that I mind looking crazy," she whispered, waving a hand over her own glass. "I'm just not about to work on every water in this place. It does taste different, though, it really does. But we'll say we're just kidding, won't we? We don't want to get ourselves in trouble here."

That afternoon, about a dozen people gathered in one of the small meeting rooms to hear Rolling Thunder talk about meditation. I might have expected more people, judging from the curiosity Rolling Thunder and his strange troop had generated, but there were several other things going on and, as this event was not part of the official program, we had had to notify people individually. And most of the people attending this conference might have expected to hear a different approach to the subject of meditation. According to the way this event had been discussed, I supposed these people were here to pick up some new meditation techniques—or actually, perhaps, some Indian methods for achieving "altered states." But Rolling Thunder began his usual talk about the contemporary disregard for original peoples and their traditional ways and wisdoms and disregard, as well, for land and life itself. To him, any meaningful consideration began with the recognition of contemporary realities. Everyone listened patiently for a time, and then, when there was mention made of increasing consciousness, someone seized the opportunity.

"That's related to meditation, right? Are you going to say something about meditation?"

"Well, that depends on what you mean by meditation. What is the meaning of meditation?"

"I'm not really sure about the actual definition. That's what I wanted to hear. I mean, it's been talked about a lot in this conference. Some of us were just interested in your view—or the Native American view."

"Well, you have to take it in steps."

"Could you give us the steps?" The young man had come with pad and pen.

"People talk ecology on the one hand," Rolling Thunder went on, determined to make his own presentation in his own way, pressing those familiar deliberations clothed in words I had heard so many times from him, "but yet on the other hand, they go on fighting against it—or at least ignoring it. I mean even the first step—you'd think—some of you people, it doesn't even occur to you. The first thing you could do is just remember every day to thank your mother. That simple thing—giving thanks to Mother Earth—every time you eat, every time you walk on the grass. Well, that may not be the first step really, for most of these establishment people. The first step is to stop—stop ripping off the Earth. But when you talk meditation, that don't mean sittin' in the dark trying to space out—not to me, anyway. We tell our people not to do that. In fact we could warn you, you don't just sit down and close your eyes and open up in some kind of passive way and say, 'Well, here I am, take me away,' or whatever."

"Then what are the steps?" another asked.

"That's what I gave you, what I just told you. If you don't think you're ripping off the Earth, or abusing the land, maybe you're not paying attention to how you live. That's the first step. Then every time you take a bite to eat, or even a

breath of air, you give thanks, and it goes on on some level—
it becomes a habit. And every time you take anything from the
Earth—food, air, clothing, anything—you give something in
return. So meditation works like that. It's not for getting
something personal for your little old self—it's a kind of
recognition and giving back. Then if you want to sit down and
meditate, at least you'll know where your head is at. What's
the point in sitting down and just throwing your mind in neutral? And then you get up and check your watch to see how
long you've been at it and you get to tell everyone, 'Oh, I do
meditate quite a bit, and I do it pretty regular.' Well, so what?
Then you just go back to the way you always were? Sittin' in
some so-called altered state every now and again, and then
goin' right back to the same unconscious way of livin'?

"So, if you want to know our thoughts on meditation, the
steps go to more and more consciousness—not into uncon-
sciousness. Our people in our traditional way, we can walk or
stand or sit—it doesn't make any difference—but we're on
the land, the real world. That's the real connection, and it
goes on from there."

Everyone appeared attentive and thoughtful. People were
jotting down occasional words or phrases—more as a gesture
of acceptance, I thought, than out of fear of forgetting.

"It goes on to where you get free of your little self. Maybe
you're sittin' under a tree and there's an eagle circlin'
above—so you tilt your head and look up. Next thing, someone's lookin' down from away, way up, and you can see hills
and meadows going on forever and hundreds of trees—and
there's that little person, sittin' under one of them. And
there's nothing like which one's you. That's not the point—it
makes no difference about you."

People stopped writing and looked up at Rolling Thunder.

"So once you give up on your seekin' and seekin' and forget about your little ol' personal experience, you might say
you understand something about meditation."

There was a long silence.

"Well, we mentioned we might arrange to have a sunrise

ceremony out here. So we might do that tomorrow morning, right out here on the grounds. That would be a step right there."

•   •   •

An equally small group gathered for the sunrise. They came down one by one and peered at each other through the darkness. They stood with their hands in their pockets or strolled about on the concrete slab between the building and the parking lot and said very little. Rolling Thunder appeared with only a few of his people, carrying the ceremonial paraphernalia in a metal wastecan from one of the rooms. They took out some feathers and a couple bags of tobacco, and, with paper and sticks, made a fire in the wastecan.

"You can all gather 'round here," Rolling Thunder said, lighting his pipe. "Just make a sort of semicircle around here this way, so's we face east." One of the young men held out a bag of tobacco so that everyone could take a pinch. Rolling Thunder stepped up to the fire. For a moment he stared at the wastecan. The meek little blaze barely came up to the top of it. He looked down at his feet and tapped the concrete with the heel of his boot. He puffed on his pipe, raised his head to the sky, and cleared his throat. "To the East where the sun rises. To the North where the cold comes from. To the South where the light comes from. To the West where the sun sets. To the Father Sun. To the Mother Earth." He went on for a moment, speaking too softly to be understood and then sprinkled his tobacco into the burning wastecan.

Then he took a few backward steps. "Now each one of you, startin' from this side, you can step up and offer your tobacco. You can say something out loud, if you like, or just speak to your own self—it makes no difference. Just be brief and be careful. Whatever you say now, that's the way it's going to be."

"Just be brief" was good advice: The sky over the Rincon Mountains to the east began to glow a soft rosy pink even as

◑

the last of our group stepped up to the wastecan. In these sorts
of ceremonies, I knew, the timing is supposed to work out.

Rolling Thunder could not help but refer to that wastecan,
and to "all this concrete" as well, even as he proceeded with
the ceremonial prayers. It may have been an apology, in part,
for petitioning the Great Spirit from our somewhat less than
hallowed setting. But it was also an impulsive venting of his
own discontent with what most everyone called progress.
"Here we are trying to follow our sacred ways standin' here
on this concrete because everyone sees fit to have their gatherings in lifeless places safely shielded from anything that
might be alive or natural. Well, the day will come when whatever it is that's s'posed to be livin' here—if it's even some tiny
little weeds—will break through and do away with all this
concrete and have their life again the way it was intended.
And those of us who hold no hostility to nature's ways and
creatures—why, we'll welcome it!"

His words and manner brought me back to that place in the
long, low rolling hills of Nevada where hundreds of piñon and
juniper trees had just been ripped from the Earth by Cater-
pillar tractors dragging spiked anchor chains. These trees
and all the diverse living things that had been growing on this
land lay scattered all over the ground slowly dying, and
Rolling Thunder's words had been for them. It had been
something like a funeral.

This was the first time I had attended a sunrise ceremony
around a wastecan in a parking lot. But every ceremony I had
ever seen—by Rolling Thunder or Mad Bear or any of their
people—had been offered, at least in part, as a healing for
Earth and Nature. So it must have been throughout the centuries, and I could suppose that only the tone was different in
the ancient ceremonies that took place before there was such
fear and sadness. None here were utterly opposed to any sort
of progress. Rolling Thunder himself had come here of his
own will and at his own expense—at 55 miles per hour over
miles of concrete highway. What is the appropriate balance
between the rights of life and nature and our pursuit of our

human adventures? If these traditional ceremonies, wherever they could endure, did not provide the answer, they certainly attended to the question. Here on this concrete we had found a most appropriate place for such a ceremony.

•   •   •

All of Rolling Thunder's entourage (with the exception of his wife, Spotted Fawn, and two young "scouts" whom he had posted in the audience) joined him on the stage. Rolling Thunder announced that his group wished to present some opening "welcome" songs that would be appropriate in this public setting only if they were not photographed or recorded. Thus, he warned, two of his scouts would be walking about to check up on everyone. His singers circled a large drum that they beat in unison as they performed the several songs they had prepared for the occasion. When the songs were over they remained in their places and Rolling Thunder stepped up to the microphone. "Well, first I better say a little something about these songs and their meanin'," he began.

I only heard the beginning of his talk. Someone came down the aisle, tapped me on the shoulder, and escorted me to a waiting telephone. It was Mad Bear in New York. "Hey, what's the scene down there, anyways?" he questioned. "You oughta see what I went through trying to track you down on the phone!"

"Rolling Thunder's giving his talk just now. They called me out of the auditorium."

"Oh, so that's it. First I got transferred, then I had to start all over again. Well, maybe you want to go back and listen."

But his voice sounded urgent and I knew he was hoping not to have to wait. "No, it's okay, I had to come a ways to get to the phone here."

"Well, let me tell you what's up and you can get back to me when you can. I've got some news. I mean this is really some news! There's going to be a big, important meeting at the United Nations and Beeman Logan and I have been invited to

attend. It's not an official U.N. function. It's a spiritual meeting held in conjunction with U.N. Day coming up here on the
twenty-fourth of October. It's sponsored by the Temple of Understanding, and it's called a spiritual summit. Well, it's the
Fifth Spiritual Summit is what it is. The first one was in Cal-
cutta long time ago, I knew about that. But it hasn't happened
each and every year. Anyways, this is going to be big—religious leaders from all over the world—the five major religions
of the world. Well, that's the way they talk about it, but we've
been informed they want us there—the Indian people. They
contacted Beeman Logan first, 'cause he's a chief and I guess
somebody there knew about him—and he contacted me.
Maybe this is an opening door for us."

"It sounds good," I responded. "I've heard a lot about Indian efforts to communicate to or through the United Nations."

"Of course, this is not a political thing. It's a spiritual
thing—a very high level spiritual thing. They say they want to
acknowledge the Native American religion as the sixth major
religion. Well, they can call it a religion if they want to. Sometimes it works out that way for us. Anyways, we'll be part of
the spiritual delegation to the United Nations. So I was thinking, you know, it might be good if you could be there. Maybe
you could be there with us. Do you think you could arrange
it? I mean, we'll have to figure how we're all going to cover
it—the expenses and all—but right now the main thing is your
plans. This is coming up pretty quick here."

"Well, let me get back to you. I can call you back tomorrow—maybe even later today."

"Yeah, I know. They called you out, and you're missing
your conference—and it's R.T. talking at that. Listen, see if
you can talk to R.T. about this. I wanted him to get this news.
I'm hoping he'll show up too. But if you can make it, you'll be
with us, okay? You can accompany the Iroquois delegation. I
gotta let you get back to that talk."

But I did not hurry back to the lecture. I used that time
and that phone to do some fund-raising. I knew we needed

help to cover transportation, food, and lodging for the Indian participants. I was armed with little more than Mad Bear's own words, but I got at least a few pledges from acquaintances on both coasts who had helped with projects in the past. I returned to the auditorium in time to hear Rolling Thunder's last sentences and a couple more songs from his young men who had apparently sat motionless on the stage during the entire talk. I was also in time to catch Rolling Thunder to make arrangements for the evening. I would meet him at his room well ahead of his scheduled session with Olga Worrall so that we could talk about United Nations Day and the Fifth Spiritual Summit.

That evening, as soon as I had relayed "the good news" from Mad Bear, Rolling Thunder called Mad Bear himself and spoke with him directly. Spotted Fawn and I sat quietly and listened.

"It's pretty sudden," Spotted Fawn pondered quietly. "It takes a lot for us to go on the road this way—especially if we take along all these mouths to feed and people to take care of. It'll take us a while to recover from this trip. Of course, we'll get something, but not what it costs us to travel this way."

"He wants to talk with you," Rolling Thunder said, handing me the phone.

"Listen, I just had a good talk with R.T. I think he's going to go. Don't say anything yet—he may not sound too sure just now. But this is his sort of thing too, you know. He won't be able not to go, you know what I mean?"

"I contacted a few people this morning," I started, "about raising . . ."

"Yeah, I know. But we can talk about that later. Is R.T. right there with you?"

"Yes, I'm here in their room."

"Well, don't talk about it anymore with them right now, okay? Just let it stew a bit. He has his own way of looking into things and working things out. Anyways, since I talked to you this morning, I got all the papers here. They sent them in the mail—all the information here. This is really big. '*One Is the*

Human Spirit,' they're calling this thing. I got back to them
to give them the names of our party. So I told them about you.
Well, I gave them your name. I said you're not one of our Iroquois people, and they asked what your function is. I told
them you're supposed to be a kind of liaison guy—is that
okay?"

Spotted Fawn tapped me on the shoulder. "I don't want to
be early, but I don't want to be late," she whispered. In a moment we were on our way to Olga's room. Rolling Thunder
had brought only his immediate family: his wife, Spotted
Fawn, and his son, Spotted Eagle. Olga had placed a mezuzah
on the door frame outside her room. Spotted Fawn checked
her watch (it was precisely eight o'clock) and knocked softly.

Olga seemed different. She was dressed in a long gown and
looked formal—almost stately. She spoke a few words in a
foreign language—Russian, perhaps, and then gave her welcome in English. It felt like a temple in this room—as though
many unseen preparations had been made. It was all like a
ritual from the very beginning. Olga greeted and seated each
of the four of us, one by one, warmly grasping hands and
speaking slowly and softly. The chairs had been pulled up toward the bed to make a sort of circle. Olga sat beside Rolling
Thunder, placed an open hand gently against the side of his
head, and held it there for a long time, looking as though she
were ready to listen.

Rolling Thunder remained his usual stern and stoic self.
He sat calmly but said nothing, and Spotted Fawn spoke on
his behalf. Olga listened and nodded. Her manner was so empathetic and comforting that tears began to come from Spotted Fawn's eyes. Sound and motion stopped and there was
only stillness. Olga sat with her hands over Rolling Thunder's
ears, but what was really happening was not visible to my
eyes. My thoughts wandered, and even time stood still, it
seemed. Something about Olga's intense but peaceful concen-
tration induced a steady flow of imagery in my mind. When it
was over, I realized nearly an hour had passed and I had
hardly been aware of watching. Rolling Thunder sat motion-

less. He was without expression—staring blankly into space.

Spotted Fawn was still silently weeping, and Spotted Eagle sat with his eyes closed. Olga took Spotted Eagle's hands in hers and he opened his eyes with a start. But she spoke calmly. "You yourself can help your father, and many others as well."

"This has gone on for so long," Spotted Fawn said, her voice barely a whisper. "We don't seem to be able to overcome it. R.T. has tried so hard. It gets worse. Sometimes I think he may lose his hearing."

"No," Olga replied softly. "No." She placed a hand on Spotted Fawn's cheek and gently turned her head. "Look," she said, diverting Spotted Fawn's attention to Spotted Eagle, "these are healing hands, see here. This man is a potential healer. This should be recognized so this can be developed." She looked at Spotted Eagle. "Do you recognize this?"

He did not answer.

"Say something!" she prodded.

Spotted Eagle looked away. "So, R.T.! How you feeling there? Can you hear any better?"

"Yeah, okay. I don't know now. Pretty good, I guess."

Olga responded to him—but she watched Spotted Fawn. "Give it time. Give it time. You'll not lose your hearing. Your hearing will improve. We shall see. Now we'll just sleep on it."

We returned to their room, and I sat with them for a while. We talked about their plans—about New York, United Nations Day, and other things. Rolling Thunder spoke only enough to change the subject whenever any mention was made of his ears. Mostly, he listened. He looked pleased—as though he were enjoying some noticeable change in his hearing.

CHAPTER FOUR

"One Is the Human Spirit"

*"The Indian people can help . . . and give great power . . .
when it comes to enhancing . . . the unity of minds. . . . This
is our gift."*

◗ I arrived in New York City nearly two
weeks before United Nations Day and reserved a couple of
rooms in the Lexington Hotel near Grand Central Station.

"Well, we may need more rooms than that," Mad Bear told
me on the phone. "Beeman can stay with me, but then there'll
be a few more people. I'm bringin' a man from Six Nations
Reserve—up Canada side—you can meet him when we get
there. And then you know that Anyas? That young fellow I
showed you his picture? He'll be coming down as our helper.
We need an assistant, you know, when we carry our medicine.
And what about R.T.? Did you get a room for him, or no?"

"I've talked with Rolling Thunder since we were out in
Tucson, and he and Spotted Fawn are definitely coming. But
they'll be bringing Grandfather David and I think a few of

their own people. I didn't know what arrangements to make for them."

"Look, you better line up at least a half a dozen rooms over there, just to be on the safe side. I'd like to try and have all our Indian people together, you know what I mean? Right there in the same place."

I "lined up" the "half a dozen rooms" just as he requested.

"You didn't need to come way out here to meet us," Mad Bear said, as soon as his smiling face appeared through the gate at La Guardia Airport. "I know my way all over this whole city. I can get from anywhere to anywhere, though I don't particularly enjoy it, to tell you the truth."

"But you like to brag about it, is it?" Beeman chuckled. And then he grinned at me as though expecting my greeting.

"How are you?" I said, shaking his hand. "It's good to see you again."

"Yep," he answered simply.

They introduced me to the others—"Three of our relations from up North"—as Mad Bear put it. Anyas I had recognized from his picture. Then there was Alex from Six Nations who was perhaps nearly Mad Bear's age and a somewhat younger man they called Crow.

"Sorry we were delayed coming out," Mad Bear said. "We had to get our outfits in shape, and our medicine. And Anyas here, he's a kind of guard—for our medicine and whatnot— so we had to complete some ceremonies so he could handle his duties."

"Let's get outa these crowds," Beeman said. "It's like a three-ring circus in this place."

"Three-ring circus, is it?" Mad Bear grinned. "Well, like they say, you ain't seen nothin' yet."

"Do you have any other luggage?"

"No, that's why we packed up these carry-on bags, so's we could walk right on outa here."

I had marveled more than once at Mad Bear's ability to get books, papers, toiletries, several changes of clothes, and his full Indian regalia including his Iroquois hat and feathers all

into one medium-sized satchel. It seemed all the others had
done the same. It made sense, since there were a number of
us, to take a taxi rather than the airport bus; and we waited
at the curb for a Checker cab with fold-down seats so that the
six of us could ride together.

Mad Bear sat up front. He had a hard time getting in and
out of a backseat and he needed more room than any two of
us. "Toidy-toid and Toid!" he called out in a loud voice, as we
pulled away from the curb.

"Right!" said the driver.

Mad Bear laughed and slapped his forehead. "No, no, just
kidding. We're going to the Lexington Hotel. What street's
that at, Doug?"

"I know where it's at," the driver exclaimed, "and it's not
Third Avenue. It's Fourth. Lexington Avenue's Fourth Avenue."

"You know, you're right," Mad Bear allowed, still chuck-
ling. "You are coitainly right at that."

"I know I'm right," said the driver. "I ain't drivin' cab no
fifteen years for nuthin' here."

"Why you talkin' funny, Bear?" Beeman asked, in a serious tone.

"We're supposed to look like we're from Brooklyn!" Mad
Bear whispered. "So don't go and sperl it!"

"Where abouts you people really from?" the driver wondered.

"Australia," Mad Bear replied. "But we're really trying to
keep it secret. We're some of those mysterious aborigines you
might have heard about." He turned around and winked at
me, holding his hand over his mouth. "Do you think you can
keep it under your hat?"

"Yeah, why not?" said the driver. "Who'm I gonna tell?"

We had signed in at the front desk and showed Mad Bear
and Beeman to their room.

"When do we eat?" Anyas asked.

"Eat!" Mad Bear exclaimed. "How can you think of food at
a time like this?"

"That don't sound like you, Bear," Beeman remarked. "But don't worry about food," he assured Anyas. "We won't be passing up any meals as long as Bear's around. Fact, we'll probably get in a few extra here and there."

"Look, give us a few minutes to wash up and change clothes," Mad Bear suggested, "like twenty, thirty minutes, then just come back and knock on our door."

But Anyas and I had barely settled in our room when the phone rang. "Hey whataya think of this? I figured out how to work this thing. Anytime I wanna contact you guys, I just call you direct, room to room, right on the phone. Just like uptown, isn't it? Anyways, come on over. We're sittin' here waitin' for you."

They were sitting in their room with their door wide open and their window raised, and Mad Bear was dressed in his complete traditional regalia. "Don't close the door," he said. "I need the air in here."

"Bear, what're you all dressed up now for?" Anyas wondered.

"Well, I put this on to straighten it out, it was kinda mashed up in my bag. It'll straighten right out on me here, and then I'll hang it up. Where are the others? That's right, they're in their own room. I gotta ring them separate. Hey, Beeman, you wanna try out this room-to-room telephone system?"

"No, Bear, I don't wanna try it out."

Just then the other two showed up at the door. "Hey, Bear, whatcha doin' with your costume on? We going to have another ceremony or something?"

"Look, I'm just trying to get this thing in shape. Come on in here and have a seat—an' leave the door open."

Beeman lay back on his bed and folded his arms under his head. "Shape, that's a good one," he chuckled. "What kinda shape you hopin' for Bear? Looks like you're stuck with the shape you got!"

"Well, you did all right here, Doug," Mad Bear went on. "These three rooms are just the ticket for the six of us. And then R.T. and them, they'll have those others. But we're going to need more, you know. There's more coming."

"We're going to need more money somehow," I started, "this is all going to . . ."

"I want to reserve a room for this young woman, this Iroquois woman we're bringing down. She's a dreamer and she sees a lot. She kinda helps us in that way, and we need her around at times like this. Her name's Sandy. It'll be Sandy and her little boy, because he'll have to come with her. See, it'll all work out. Even the money part. We'll just occupy all these rooms and somehow it'll have to work out, right?"

In our meeting that evening, I learned more about how Beeman Logan had been contacted by one of the people who was helping with the coordinating of this spiritual summit. Beeman had contacted Mad Bear and Mad Bear had contacted me and several others including some of his own people. Through me he had gotten in touch with Rolling Thunder and Rolling Thunder had contacted Grandfather David. I got the impression, in hearing how all this unfolded, that it was the well-known Sufi leader, Pir Vilayat, who had initiated the process that led to the American Indian presence at this affair. The man who had called Beeman had been in touch with him before on some other occasion, and now one of his daughters was a participant in Pir Vilayat's "Cosmic Dance," which they were preparing to perform at this conference.

I recalled how Mad Bear had described the four previous spiritual summits when he had contacted me out in Tucson. He had told me about the "recognized" five major religions of the world and the increasing importance of mutual understanding and communication among them. By some sort of general and mutual reckoning, there were said to be five major religions on the Earth: Buddhism, Christianity, Hinduism, Judaism, and Mohammedanism. The sacred way of the Native people of this hemisphere was a theology in its own right, I knew, as ancient and vast and major as any other. But it was indeed something other than any of these other five religions.

It was good, it seemed to me, and right, that the Native

tribes of the world should begin to be recognized by the world at large through an event such as this. It was more than a matter of civil rights and charity—more, even, than the survival of a race and a culture. It was a matter of the sharing of primary and fundamental experience and knowledge for the benefit of the planet.

I learned also, on this night, that Beeman and Mad Bear had spoken with organizers and had arranged to offer an opening prayer and blessing on the first of the three days of events to be held at the Cathedral of St. John the Divine prior to the official United Nations reception on U.N. Day.

"It's only right that it be done this way," Mad Bear said. "And it'll mean a lot to the power of this occasion. The Indian people can help a lot in this way, and give great power and potential to all the rest—especially when it comes to enhancing the gathering together and the unity of minds of the various different people. This is our gift. This can be our offering if we would be used and acknowledged for it. It is especially important for this spiritual summit that we do it as it should be done. The Native Americans are the hosts of this land, and the Iroquois are the keepers of this Northeastern gate. It has always been that way, and it always will—or should. It has always been our place to welcome others from the four directions and from across the great waters—to welcome visitors to this land and give them our blessings. That's the way it was meant to be and still is meant to be."

"Yep," said Beeman, nodding his head. "That's our sacred instructions. And we're willing and able to be the unifying people. The very first organized unification of sovereign states originated here with the Iroquois people. And the United Nations headquarters stands to this day on the ancestral land of the Iroquois. And that's not by chance, neither. That's the way it was meant to be. So we have to carry out our offering and welcoming and we have to get hold of some container or some vessel so we can have our sacred fire, however small it might be—right up on the stage—right there in the gathering place."

"That's right," Mad Bear agreed. "We'll look into that first thing tomorrow, and it'll be taken care of."

On the following morning, Rolling Thunder arrived with Grandfather David Monongye, Spotted Fawn, and several others. Later, two more elders from Hopiland arrived—Thomas Banyaka and a man called Harold who Mad Bear told me was a member of the One Horn Society and a custodian of records and prophesies. Then came some more of Mad Bear's friends—a few of his younger Iroquois "relations." By the first day of the week of events leading up to United Nations Day, I had rented a dozen rooms, and nearly twice that many Indians walked in and out through the lobby in their colorful regalia.

The three-day program of performances, speeches, and panel discussions began with the American Indian blessing offered on the stage of the giant hall of the Cathedral of St. John the Divine by the Iroquois delegation. On the platform stood Chief Beeman Logan of the Onondaga Nation, Mad Bear of the Tuscarora, Alex Jameson of the Mohawk, Anyas Smoke of the Seneca, and others. The ceremonial fire burned in an old-fashioned cast-iron cauldron partly rusted with age.

Beeman Logan spoke in his native tongue, and only a few of the hundreds attending here could have understood what he said. But this was not a speech or a performance: It was a prayer—a communication to the Great Spirit.

After the Iroquois ceremony, I sat with Mad Bear and Beeman among the American Indian delegation. What followed was a performance by an all-female koto orchestra from Japan. Twelve middle-aged women marched up to the platform carrying their kotos like trays in front of them and sat on their knees in three neat rows. They sat stone still until the hall was completely quiet and then bowed in unison and began to play. It sounded as though twelve people were playing one koto—or, rather, as though one person were playing twelve kotos. They were twelve ladies with twelve white gowns, twelve instruments, and one mind.

Anyas, who was sitting directly in front of me, turned

around in his chair as they filed off the stage. "What kinda music did they say that was?"

"Well, it's Japanese. Those instruments are kotos."

"I mean what's the name of the music?"

"I don't know—it's traditional Japanese koto music—probably quite ancient."

"I'd like to get some records of that stuff. It sounds good—like some of our own traditional music in some way."

The twelve ladies stood and filed off the stage with elegant grace and precision. Then, with only a little shuffling and re-arranging, there appeared before us a panel of five speakers, seated in a row behind a long table with several microphones. These were also from Japan—mostly monks, it appeared to me. One appeared to be a Zen monk in gray and black robes with a very broad, bald head and a gentle face. Then there were two others from perhaps different Buddhist orders (though they wore somewhat similar robes). These three spoke in turn—in English—giving greetings from themselves and from all whom they represented, offering words of encouragement and unity, and making some humbly stated generalities about the commonalities, in both essence and purpose, of all the world's religions. The fourth man said nothing at all. He only turned to look at the small person in the business suit, sitting somewhat stiffly at the end of the table.

This last man's head was not shaved like a monk's, but he was nearly bald anyway. He wore glasses that made him look strict and old-fashioned. His speaking seemed old-fashioned too, at least to me, and not very impressive. He spoke Japanese in a manner with which I had become familiar in my many years in Asia. It sounded like the slow, formal, old-fashioned form of speech with lots of throaty "ah's" and "ahems." The man on his right was his interpreter, and he repeated each sentence in English, one at a time, carefully including a representative number of "ah's" and "ahem's." The interpreter looked a little younger and a little larger and he had a little more hair; but he also wore a business suit, and he spoke in the same slow, halting manner.

◐

Mad Bear was impressed and stuck an elbow gently in my ribs. "That man with the glasses up there, that's a very powerful man. I mean he's got real power—real power. Can you see his serpents?"

"Serpents?" I asked.

"That man has serpents about his head. Don't you see? You should try and see, because you might be gettin' close to seeing these things."

Sometimes in these instances, I wanted so badly to "see" what Mad Bear saw that it was almost a temptation not to admit the truth. But I told him I could see nothing of what he was describing. It was not that I wanted to impress either him or myself; I just wanted to share in the experience.

"Well, it's a rare thing to see a man like that one. He has serpents going all around his head. Boy, I get a strong sense of his power and his connections, and I would sure like to talk with him. Sometime we'll get the chance. You watch, we'll get a chance to meet that man."

That evening, when we returned to the hotel, we found Sandy and her little boy waiting for us in the lobby. I wondered how she had known to come here. Mad Bear had told me there was no phone at her reservation home and that they would have to get a message to her. There had not been time for mail to reach her—and even if they had managed somehow to send a call, how did she know to find this hotel? As always, it was pointless to press the question.

We procured yet another room for Sandy and her three-year-old son and, as soon as they were checked in, we gathered once again in Mad Bear's and Beeman's room. The Iroquois contingency had grown. Mad Bear sat in the largest chair in front of the open window and Beeman sat beside him. Alex, Crow, and I sat in chairs we brought from our rooms, and Anyas and the other young people sat cross-legged on the beds and wherever they could find a space on the floor. Bundy, Sandy's little boy, stayed on the floor just in front of his mother, looking serious, and he neither moved nor made a sound.

◑

Mad Bear lit his pipe and leaned back and Sandy set her mind to her work. She described the events that had taken place at the cathedral as though she had been there, adding her own comments and interpretations, giving her in-depth perceptions of the people who had spoken and various other people who were there. Then she offered some insights regarding events to come. Mad Bear and Beeman began to ask questions about these events, about what was expected of them and what might be expected from the other delegations. She responded to each question without hesitation—either giving a direct answer or promising to supply the requested information after "looking into it."

"Are you a medicine woman?" asked one teenage boy who was sitting on the floor.

"I wouldn't say I'm a medicine woman," she responded. "At least not until I pass the age of seventy. Then I might say it."

Over the days that followed, Sandy did not go to the cathedral with the rest of us—at least not in any manner that I could observe—yet, every evening when we returned, she related her many observations regarding that day just as though she had been there with us.

• • •

The first day of the program was filled with speaking presentations. Sometimes the speakers sat in panels, but mostly they presented alone. There was a spectacular display of rabbis, priests, nuns, monks, and swamis moving about in this enormous cathedral, all in their exuberant robes and regalia. The Dalai Lama had been invited to attend, but there had been objection on the part of the official Chinese delegation to the United Nations, or so it was speculated. But there were other Tibetan monks and lamas here. Margaret Mead and Jean Houston were cochairpersons for the event—and they had both spoken at the opening-night reception. There was a compassionate and moving presentation by Mother Teresa. There were impressive-looking spiritual leaders who were not familiar to me but who were obviously people of great note and authority. All the American Indian delegates walked about in their full regalia and seemed to generate considerable attention and curiosity. Perhaps it was partly that, until this date, there had been little Native American presence in such global occasions—but it may also have been that these religious people knew something of the oppressive atrocities committed onto American Indians over centuries of history in the name of religion. Most of the speakers, though many were from distant places and no doubt little involved with the cultural affairs of our country, tendered very pointed recognition of the American Indian delegation, often saying something like, "We are all pleased to finally acknowledge this great and ancient people and culture as a major world religion."

As the program unfolded, the participants formed various groups concerned with specific tasks or issues, and I had more opportunity to browse around and talk with people. The summit conference created the Plenary Committee for the Spiritual Advisory Council to the United Nations, and Mad Bear was selected to be the American Indian representative to this committee. Except for our comings and goings, or when we were back at the hotel, he was often out of sight. It had become my cause—or perhaps it was my job—to involve myself with the financial concerns of the American Indian contingency—and I appreciated having the time to do it. I also enjoyed talking with Alex Jameson, an Iroquois colleague of Mad Bear's from the Six Nations Reservation in Canada. As our conversations became more interesting to him, he increasingly pursued them, and we often sat together for meals or walked together around the cathedral. He wanted to talk about the sacred objects and deities of distant cultures and about yoga, meditation, and karma. He was a quiet and gentle person, full of questions, and full of listening—but I knew that he possessed an awareness and a caring that was itself an offering and a teaching.

Once Alex and I climbed the long stairway to the front entrance of the cathedral to find a group of people standing at

the top of the stairs gathered around two young men from India dressed in white. They carried the fly whisks and wore the
face masks over their mouths that typified their particular
sect. They were Jain monks. Someone had apparently
stopped them as they were about to enter the cathedral to ask
about ahimsa, a principal Jain doctrine. The onlookers appeared to be local people attending the conference—most of
them college age. And there was a man in a large black hat
standing slightly aside and listening with a frown on his face.
We had seen him before inside the cathedral—several times
trying to interrupt the program. He looked Indian.

"Do you know this man?" I whispered. Alex shook his
head.

"It means harmlessness, you see?" proclaimed one monk in
a rather loud voice. "We are dedicated to striving for that—
that is the only perfection one can achieve."

"It must be difficult for you in a city like this," someone
said. "I don't know how much you've seen here. There's a lot
of violence . . ."

"Yes, we know but, you see, it is pointless, achieving nothing," said the other. "Violence only begets more violence. We
believe in a goal of absolute nonviolence . . ."

Suddenly, the man in the black hat sprang toward them in
a threatening manner. "Hey!" he shouted. "I like violence!"

Quickly Alex stepped forward and stood very close to the
man's face. "If you're going to talk like that," he said gently,
shaking his head, "or even think like that, I don't know how
you're going to be able to stay up here at the top of these
stairs."

Instantly, the man stiffened and looked over his shoulder,
nearly falling backward. Alex was between him and the
monks, and the man was standing with his boot heels at the
very edge of the top stair. Alex stepped back and the man
turned around and hurried down the stairs. We did not see
him again that day.

• • •

◑

The proceedings at the Cathedral of St. John the Divine were
as much an ecumenical service as a conference or a meeting.
Beyond the elegant formalities of presentations, panels, and
papers, there was colorful ritual and ceremony.

Because the Native people's presence had been arranged at
the eleventh hour, their participation was prepared almost
extemporaneously as events unfolded. Several Native elders
were placed on the program. John Fire Lame Deer was seated
on a panel. He gave a lengthy presentation and answered
questions from the audience. It was arranged that Grandfather David would offer a Hopi prayer and blessing, and
Leonard Crow Dog, who if not an elder by virtue of age was
an elder by virtue of his lineage and leadership, would perform an opening role in Pir Vilayat's "Cosmic Dance."

In spite of what Spotted Fawn had said to me in Tucson
about the cost of being so much on the road, she and Rolling
Thunder had arrived with several of their people and had
managed to provide not only for all of them but also for
Grandfather David as well. Rolling Thunder had seen to
David's arrival and to his care, and he was concerned that
David's presence and position be acknowledged.

"Well, uh, I would do a prayer offering on behalf of our
people," David responded when Rolling Thunder arranged a
discussion with the appropriate persons. "Yeah, I'd, ah, I'd
be willing to do that. I'd like to sit right on the ground like I
do—not stand up on some stage like a speech or something—
well, just sit down and send the prayer in the right way."

In the evening, when the time came for David's offering, he
did sit down—right on the floor among the audience in front
of his chair. He had to be helped. There was a blanket for him
to sit on. His Hopi cornmeal, tobacco, pipe, and other objects
from his bag were placed appropriately before him, and he
was helped to light his pipe. Holding his sacred cornmeal, he
gave his prayer in Hopi, and he did not interpret for himself,
as I had seen him do in the past.

As I watched and listened to Grandfather David give the
prayer he had done countless times over the decades, I

thought about how this old man, now well over one hundred
years old and totally blind, had been brought nearly dead to
Rolling Thunder's Nevada home. More than a year had
passed since then, and it had been an active year for David. I
recalled Rolling Thunder's telling me that if David could continue to be who he was supposed to be, he would recover, but
that if people stopped listening to him, he would perish. Now
people were listening—and it mattered neither to them nor to
David whether they understood his Hopi-language words.
They understood David.

CHAPTER FIVE

Greenbacks, Gold, and a Bottle of Whiskey

"Now we might have a chance to do some medicine that might help out a little."

◑ Early one morning during the Fifth Spiritual Summit, Sandy knocked on Mad Bear's door and gave him an account of a dream she had had in the night. Mad Bear came excitedly down the hall to awaken me. Sandy had felt she ought to tell Mad Bear before he left for the cathedral that morning, and Mad Bear could not wait to tell me: She had dreamed of the man with the serpents about his head. "There is going to be an important opening for all of us in intercultural relations," she had told Mad Bear, "but it will be only an opening, and we will have to follow up somehow. You don't have to know who this man is, though. And you won't have to look for him when you get there this morning. I see him coming to you—he'll approach you directly and initiate the whole thing. This will be the first thing that happens when you enter the cathedral this morning. We don't know who this man is, but he's a somewhat slight man—an Oriental man, I think. He has a suit and he wears glasses, and in my dream I see this man with spirit snake-beings circling about his head."

Mad Bear, of course, did know who this man was, and he could not stop talking about him—all the way through our hasty breakfast and our uptown trip in the van. "We know who he is," he went on repeating, "and now we'll find out something more about him. We were hoping something like this would happen, right? Didn't I tell you?" He was certain that the man from Japan would approach him as he entered the cathedral—the first thing to happen, just as Sandy predicted. The moment the van pulled up to the curb, Mad Bear hopped out and bounded up the stairs.

The man from Japan was nowhere in sight. The first thing that happened the moment we arrived was something other than what Sandy had predicted, and something quite different from what any of us could have expected. There were three angry men standing in the lobby waiting for the first Indians to arrive, and they confronted Mad Bear and Beeman Logan in a most ungentle manner.

"Now you'll just hold it right here, and we're going to talk about this," they said holding several large sheets of paper in front of Beeman and Mad Bear. Somehow it felt as though under their coats they wore holsters with pistols. "This is going to stop, this is going to be stopped right here and now. This is no light matter, when the United Nations is involved like this, and we are going to take this very seriously—very seriously, indeed!"

I looked over Mad Bear's shoulder. "These were found outside here," they went on, not allowing anyone a chance to respond. "Right outside here on the grounds. We don't know who is responsible, but we're going to find out. Where else have your people been putting these things around? If you know, you say so. We'll find out, and we're going to get to them, and it's all over. It's all over for you people."

Mad Bear now had one of the papers in his hand. He was

looking at it with a frown. They were hastily made up posters calling for a mass American Indian demonstration of protest at the United Nations on United Nations Day.

"Now, we just can't have this kind of thing here at the cathedral or the U.N. or anywhere else. If this is your attitude, if this is the way you operate, why you people are just going to have to leave here. I'm afraid I'm going to have to ask you people . . ."

Mad Bear finally interrupted. "I have to tell you that none of our Indian people made these signs or had anything to do with this thing. None of our people who are participating in this spiritual summit have anything like this in mind or would even consider such an idea. This is directly contrary to our purpose. We're spiritual leaders with spiritual responsibilities, and we're here on a spiritual mission. We are all pleased to be here and we're pleased with the way things are going. We disapprove of this thing as strongly as you do. It hurts us more than anybody. In fact, it would be my guess that this might have been something aimed against us, to work against our purpose here. I think I might even have some idea who could be behind this, though I shouldn't say just yet."

The men were reluctant to be convinced. They looked at Mad Bear suspiciously, as though he were making some skillful sort of cover-up. Two young Indians who had arrived with us had been walking out around the cathedral grounds and the surrounding streets while this talk was continuing, and they returned with many more such posters. The expressions on the faces of the three men turned now to genuine anger, and the man who was doing all the talking started up again. "Now, see, this is continuing to go on. You people just may be arrested! This is inciting . . ."

"But we're not the ones doing this . . ."

"This is inciting riots and you people are subject to arrest . . ."

Up walked the Japanese man with the business suit, the bald head, and the glasses. He had been nowhere in sight, but he seemed to know exactly what had been said. His words

sounded stern and insistent, and immediately, his interpreter
put them into English. This time his interpreter was a young,
attractive, Japanese woman. "These people have told you
they're not involved with this thing, and why do you go on
with it? The Indians are not causing any problems here, and
you are causing problems for them. Now, we're about to have
an important private meeting, so stop this unnecessary talk
and leave the Indian delegates alone!"

Somehow, this was totally effective. Apparently, there was
something about this man's presence or position that was per-
suasive enough to close the matter, and the three men simply
turned and walked away. (Or, I wondered, could they perhaps have seen the serpents?)

"Now that that's over," he said to Mad Bear, through his
interpreter, "I would like to have a talk with you before this
morning's activities get under way."

"I knew this was going to happen," Mad Bear beamed.

"Of course," he replied. "Let us quickly find a place to
talk."

We found a small room in the basement with about a dozen
folding chairs stacked in one corner. We arranged seven
chairs in a circle, closed the door, and sat down. At first, the
talk was rather trivial. Polite greetings were exchanged, and
then introductions. The man from Japan had the title of rev-
erend, at least in English. He was a high Shinto priest whose
headquarters was in Tokyo. The young Japanese woman was
a journalist who lived and worked in New York City.

Mad Bear said a few words about Beeman Logan and himself and gave the names of the rest of us.

"Now," said the Shinto priest, "there is something I am interested to say to you and your group."

"First, I'd like to make just one comment here," Mad Bear
interrupted. He looked around at the rest of us, as though
about to share something personal. "I've noticed this man
from the very beginning and was hoping for this chance to
talk. This man has power, and I see something powerful about
this man. This is just for the information of the rest of you

here." He looked at the priest directly. "And one of our people—you may not see her with us, but she is with us—she sees many things, and she told me just this morning before we left—she spoke of you just as I had seen you—and that we would have a meeting that could be an opening door."

Mad Bear paused for the interpreter to translate. The Shinto priest nodded, understanding, but otherwise there was no reaction.

"I just wanted to say that we're sure happy to meet you and to have this chance to communicate."

"We must not be gratified," said the priest. He paused, and we sat for a moment in silence. Perhaps he was waiting for some agreement from the others. "This is a nice program here," he went on, "and we have seen so many nice people. There has been such nice pageantry and much is yet to come. We will continue to see all these beautiful costumes and ornaments. And the climax of this whole affair will be the ceremony at the United Nations on Friday morning. It will be just that, a ceremony. And if it is satisfying in itself, then it will be less than useful. We may all go home and we may say, 'Ah, we had a nice summit, and we prepared a good statement. Next year, perhaps, we can meet again.' But our work here is something other than a pleasant experience. If our work is only to be satisfied, then we should leave this place with only memories and the hope of enjoying something similar again sometime."

Mad Bear only nodded and said nothing, but his agreement was unmistakable.

"Now, what is the real purpose for which we have all gathered at this time?" the priest continued. "What is the usefulness of our encounter? What are we to do with this occasion once we have parted and gone our separate ways? We must resolve here and now to maintain this connection—to maintain the communication. We must expect to act together—in a powerful unison. So we must plan to travel continually—to meet and join forces. The duty of the religious leaders and spiritual representatives of the people is not to perform ceremonies, only. It is to guide the people to save their world. This cannot be done by any other leaders however they may hope to help. It will not be done by executives or politicians. It must be done by those who will be inclined to come together for no other purpose than to represent the hearts and minds of everyone. The divine order caring for this planet approaches us now. They are closer to this incarnate plane of our Earth than they have ever been before. Yet they require of us who are in physical form to do the physical work. It is our karma, anyway, and now it becomes our opportunity. For this we must travel—we must get together physically. We must travel because it must be done cooperatively—jointly and with teamwork among cultures. It is not to the point to communicate technologically. We must know each other. We must have close personal contact and a direct and ever-building awareness of our group unity."

Both Chief Beeman Logan and Mad Bear agreed out loud. This was indeed their work—or at least their goal—that the Shinto priest was talking about. They had long been traveling in their own country to unite their people behind this cause, and as they worked for intertribal unity, they dreamed and talked about intercultural unity. They had long striven to communicate with people of other lands through the United Nations, and they had traveled to distant shores to meet with people of many races and cultures. Mad Bear had often spoken to me about the global responsibility of all spiritual spokespersons and representatives.

"So then it is up to us," said the priest. "It is our work, and either we will do it, or it will not be done. If we can agree that this entire event—even our official reception at the United Nations on Friday—is nothing other than a stepping-stone, if we can resolve here now that we will continue after this event and this gathering has ended, then we will have succeeded in our meeting here this morning."

"Well, we can consider that accomplished," Mad Bear said. "But at some point, we are going to have to plan just how we are going to carry this out."

◖

The words of the Shinto priest had hit home with Mad Bear. No idea could be more exciting to him, I knew, than the idea of medicine people all over the planet joining forces. But to Mad Bear, it was never inappropriate to talk about the strategies and practicalities. The cooperative effort of the spiritual leaders of the world would require the wherewithal to travel and communicate, and the Indians had questions about the almost unlimited amount of money that would be needed to carry out this work. One of our party felt compelled, while they were on this subject, to speak to a more immediate problem: Many of the Indians who had barely managed to get here were now out of funds and yet had to spend the rest of the week in this big city and then somehow make it home again.

But the Shinto priest was hopeful. Money, he was certain, whatever that was to mean in the future, would definitely serve to help carry out this work and not stand in the way of it. If millions are needed to bring together this planet's healers and helpers for their collective work, then millions will appear. "And if it should require hundreds of millions," he claimed, "then hundreds of millions will appear—or if hundreds of billions, then that will become available." Whatever power and resource is required will be liberated for this purpose, he told us, as a result of the upcoming inevitable changes in the planetary economy. Something to help with the immediate needs of the Indian representatives now gathered here would become apparent tomorrow.

On that positive note, we closed our brief basement meeting, shook hands, and went upstairs to observe the day's events in the main hall of the cathedral. On the following morning, the Shinto priest took Mad Bear aside and gave him a solid gold medallion, a bottle of whiskey, and ten crisp one-hundred-dollar bills. Through his interpreter he told Mad Bear that the money needed to carry out the eventual work of which he spoke would be long in coming and yet it had already become an inevitability. The gold medallion was a special gift for Mad Bear, he said, and the money and the whiskey were for the Indians here to do with as they wished.

"Look at this!" Mad Bear exclaimed, returning to where I waited beside the front steps of the cathedral. He showed me the money, being careful to be inconspicuous. "Can you beat this? This'll go into the Indian fund. A thousand bucks! All in brand-spanking-new bills. I almost hate to hafta put it in that drawer. But what puzzles me, he gave us whiskey. A bottle of whiskey for the Indian delegation? Now that's a mystery, just what the meaning behind that is, we're going to have to put our heads together and give it some thought. I just thanked him for it, and tried to keep a straight face. Then I got to thinking about it. There might have been some purpose in it—something symbolic that he understood. Whiskey symbolized the downfall of our people, in a way, and it's responsible for weakening our culture and holding down our people even today."

"Where's the whiskey now?" I asked.

"Well, it's nowhere now. Still it might provide an opportunity of some kind."

Anyas and I made the trip back downtown to the hotel to add the money to our drawer behind the cashier's cage. When we returned to the large hall of the cathedral and took our place beside Mad Bear, the morning's proceedings had already begun. Mad Bear whispered in my ear. He had spoken with the Hopi elders, and together they had arrived at a plan that might provide some good medicine for this alcohol issue.

"But you told me the whiskey's already gone."

"Well, at the moment it is. We've put it out of existence. But we can't just leave it at that. So we'll have it back when we're ready to do our ceremony. That'll be the last thing we do here. I mean, we can't control all the booze in the world. So just to make one bottle of whiskey disappear—that doesn't serve any purpose. But now we might have a chance to do some medicine that might help out a little—at least for our people."

• • •

◐

Each day of the summit conference more delegates had arrived from out of state and out of the country. The Indian delegation had grown and we had booked nearly one dozen rooms in the Lexington Hotel. Most of the Indians brought only themselves and had no funds for food or lodging. Unlike most of the other delegates, the Indian leaders represented no organized religious order with property, status, collections, and treasuries. For many days I had busied myself with fund-raising and, fortunately, we had acquired many supporters. Participants and attendees had learned of the Indians' needs, and those I had contacted earlier by phone had mailed checks.

Sometimes people found me during the events at the cathedral and handed me donations for the "Indian fund." One day, by midday, I had received the results of several local groups' collections and, during the lunch break, I looked for Mad Bear among the crowd. "I have over a thousand dollars in my pocket," I told him. "I think I'd better go back down to the hotel and put this in the safety box."

"Okay, but then you take Anyas along with you."

"Well, I'll be okay. I thought I'd take a taxi down there and then come back on the bus or the subway."

"But still you take Anyas. That's our way—we never go alone. There's never a need to. Anyas knows that and he's used to it. That's partly what he's here for."

I looked long for Anyas, and when finally I found him, he did not want to leave. "I have to take care of this," I insisted, "and now's the time to do it, before the afternoon starts up again."

"No, I'll go," he said, "just wait, I just want to wait. I was talking to someone over here somewhere, and I got distracted."

"But you can find them as soon as we get back. It won't take too long, just down and back."

"No, that's not it. It's just that I got distracted . . ." He looked about anxiously. He seemed puzzled and disoriented.

At my urging, he left with me. I could have done this alone,

but I wanted to follow Mad Bear's wishes. We went downtown
by taxi and came back on the train. Anyas looked increasingly worried, and I questioned him. Finally he admitted to
me that he had lost Mad Bear's medicine case. It had been his
job to carry the medicine case whenever Mad Bear was moving among the people, and now Anyas had lost it. It was a
grave situation. I knew it was crucial that the medicine case
be protected and that others be protected from it. It had been
"doctored," as Mad Bear had put it, and Anyas had been doctored so that he could handle it.

"Don't tell Bear," Anyas kept saying. "We got to find it. I
know I just set it on this chair behind me when I was talking to
someone. Then I turned around and it was gone. I can't understand it. Just don't tell Bear."

"We've got to tell him," I said. "We can look, but if we
don't find it, we really have to tell him. You know what could
happen if someone got their hands on that satchel and what's
in it."

"I'm scared," he confessed. "We just gotta get it back."

But before we could find it Mad Bear found us. Anyas had
no medicine case, and immediately Mad Bear knew. He
watched Anyas as Anyas tried to explain. "Stay with him,"
Mad Bear instructed me. "Something's wrong with him, something's been done to him. I think I have a feeling what's going
on here." In a moment he was out of sight.

I stayed with Anyas until the end of the afternoon and
everyone left the cathedral, and the two of us went back to
our room. Immediately, Anyas lay down on his bed. "I don't
feel too good," he muttered. I reminded him that we all had
tickets to the closing banquet that was to begin in a couple
hours at the Waldorf-Astoria, just up the street. Anyas
jumped up, held his head as though he were dizzy, and fell
back on to the bed.

"What's the matter?" I asked.

He did not answer. He only stood up, took off his clothes,
and got under his covers. Then he got up, got dressed, and lay
back down again. There was a knock at the door. "I don't

know," Anyas mumbled. "I don't know what . . ."

"Something's wrong with Anyas," I whispered to Mad
Bear, standing in the doorway. "He keeps lying down and getting up and . . ."

Mad Bear pushed me aside and stared at Anyas and Anyas
tightly closed his eyes. Mad Bear walked up and glared at him
as though he were trying to peer right through his belly. Then
he motioned me toward the door. "Leave us a moment," he
said. "I've got to work here."

After only a few minutes, Mad Bear came out, and we went
to his room. Sitting on his bed was his medicine case. "He'll be
all right pretty quick," he told me. "But we'll let him stay in
so's he doesn't have to deal with all the people at the banquet.
Anyways, I got my bag here. I had to use a little medicine and
track it down myself. I found the guy—a white guy, and he'd
had his hands in it so I had to work on him. At first I suspected that Indian-looking guy that's been wandering around
up there looking like he's trying to cause trouble. You've seen
that guy in the big black hat? Just like in the movies. Funny
thing, nobody knows him. Between all of us here from our
various tribes, we should know just about everybody. Anyway, he may not have had anything to do with it, although I
think he's up to no good. I'm not sure if he did or not. That
young white guy had to have help some way. Somebody or
something got to Anyas—I mean, got hold of him, you know
what I'm saying. That's how he lost his bearings—or got over-
shadowed. Couple times you guys came down here right?
Maybe he seemed all right to you then, but I don't think he
could have found his way by himself. So it wasn't his fault, really. Yet, if he'd been on guard, really diligent like he's been
taught, it might not have happened. He'll learn. Eventually,
he'll be able to deal with this stuff. At least I hope so, because
he can't escape the challenge. Not with the path he's already
set out on.

"Anyway, this other young guy—and he might have some
others working with him—you know what I found out? Because he was after my medicine and I had to have quite a talk
with him. He's the guy responsible for those protest posters

that they found put up all around the cathedral. None of our Indian people had a thing to do with that—not any part of this spiritual delegation, anyway. This young white guy, he doesn't strike me as being evil, really. I had a heavy talk with him and he's leaving. I think he's sorry, in a way. He's not really mean-hearted. But I think he's disappointed too. He's after something for his own ego—power or control or what have you—a little limelight and recognition. So something's got a hold on him too. This kind of ego thing—this makes it easy. These people, when they go for power and glory and like that, they become an easy target. Then they end up serving some agenda of some other devious outfit that they're not even really part of—just being used. Most people don't know that—how it works."

• • •

The Iroquois delegation, with the exception of Anyas, walked together to the Waldorf-Astoria Hotel. A lavish banquet, held in the Waldorf's extravagant banquet room on the eve of the official United Nations Day reception, was the consummating event for this Fifth Spiritual Summit Conference. It was a monumental affair with all the religious delegations and their associates as well as hundreds of others who had bought tickets to attend. At his request, I sat beside Mad Bear—to his immediate right, as usual—while the others who had arrived with us split up to join various other tables. Our hosts were encouraging everyone to "mix it up," reminding us that this social event provided, at last, an opportunity to really get to know people from other countries and cultures. Mad Bear and I began an immediate friendship with a Hindu delegate at our table as we waited for the seats to fill.

If this was a social event, it was also an elaborate one. Enormous arrangements of roses and candles formed the centerpiece on each of the many large, round tables. At each place setting was another candle—a small, white, votive candle in a clear white cup painted: "One Is the Human Spirit." And there were printed programs listing the order of proceed-

ings including the opening prayer and blessing, the musical
entertainment, the speakers who were to offer their after-
dinner remarks, and a closing candlelight ceremony. As the
waiters began to light the centerpiece candles, someone
stepped onto the speaker's platform to instruct us that we
were to save the little votive candles—one for each person—
for the closing ceremony.

"Then what about these other candles?" Mad Bear whispered. "They're sitting right here burning in these flowers.
What kind of a setup is this?" But the lush, red roses looked
impressive, I thought to myself, and they smelled beautiful.

The first event of the evening—even before the banquet
was begun—was an Iroquois prayer conducted by Chief Beeman Logan and Mad Bear. Again, as at the beginning of the
week's events at the cathedral, the Iroquois people were recognized as the caretakers of this Northeastern land—if not in
a political sense, at least in a spiritual and historical sense.
The peoples of the Indian Nations were thus acknowledged
hosts of the peoples from the four directions and from across
the great waters. And again, after only a few introductory
words in English, they each spoke in their own languages—
because these were prayers and invocations—and there was
no translation.

Dinner music was provided by Ravi Shankar and his two
musicians and, as they began to play, the waiters began to
serve the meal. It was not long before we noticed that the candles at our table were burning our roses. Mad Bear had been
right. It was an impractical arrangement. Then the music was
momentarily interrupted and an announcement was made
from the speakers' platform that all the centerpiece candles
on all the tables should please be extinguished. "It has just
been brought to our attention," said the speaker, "that the
candles are drying out the leaves and petals of these poor,
beautiful roses, and the flames are now beginning to scorch
them. As you know, this is a meeting of compassion and understanding, and so I'm sure we ought now be willing to sacri-
fice our decorative candlelights as a decent gesture of mercy

and thoughtfulness for the roses."

"But the roses are dying, anyways!" Mad Bear called out—rather loudly, in fact, as though he hoped his voice might reach the man behind the microphone. Several heads turned. A few people nodded in acknowledgment, but most simply stared at him. "I feel like going up there to that microphone," Mad Bear said to me, "and reminding these people what they're trying so hard not to notice. We're ignoring the fact that these are not flowers here. They're pieces of flowers cut off from their roots and brought in here to die right in front of us while we're eating. People make an effort not to notice. You can sense the dying if you attend to it. It's the first thing I noticed when we walked in here—hundreds of flowers dying in this room. Well, I'm not going to say anything, but I'd sure just like to bring it to people's attention so's they'd have to think about it."

I glanced at our Hindu friend sitting beside us, recalling the many leis and garlands I had seen presented to the babas, gurus, and swamis in India—and the thousands of flower blossoms laid down in brilliant profusion along the pathways and hallways of temples and ashrams.

"Bouquets and cut flowers might not be so wrong in themselves," Mad Bear continued. "These things can be done, I guess, at least if they're done for a sacred purpose and in the right way—with an offering and devotion—and if the living plants agree. I myself gather herbs. These things can help us, but they are living beings. Well, at least somebody noticed something here, and thought about it a bit. It's just that people—most all people in the modern world—quit paying attention to living things. They make so much noise, they can't hear things like flowers. They probably wouldn't hear them anyway—they probably wouldn't even listen. People work hard to achieve insensitivity. It takes a lot of practice to build up these attention blocks. Your people actually work at this—that's what gets me!"

• • •

The week's events came to a close with a formal reception in
the United Nations building in which representatives chosen
by the conference delegates met with top U.N. officials to present their communication. Seating in the reception room was
limited to these chosen representatives, and most of the delegates and the rest of us sat in other rooms to watch the proceedings on closed-circuit television.

Since it is evident, the communication pointed out, that
what we have achieved in technological developments and in
international trade and global economy are not in themselves
sufficient to ensure the safety or well-being of either our
planet or its inhabitants, it is essential that we employ the vast
resources of our religious and spiritual experience and knowledge. The communication proposed that this international
body recognize these representative delegates as an "unoffi-
cial" advisory council attached to the United Nations as a resource for spiritual guidance.

We could see on our screens the various faces and costumes
of the delegates and officials as they made their speeches, but
Mad Bear later described to me something that the cameras
had not shown—something that, in fact, had not been noticed
by most of the officials in the room.

"You know, something weird happened in there, though it
didn't really surprise me. Just as we were getting started, this
guy shows up. You remember that strange man I pointed out
to you? He looks Indian—well, he is Indian—but none of us
know him. We still can't figure him out. Anyways, he shows
up in there. Where he came from, I mean, how he got in
there, I've got no idea."

"I know who you mean," I said. "I've seen him several
times. Alex talked to him."

"What did he say to the guy?"

"Well, he was trying to start trouble when those Jains were
up there in front of the cathedral. I guess you could say Alex
told him to leave."

"And he actually left?"

I reflected on the man in the black hat standing with his

back to the stairs. "Yeah, he left. I think he just wanted to get some attention."

"Yeah, well, the man's not nobody. I mean, whoever he is, the man's got medicine. No one had gotten up to speak yet, but a couple of our main speakers, they started coughing. I looked and spotted him and right away, I knew what he was up to. I started fishing in my pockets for my bear medicine, but I couldn't find it. I generally carry a little on me. You know, those little sticks like I gave you a piece to chew before that meeting. But I couldn't find it. Well, Swami Satchitananda, he was sitting right on the other side of me and, you know, he picked up on this whole thing. He took my arm and plunked this little jar in my hand. It was that Chinese stuff, some of that so-called tiger stuff. You may know the stuff. Comes in a little jar. Fantastic smelling—the vapors penetrate right into you."

"Tiger balm," I said.

"That's the stuff! And I knew just what to do with it. I opened the jar and handed it to the ones who needed help and told them to quick rub plenty right into their necks. You know, there's really something to that stuff. Either that or he'd done something to it. But then, I found my own medicine—just a little piece in this top pocket, and I broke it so they could share it. I told them how to bite down on it. That man gave me a hard look, and then he left—just walked out as though he'd lost interest in the whole . . ."

He stopped himself and looked around. I thought perhaps he suddenly sensed that the strange man was listening. But no one was around. "Just a minute," he said, walking away. "You wait here. They're looking for me, but they don't know where I'm at. No problem, I can find them easy!"

I waited, wondering whether that man might be doing something to Mad Bear. But when he came back, he was grinning. "Look, we gotta go. You hang around here. We got a little something we gotta take care of, and now's the time to do it—just some of our own people and the Hopis and all. We're taking Grandfather David."

I supposed it had something to do with what he had just been telling me, but I decided not to ask.

"No, it's not that," he said, responding to my thoughts. "It's that other affair we were talking about before. We've still got to deal with that thing. So, we're going to bring it back so we can send it off. That was our decision. I'd like to take you along, but then, some of the others might . . . Anyways, I'll tell you later. And you can join us this evening with Grandfather David. We're all getting together down in his room—our whole Indian delegation."

● ● ●

Old Grandfather David talked for hours that night, and the longer he talked and the later it became, the livelier David became. It seemed, in fact, that he grew younger as the night wore on. Mad Bear and I had been among the first to arrive. We had knocked on his hotel room door and were let in to wait with the few others already there while those who were caring for David were helping him to rest and dress in peace in an adjoining room. Nearly a dozen of us had crowded into his room by the time he was brought in to join us, and he had had to be carefully guided between bed, chairs, feet, and crossed legs.

It began as a group conversation. People talked about events of the past few days, about that whiskey bottle, and the ceremony on its behalf that had taken place that afternoon down by the water. The disposition of that bottle had been partly David's idea—and he had joined in the prayers with the others at the edge of the Atlantic, and administered the final invocation and cornmeal offering as they had set the bottle afloat across the great waters. It was over this very ocean, from that strange land to the east, that the Native people had first received the catastrophic "gift" of firewater. David, I knew, could not in his blindness have seen the bottle as it bobbed in the water and was taken by the undertow, but perhaps in his own mind he held the strongest vision of the ritual.

◐

That evening, at first, David joined only intermittently in
the group conversation. He sat stone still in his chair, mostly
staring into space and occasionally turning his head in the direction of the voice he was listening to. I wondered if he had
some sense of how many people were packed into his room, if
he had any mental image at all of this circumstance or, if so,
how it all "looked" to him. But somewhere in the midst of all
the chatting, he seemed to grasp that he had a room full of listeners and that many eyes were upon him, and he began to
speak. This time, it was neither a lecture nor a prayer. He
simply talked, and whatever message was conveyed was im-
plied by his manner as well as by his words.

He talked of his childhood and his earliest encounters with
"the white folks," and he talked of his wife and his own family, about his life in Hopiland, and about his many travels.
These were stories, all stories, and most of what he chose to
tell was as funny as it was true. He had, no doubt, told these
stories many times over the decades, but if anyone here had
heard them before, he or she laughed at them again. He had a
sharp sense of humor and a sharp memory as well for a man
over one hundred years of age.

Grandfather David sat up in his chair and folded his arms
across his chest and patted his shoulders with his hands.
"Well, and uh, I'm talking English too, and that's not even my
language. If I was to talk Hopi, well, you might just enjoy the
heck out of it. You'd get it from my real view of it—except, see,
you wouldn't understand it. Now, you see, well, we can all understand one another. Well, it might be a good thing, after all.

"You know, when I was a young boy, I was a hostile. That
was our label, the name we were given. That was one of my
first English words. But I didn't get the meaning. Well, I
thought it mighta meant 'peace' because, we Hopi, that's our
name for ourselves. Hopi means peace. Well, Hopi sounds a
little like hostile—but not too much. So, in English, we knew
one word, and we called ourselves the hostiles. But then,
pretty soon, see, it didn't make any sense. Well, if we were so
nice and hostile, how come they were trying to run us off?

Then later, we understood. With that 'hostile' notion, if they believed it, they could get us out and take the land, and not even share. We never heard of such a thing, and we weren't prepared for it. Yet we are still there—just where we always were, thousands of years, before that Bering Strait or any crossing—that's our history.

"So we refused to learn English or to learn their ways. We didn't want to be taken over and, uh, done away with in that way. Those days, nobody learned English. We resisted. Only I had to learn it because I was supposed to be spokesman. I was one of the only ones. People heard me speak and they were surprised. That was in the eighteen hundreds—long time ago. They used to talk in front of me—terrible talk—and I understood. One day, I was walkin' pretty far and I walked up to this old trading post. It was run by white folks, and a fairly good-size place. I wanted to buy one of them lanterns they used to have, so I went on up. One old guy was sitting on a stool outside, just sitting by the door. There was a blanket hanging, or a curtain or something, for a door, and he hollered inside when he saw me coming. Then I could hear him when I got closer. He said, 'Just some old Injun. Never saw him before. He looks about as stupid as all the rest.'

"Well, so I played along and I went up and pointed at that hangin' door and said 'ugh!' That's what they used to say to us when they thought they were speakin' our language. 'Ugh, ugh!' So we went on in and there was another man and woman in there, and they all said I looked about as poor as I looked stupid. But I saw a lantern on the shelf and I pointed to it. They mistook me and handed me this funny hat that was up there. So I put it on backward and said, 'ugh,' and took it off. Then they were saying things like, 'These Injuns don't know what they want. Tell them it's pretty and they'll buy anything. Only this one looks like he doesn't even know where he's at or what he's doin'. Probably got no money anyway.' So I said 'ugh, ugh,' and I walked on out.

"But I went on back the next day to buy the lantern. Same folks were in there, and I went on in and I spoke to them and

said, 'How are you folks this morning? I guess you might remember me, I'm a hostile from way over beyond the Third
Mesa, and I've come all the way back over here with money to
buy that fine lookin' lantern up there on the shelf.' Well, they
didn't know what to do. They looked like they'd been stuck
by lightning. So I said, 'Well, you folks seemed so nice and
friendly, it seemed a shame not to understand your kind
words. I know you folks aren't too keen on learning my language—it's too difficult for you folks. So I went on home last
night and learned yours. And without a lantern too. I studied
all night—kinda hurt my eyes. So now we can be friends, just
like brothers and sisters.' Seemed they didn't really want to
talk, anyway. But I did get to buy the lantern. That was a
long, long time ago."

He paused and pulled a large, round watch from his
pocket. "Well, speakin' of time . . ." He glanced at his watch
and jumped to his feet. He looked at all of us sitting there regarding him. "Why didn't you tell me? You wanna let me keep
you up all night? One-thirty in the morning! I coulda gone on
all night. Well, uh, I mean, it looks like I already did. You
shoulda' stopped me."

Mad Bear grinned and gave me a poke. Whenever there
was an excuse to do so, he seemed to be sitting close enough to
get an elbow into my ribs. "He can see!" he whispered loudly.
"David can see!" People said goodnight to David and to one
another and left to return to their own rooms—all except for
Mad Bear, who persuaded me to join him for his usual bedtime snack. As we sat in the restaurant across the street, he
continued to talk about David: "Did you see that, how he did
that? Wasn't that something? He just opened his eyes and
looked at his watch and he could see the time. And did you notice his color, his posture, everything? I mean, he really came
to life. Energy! That's what it is—all that good energy! Shows
ya how those kinda things work. Shows what can happen, just
given the chance."

● ● ●

◐

It had been a significant week for the American Indians, significant, it seemed to me, in many important ways. American Indian leaders had long been interested in the United Nations, long before its existence, in fact. Ancient prophesies foretold of the tall building of ore and mica where nations would gather in the land of the Iroquois on the island now called Manhattan. Their hope of participating in that assembly was more than a dream. It was an instruction. Treaties are, by definition, pacts among sovereign nations; and the state of these treaties and of the American Indian nations was an international issue, in their view—one appropriately dealt with by the United Nations. In addition to their human-rights appeal to the United Nations, they had a message to communicate in this building of ore and mica—a message that would benefit all the people—a message regarding their own mission and the righteous and honorable custodianship of the life and land of this planet. If there would continue to be a working spiritual advisory group to the United Nations of which traditional American Indian spiritual spokespersons were to be a part, then the recognition of this mission as well as recognition and relief for the Native people would be sure to follow.

Politicians and their various mechanisms may come and go, I thought, but the spiritual paths endure forever. The traditional American Indians were a unified presence here. They were one people, one sacred way. In their own meetings throughout the week, they had agreed upon the importance of presenting themselves as being of one mind. Every resolution and communication was issued by the united voice of a united delegation—a delegation that represented many sovereign nations and tribes and an ancient and enduring culture and tradition.

Mad Bear had seen an opportunity and had made the best of it. "You know, I had a good talk with the One Horn and the rest of the Hopi elders and some of the elders and spokespersons of other tribes here. It seems they all agree that this is the right time for communicating and sharing with all others— with the peoples of all colors and cultures. This is what I've been hoping for—working for—this acknowledgment and agreement. All the signs point to the correctness of this. Our sacred instructions have told us that when the time is right we are supposed to communicate, even reveal the records that we have been safekeeping. The One Horn Society is important in this because they are the keepers of the records. That's why it meant so much to me to see a One Horn way up here in our Iroquois country, especially at this time. I asked him if he thought now was the time to release the prophesies, records, and instructions over which his people have maintained custody for all these centuries. You know what he said to me? He said, 'It might be now or never. If we don't do it now, I don't know when we would ever have a chance again.'

"It's good," Mad Bear mused. "It's good that it can be seen in this way. All these other populations here, all these other races and cultures, the ones we called the invaders, I think that's why they came here. They're here for this learning, though that's not recognized even to this day. Everything has its spiritual purpose, but it doesn't always unfold. Now the time is getting short. There will always be us—our people and our records and our sacred instructions—but there just might not be the other peoples, maybe not much longer. With their self-destructive ways, I doubt whether they can survive on this land."

CHAPTER SIX

The Best of Both Worlds

"Most people get confused between foresight and fate."

◗ When United Nations Day was over and subsequent press conferences and interviews concluded, all the contingents, guests, and participants returned to the four directions and across the great waters, as the Native residents had put it. With the coming of November, the air turned crisp and the days grew shorter. Though there were still crowds in the streets, the restaurants, and the hotel lobby, the city felt almost lonely when all the delegates left. The various representatives had been dispersed throughout the city, but the Lexington Hotel had accommodated almost all of the American Indian delegation. They had dominated the lobby and the coffee shops, and the impression endured with the hotel personnel. "Our Indians looked so majestic," they would say. "Do you think they'll be back?" Or, "I saw our Indians on the television! Those were our Indians, weren't they?"

Somewhere out in the cold Atlantic Ocean floated one costly bottle of whiskey and, if the ritual had been successful, or if it had been meant to be, it would one day reach some European shore. Perhaps it would sink on its way, perhaps it would freeze. Or perhaps, once again, it would simply cease to exist. It had seemed a strange sort of objective for which to make medicine—to send one bottle of firewater back in the direction whence its kind had so long ago arrived to plague the indigenous peoples. Still, it had been done with dispassion and as a symbol of detachment and may well have served as an evocation of volition.

In lower Manhattan, there is a small piece of raw, untouched ground surrounded by a fence with a sign claiming it to be a single preserved sample of the original native land. Looking through that fence at the curious cluster of growth— primitive trees, shrubs, and weeds that now appeared foreign in this city—one could contemplate distant centuries and the people who then walked upon this ground. Life must have been much different back when the Indians had Manhattan— or whatever they called it then. Mad Bear had carried with him from his "trading post" some ancient beads and medals that had originally been brought over from across the great waters—trinkets that had been handed down from the days of the newcomers. These were some of the "handful of beads" with which the Europeans were said to have purchased Manhattan from the Indians—the Indians being savage and backward and having little understanding of the value of the land. This fiction was almost a laughing matter to the Iroquois delegation who looked over those antique items and talked about that part of "history"—except that it was not actually funny.

"I hope you don't believe it," one of them had remarked to me. "Your history teachers like to think our people were stupid. Imagine our ancestors jumping up and down: 'Oh, boy! Shiny objects!' They were not that stupid. Our people were looked up to in the beginning. We got along good in the beginning. If our ancestors had turned their backs on the first pale-faces, they never would have made it. The newcomers had

almost nothing—they were fleeing from their homeland—and
we helped supply their needs. They gave us what little they
had to give, and we accepted these simple trinkets out of
friendship—and it was not in exchange for land or in exchange for anything. We never thought about selling land.
That's a disrespect to the Earth, if you think about it. But
now—we are all now forced to participate in it. Our people
never would have dreamed up such a notion."

Over the past week, the Iroquois had several times conducted their official welcomes. They had not only been
invited as delegates, but had also, in a sense, been acknowledged as hosts. Now Beeman, Mad Bear, Alex, Crow,
Anyas, Sandy, Grandfather David, Rolling Thunder and his
people, and all the others had returned to their homes in the
West or in the North and left me in New York to wind up our
remaining business. I closed out the safety deposit box and
settled the accounts for more than a dozen rooms. Only my
room on the twenty-third floor was retained—on a special
weekly rate—which eventually became nearly two months.

One evening, I was invited to join a New York literary
agent and some of his friends for dinner in his apartment in
upper Manhattan. As we talked, we moved into the living
room and sat with our coffee in front of a large window that
looked out upon perhaps hundreds of other windows above
and below us. One of our party called our attention to this
scene.

"You know, this place was Indian territory once. Manhattan used to belong to these Iroquois people you're talking
about. Their spirituality may endure, and I think it's pretty
much right on. I mean, I have no argument with their beliefs,
and I admire them for hanging on to them. But, obviously,
their culture is long gone."

Someone else said, "Everything's got to give way to
progress sooner or later. Maybe it's not even progress. Technology marches on and, sooner for later, it takes over everything in its path."

I looked out through the dense concrete forest of residential skyscrapers. "I don't know, I said. The Indians are always pointing out how the grass keeps growing up right through the concrete, breaking it up—eating it, actually. It may look like the concrete has the upper hand at the moment, but it's really very temporary.So are the cities, and so are we.

"We're so dependent," I went on. "What happens if we run out of water, or if it's shut off, for whatever reason, for a month or so? We've had so-called brownouts here, but what if there's no electricity for a month, or there's a gas shortage and all the trucks and buses stop running? I love this city myself, in spite of what Mad Bear says. But, the point is, we've got ourselves in a pretty vulnerable situation. The traditional way of life on the land is here to stay, no matter what happens to the rest of us. A collapse or a failure in any of our intricate and complex systems would cause panic and havoc and horrible suffering, while the Indians out on the reservation would go on just about the same."

"Maybe," someone said. "But give me this lifestyle any day. I wouldn't want to live out in some teepee or wigwam trying to chase after something to eat or stomping around a fire, slapping my knees, trying to keep warm."

"I don't think I would either," I said."I don't know, I've never tried it. But, some of the best times I've had and the happiest people I've ever met have been out on the reservations or in little country villages."

"Still, without technology," he replied, "you could never travel to all these places."

"I know," I answered. "I'm not saying I don't approve of technology. I'd like to see even more. I'd like to see more people travel from continent to continent—to reach out across the planet and even into the cosmos. But, you know, that's a significant part of the Native American vision. It's in their historical records and in their prophesies, too. Maybe what we're growing toward—if we can make it—is the best of both worlds."

· · ·

◐

In mid-November, while I was still in New York City, one of
the Grateful Dead came to town, and he reached me by phone
to tell me about the Rolling Thunder Revue. "Bob Dylan and
Joan Baez and a bunch of musicians just put a concert together to take on the road. They're calling it the Rolling
Thunder Revue. They've got a film crew with them 'cause Dylan wants to make a movie. They're only releasing their publicity as they go, but I've got their whole itinerary. They're
heading up this way now, and they have a concert coming up
in that big convention center in Niagara Falls. Dylan and the
whole bunch will be checking into the Hilton up there next
week. I thought I'd let you know that so maybe you could
make it up there."

"I've heard about the tour," I said, "but I didn't know
where they'd be performing." (I had already heard about the
Rolling Thunder Revue from one of Rolling Thunder's acquaintances—a man he had once met on the railroad. This
man had worked with the Grateful Dead and other groups
through Rolling Thunder's introduction. He had been with
Rolling Thunder's party during the first days at the U.N.
Then he announced that he was leaving to join this Rolling
Thunder Revue as road manager.) "I'll be around Niagara
Falls anyway," I told him on the phone, "because I'm going
back up to Mad Bear's from here."

"Well, they just worked out their agenda. But they'll be
right up there at the Hilton. You ought to get in touch, you
know, give Dylan your *Rolling Thunder* book. That's probably where they got the name for this thing." Rolling Thunder
had developed an acquaintance with a good many musicians.
One of these was Ramblin' Jack Elliot, whom I had seen more
than once at Rolling Thunder's place in Nevada. Ramblin'
Jack was part of this tour, I had learned, and I supposed the
idea for the name may have come from him.

Before I left New York, I spoke with Mad Bear. He was en-
thusiastic. "We oughta go," he had said. "I mean, maybe we
oughta take in the whole thing." But by the time he picked me
up in Niagara Falls, I was discouraged. I had taken the usual

airport bus from Buffalo and had disembarked at the Hilton Hotel. I had mentioned all the names I knew—I had even mentioned Rolling Thunder Revue.

"No, there's no one here by that name either," I was told.

"No, but that's the name of the tour."

"Well, there's no one by that name here."

I could have guessed that the musicians would not have registered under their known names. It was possible that they were all listed under the name of the road manager but, though I had twice met him, I could not recall his last name.

"Well, don't worry," Mad Bear reassured me, as we drove back toward the reservation. "It'll probably come to you what that fellow's name is. We'll think of something. Or else we'll just go hang out by the back door, and I betcha we'll be able to grab 'em coming in or out. I sure wouldn't expect us to compete with that mob just to get into the concert—and there's going to be a mob because they've really got the word out now. I mean, to hear my nephews talk, the whole human population is nuts about their concerts. Anyways, we're the only ones who know where they're staying. Just think, all these people and we got the advantage. And we're not even fans of these people. At least I'm not—not yet, anyways. Although, that's not saying I won't become one if I get to go to their concert."

We pulled into the driveway, and Mad Bear jumped out to unlock his garage door. "Oh, that's right!" he said, snapping his fingers. "I can't pull the car in—we've got to let your bed down. Well, come on in through this way and we'll get your sleeping quarters squared away. Have you eaten? I bet you're nice and hungry, aren't you?"

Well, I'll bet you are, I said to myself.

"You know, I was thinking, if we don't make contact with Dylan and them, we oughta drive out and see Sandy—you know, who we had down there with us in New York. Just say 'hello,' I guess, no particular reason. It's a pretty fair drive out there, but she's been on my mind a couple times. She just popped up again, like maybe she's trying to tell me something.

Since we can't call her, I was thinking maybe . . ." He sat
down and closed his eyes for a moment. Then he opened his
eyes and softly spoke the name I had been struggling to remember.

Perhaps Sandy had somehow helped? I did not take time to
discuss it or even give it much thought. I went to the phone,
called the hotel, asked for registration, and gave the name
that worked—and instead of, "There's no one here by . . ." I
heard a ringing and then, "Hello?"

On the day of the concert, we drove to the Hilton Hotel. I
had a book for Bob Dylan and Mad Bear had something in a
little sack. I had spoken again to the road manager before
we left the house and he was waiting for us in the lobby.
"C'mon," he said, "they're all over there already."

I was sure that a couple of unexpected gift bearers would
be a little less than welcome just before the concert. "I was
just going to give this to you and let you give it to Dylan," I
told him.

"No, no!" Mad Bear quickly piped up, pulling on my arm.
"Let's go on over there and see 'em!"

We walked to the convention center. There were mobs of
people indeed, mostly young people, stretching for blocks.
There were more than could fit into even this huge place.
There were also mobs of police, it seemed, but not enough to
keep more than a semblance of order. People were pushing
and shoving and trying to climb up and over the tall fence that
surrounded the convention center—only to be pulled down
by one another if not by the police. We were escorted inside.

On several sofas in one backstage room sat Bob Dylan,
Joan Baez, Joni Mitchell, T-Bone, Ramblin' Jack, and several others I didn't know. We were introduced and I presented the book. "And this is a little something I put
together," said Mad Bear, handing Dylan his little package.
"You can use this in your pipe or whatever." Dylan put his
nose in the bag and sniffed. "No, it's not what you might be
thinking." Mad Bear laughed. "But then it's not nothing either, that's for sure!"

Before long, Mad Bear and I were on the stage—seated behind rows of mikes, drums, cables, lights, and amplifiers. We could hear very clearly, and we could even see, in a sense—a sort of rear-end perspective. In the distance beyond the stage, barely visible across the bright lights, stretched a sea of undulating bodies. Mad Bear kept making comments in my ear. "We brought something for Dylan only, and here we are kind of like their guests. That's too bad, we ought to have a little something for all of them." It was a while before Dylan made his grand entrance, and then the focus and the reverie was centered on him. At one point he announced: "I'd like to dedicate this next song to my friend Mad Bear right here," and he turned and waved an arm in our direction. Mad Bear clasped his hands together and shook them high above his head. Apparently, we were more visible where we sat than I had thought. In any case, the crowd roared—including those, no doubt, who had no idea what this was all about.

"Well, I'll think of something," Mad Bear said. "We'll have to come up with something." He took from his wallet a small folded receipt and scribbled something in the corner. I supposed he was making a note on some gift idea. He tore off the corner and handed me the tiny piece of paper. "How's this? You think it'll work? It's kind of sloppy, but we don't have anything else here. I sure hope it'll go over okay."

I squinted to read the words: "You and the whole bunch of you are all invited out to the reservation for a big Indian feed tomorrow afternoon. R.S.V.P. Your friend, Mad Bear." I handed it back and only nodded. A big feed? I knew that "the whole bunch," if it included all the backup musicians and crew, added up to over fifty people. It needed some discussion, but this was not the place for it.

The necessary conversation occurred early the following morning over the little percolator. At the first opportunity, Mad Bear had handed the strange little note directly to Dylan right there at the back of the stage. "I sure hope you'll pardon the informality," he had said. "It's not a very proper invitation. This little piece of paper is all we had here, but don't

take it as an indication of the feast to come." Of course neither Dylan nor the several others who stood looking over his
shoulder could "R.S.V.P." on behalf of the entire crew. They
would have to let us know. Before we left the convention center that evening, we had learned of their acceptance, and in
the morning the arrangements were begun—arrangements
that consumed the entire day. There would be not only the
entire crew of something over seventy but also more than
seventy Indians as well. They would be coming from all
around—and many of them very soon so that they could get
started with the preparations. Several of the tribal chiefs
would be waiting in their cars at the edge of the reservation to
meet the Rolling Thunder Revue caravan of vehicles and provide a befitting escort to the Tuscarora school gymnasium/
auditorium. Mad Bear had managed to procure this community site for the banquet, and nearly a dozen clan mothers
had agreed to cook and serve. But what was being danger-
ously left until the last minute was the matter of procuring
some food for this banquet. Not even Mad Bear's kitchen
could possibly have on hand sufficient provisions to feast
nearly two hundred individuals.

"I know," Mad Bear said. "We've got to get the food lined
up—and plenty of it, I mean more than plenty. The food!
That's the foundation of this whole thing. But we did have to
confirm that we could really pull it off first, before we stuck
our neck out on two-three tons of food. Anyways, I had an
idea in the back of my mind the whole while. We can give our
whole big order to the Thank-you Store out here. With a huge
order like this, they'll be happy to extend us a little credit.
That's what I'm hoping. Well, a whole lot of credit, when you
think about it. But it just hit me they may not have too much
time to put it all together. We'd sure as heck be embarrassed
if we got everybody in there and nothing to put on the tables.
We better get on the ball here. First we gotta make our list.
And there's no holding back, not on the food, not at a time
like this."

We carried our coffee to his desk in the front room and he

picked up a pen, licked a finger, and vigorously leafed through his tablet for a blank page. He was having fun. "Let's see, meat, potatoes—probably fried potatoes, cooked vegetables, salad, soup, dessert, the whole works. What else? Just some of everything, I guess. Every kind of meat and vegetable. Well, I guess I'll feel better if I get aholda the store first—make sure what they can handle here." He picked up the phone. "Course the deer meat, we'll have to get that through some of our people. Thank-you won't have the deer meat. I was thinking venison soup. That always goes good. Hold up, it's ringing."

He made his pitch to the owner in his typical Mad Bear style: "Hey! How you doing? Listen, we need your help on something here. Lemme tell you what's poppin'—I mean, this is really big! We're going to need a pretty hefty order here, and we were hopin' you might let us square away our bill a little later—I mean, it being Sunday and all. Lemme tell you what's up." I listened as he described the upcoming event, exaggerating only a little. They put the entire shopping list together on the phone, with Mad Bear repeating the owner's words aloud, giving consideration to what this little store could supply on such short notice, and glancing occasionally at me for my nod of approval. The owner and his teenage son would gather up the whole order and bring it out in the truck as soon as possible. "Like I said, you're certainly both invited," Mad Bear repeated. "I mean, you're part of this whole thing, now. Of course, though, we'll naturally take care of everything. But, I mean, what the heck. You're really helping out here."

Mad Bear tossed the receiver into the air and turned to grin at me. "Great!" he exclaimed. "They're not only okay with it, they're excited! I could have told you. See, our Indian people, they don't have a notion about these famous performers—got no reason to—although they take our word for it. Our people—they just always show up whenever we have a gathering for any reason. We're a community people. But this guy, he knew all these names and he knew about the concert.

And his poor kid, he couldn't even get into the concert. You know what he told me? He said, 'Wait till my son learns about this, he's going to fall over backwards!' "

Mad Bear and I walked across and down the road to the white wooden building where the reservation kids went to school. The large center room that served for gymnasium, auditorium, and a few other functions including town hall took up most of the floor space. A narrow balcony with chairs and a railing went halfway round the room. People began setting up tables and covering them with smooth, white butcher paper. I supposed that though this particular function was a first, these reservation people had experienced many feasts in this place. The father and son from the Thank-you Store arrived with their truckload of provisions about the same time as the women arrived to set up the kitchen, and preparations were soon under way.

"Well," Mad Bear acknowledged as we walked back toward the house, "I know I raised a few eyebrows on the other end of the line when I called our people on this thing. I know a lot of them were thinking, 'Here goes that Mad Bear again, drumming up some kind of big-deal monkey business.' Anyways, it's all coming together good, that's what we had to look in on. But I'll tell you one thing. Our people are going to get a pretty good kick out of this—and not just the young ones either. Even the elders will be tickled. You watch, they'll be talking about it for many moons, as we used to say. Well, now we got our own preparations to buckle down to. I'm going to put together a little something for each and every one of those guests."

He did. I had doubted it at first, knowing how many guests would be arriving. But he apparently put together hundreds of dollars worth of little somethings. However "tickled" all the others might eventually become, Mad Bear himself was unmistakably excited. He nearly emptied his "Mad Bear's Trading Post" display cases. Some of these bone and turquoise pieces were costly items—and the historical keepsakes, I knew, were absolutely priceless. We discussed what would be appropriate for whom. The most special items went, of course, to the celebrities; but there was, indeed, something for everyone, including the drivers, the film crew, and the stage crew, if only a small packet of tobacco or medicinal herbs.

A long caravan of buses and cars pulled up to the old schoolhouse. Performers and crew of the Rolling Thunder Revue, the Indian escorts, and all the others who had joined the caravan piled out of their vehicles. There were seventy-five members of the Rolling Thunder Revue and about an equal number of Indian men, women, and children. Most of the clan mothers and their helpers were already inside, busy with the cooking.

The traditional Indians were constantly holding community affairs—tribal and intertribal meetings, powwows, potlucks, socials, and ceremonies—and they, especially the clan mothers, were adept at short-notice organizing. The "whole bunch" had been invited and the whole bunch had come—sending word ahead to reconfirm their number out of concern that there were too many of them. They had no doubt expected to meet some Indians and to be offered some food. What they got was song and dance, a banquet feast, and many gifts. The long rows of tables with their crisp, white paper filled more than half the room. There were folding chairs around the tables and also in the narrow balcony. The remaining floor space became a stage, and the Indian hosts wasted no time initiating the festivities. As soon as everyone, or nearly everyone, was seated inside, the Indian children began their dances with one of the elders announcing each one in turn—"Turtle Dance, Duck Dance, Alligator Dance"—and looking as though they had been rehearsing all day. Sometimes the girls danced and sometimes the boys, and sometimes they danced together. Some sang and some played drums.

After many offerings, they asked their guests to return the favor: "So these are a few of our traditional dances and songs we have shared with you. And now, we hope you will share some of your songs with us and our people."

The performers looked surprised. They had not thought

they had come to work. "We can't," one of them hastened to say. "We need our instruments, and we didn't bring them." But Joan Baez jumped up and began "Swing Low, Sweet Chariot" and, after a few verses, almost everyone joined in. If the others were inclined to follow, they were still reluctant. Joni Mitchell would be happy to sing, she said, but she really needed her guitar.

The boy from the Thank-you Store called out: "I've got one here!"

"That's right," said the father. "My son's guitar is out in the truck. Go and get it!"

So then there was a guitar, and the others were induced to contribute. Bob Dylan had been the last to arrive and he was the last to sing. He had looked subdued, even reclusive in this crowd—until he began to perform. He sang "Hurricane," and there was no way to remain restrained with it. The energy and charisma that he had used to fill huge concert halls and auditoriums bounced around inside the old schoolhouse and charged the air. Until then, the group had been rather formal and quietly attentive, but as people got up to fill their plates, the room was buzzing with noisy excitement.

I talked with one of the filmmakers who sat down beside me. The filmmakers had come prepared to work. The Rolling Thunder Revue was using the tour, in part, to produce a feature film to be called *Ronaldo and Clara*, and the camera people were always ready for any opportunity to capture some potential footage. The man asked me whether Mad Bear would be willing to be interviewed or at least to say a few words on camera after supper. He thought it would be appropriate to do it outside among the trees. It would be dark, but there was a full moon, and they could manage some interesting lighting effects. I told him I was quite sure Mad Bear would agree, and we could ask him after supper. He suggested we might ask Mad Bear if he would make some "Indian-type comments about the Moon or stars or something . . ." Then he noticed the ring on my finger and he interrupted himself. "Where did you get that ring?" he asked.

His question surprised me. I had worn that ring day and

night ever since I had first put it on and, though I had never worn a ring before, I had quite forgotten about it. "Well, I don't know," I said, "it's kind of funny." That was hardly an adequate response, but I didn't feel like discussing it.

"But just how did you come by it?" he persisted.

I hesitated. How could I explain it?

"You don't want to tell me, right? It's strange to talk about it. But it doesn't have anything to do with Mad Bear, does it?"

"No, I don't think so. I've never talked to him about it. I'm not sure he's ever even noticed it."

"But tell me about it. I have a reason for asking."

"Well, like I told you, I found it," I began. "But not like on the street or in some public place. I found it in my own drawer in my bedroom, a drawer I used often, every day. Still, I found it, because one day it was just there, in a bowl with some change and things."

"So why not say it? It materialized!"

"Yeah, that's what it seemed like . . ."

"That's what it was," he interjected.

"Because," I went on, "one day it was just there. And there it stayed, and I didn't touch it. Couldn't. Maybe I thought, or hoped, it would disappear. But at one point, I decided it was not going to go away and that if in three days exactly from that moment it was still there, I would pick it up and examine it. Then when I did pick it up, I decided to try it on, convincing myself that if it fit, I might as well go ahead and wear it. Well, it fit beautifully, like soft liquid on my finger, and I've never taken it off."

"Yup," he responded. "I guess that's the way it works. But I still don't know what it means. I have to tell you, I have the same exact ring—except I think I've had mine a lot longer. Yours is the only other one I've ever seen. And I got mine in the same way exactly—in the drawer, suddenly materializing, the three days waiting, the perfect fit—the whole bit. Maybe eventually, you'll take yours off like I did. Mine's home now. Sometimes I wear it. I don't know if I should. Sometimes it disappears and it's nowhere around, and then I come across it again, like right on my dresser or kitchen counter or some-

thing. Then I try to tell myself I must have left it there. But
for weeks, without my seeing it? It's too weird. Maybe we
should talk to Mad Bear about these things. Prob'ly he'll
know about it."

I was not anxious to broach the issue with Mad Bear. For
one thing, if he did have any thoughts, he would not likely ex-
press them on this night. I was too familiar with his Indian
technique for avoiding answers. In any case, the chance did
not present itself. As soon as all the feasting was winding
down, the giving of gifts began.

Mad Bear had what he called "a little something" for every
one of the guests and distributed these around. I walked
around and talked with the performers. Bob Dylan wanted to
ask me about Mad Bear. He asked me something like how or
whether I had experienced the authenticity of people like
Rolling Thunder and Mad Bear. He was still sitting at his chair
at the table and I sat on my haunches beside his chair. Our
conversation was interrupted when some young person threw
a mousetrap down upon him from the balcony, striking him in
the wrist. He looked first startled and then hurt. Without
speaking, he stood up and walked out. Many of the young people followed, shouting and grabbing at his clothes. I felt sorry
for him. Another performer had only recently remarked how
comfortable she felt in this atypical group who treated them
like ordinary folks and yet so hospitably—and this was the
only uncomfortable incident. I walked along as though I
wished to help the situation, but there was nothing I could do.
Dylan went into one of the large vans and closed the door behind him. I walked between the buses to return to the building. I saw a couple of people pointing large cameras and lights
at Mad Bear as he stood under a tree, and I stopped to watch
from a distance. I noticed the silhouette of a performer behind
the curtain in a window of one of the buses. He could not know
that I could see him. He was holding in front of his face the
medallion that Mad Bear had given him and had placed
around his neck, and he was kissing it. I walked back inside.

• • •

For the several days that I remained at his place and, no doubt, for several days thereafter, Mad Bear talked constantly about the "big feast and social," as he called it. Though he ran up a huge account on behalf of his tribe—a debt for which he would likely be held responsible—and had given away what seemed like nearly half the precious items in his museum and his "Trading Post," he was pleased. "Good one," he kept saying, "good one! I'd say we really pulled it off." And when neighbors came around to visit, they talked about it also.

"We've got to do something about these young-uns, though," one elder remarked, and he and Mad Bear shook their heads and talked about how the young ones had changed. Except for the one incident with Dylan, I thought the kids had been remarkable.

"But the young people are different nowadays," Mad Bear claimed. "They don't have much sense of community, seems like. Not that children should be seen and not heard. We don't think that way."

"Well, maybe I'm beginning to," said the old man.

"No, kids should be kids. They don't have to act like adults, just interact with them, and in a good way for everybody. Now they just go their own way. Nobody gets to really enjoy each other. Used to be, they were more connected, especially with the elders. They'd relate with them, and there'd be this group spirit. It used to be a wonderful thing."

"Wonder what their kids'll be like?" the old man mused. "The new generations? I don't know. Things're changin', that's for sure, goin' every whicha way. No more guidance. And maybe one day . . ." He paused and shook his head again. "Maybe I gotta come back as one of these kids."

Mad Bear also talked, during those several days, about his "project." We sat at his table with his little percolator and his endless snacks and doughnuts and discussed where we might go first and when. He wanted to travel to the various tribal nations, especially to those in the Southwest, to the keepers of the records and prophesies, to meet with the traditionals and spokespersons, and gather some sort of collective commu-

nication regarding the coming Earth changes and the planetary transition, which was already in sight. From traditional
spokespersons of ancient tribes whose rock writings, stone
tablets, and oral histories spanned thousands of years, he
wanted a vision of what lay ahead, beyond the inevitable
transition. "When do you think we can get started?" he kept
asking.

On the morning I was packing to leave, Mad Bear got a call
from the Thank-you Store. I overheard him talking about the
bill and arrangements to pay, and he and the owner went on
for some time, talking mostly, it seemed, about the event itself
and all the performers.

"How much did all that come to?" I asked when Mad Bear
had hung up.

"They don't know for sure yet. They're still figuring. I
think they'll give us special consideration on some of it. But
that's not why he called. He was thinkin' we might drop over
there and talk to his son—or to the other kids, I guess—his
friends from school. You know what that kid did? He hung his
guitar on the wall with a kinda plaque or something that said:
'Bob Dylan, Joan Baez, Joni Mitchell, Ramblin' Jack . . .'
and he listed the whole bunch of 'em ' . . . all played on this
guitar.' Well, of course, none of his friends from school over
in town were there on the reservation. They couldn't have
seen it, and they couldn't have known. Well, they don't believe him. They just don't believe him. His father backs him
up on it, and then they think they're both kidding. 'Course,
you'll be leaving, so you can't go over there. I might drop by
after I get you to the airport. But then, I don't know what help
I would be convincing those kids. You know me, I'm always
grinning anyways. I can't stop laughing, even over the truth!"

Mad Bear drove me all the way to the airport in Buffalo.
"So, when do you think you'll be able to head back this way?"

"I don't know," I answered. "What needs to happen now is
some research for putting a feasible budget together, for the
travel, mostly, and then the fund-raising. We'll see how it
goes."

"Maybe we should've pinned down a little more specific plans for the budget. I mean, have you got enough to go on? We didn't lay out our whole itinerary, by any means."

"No, but I think we decided we'd just bite off what we called the pilot project first—the first trip Southwest. Then, based on that, we could generate the rest of the objectives and the itinerary. I've got enough to start on from our side. The question is just how to go about it."

"Yeah, that part I don't know about. 'Course, we can always talk on the phone if we need to put our heads together on any more of the planning. Did I tell you my latest dream, by the way? I've been telling you my dreams, right? Well, this was a simple thing, really, not much to it. I just saw us heading down South, down toward the Mexican border. We had this cute little caravan. I don't know who all was along. But I dreamed we were in three Jeeps. They were all identical, dark green, real sharp, and they were ours. You know, for the work. And they had printing on both sides, on the door panels there, with the name of the outfit like you and I talked about. Three Jeeps. Think about it. We get those and we're off and running!"

Right, I thought to myself. Dream on. We'll be lucky if we get a little gas money.

"You know, there was something else I was thinking about," he went on. "We ought to make a little trip out there to Virginia Beach, to the Edgar Cayce people. I've read up on all those Cayce readings, 'specially the prophecies. I've got copies of a lot of that stuff. And Nostradamus, too. Did you ever read up on the prophesies of Nostradamus? What somebody oughta do someday pretty quick is go all across this country—or the world, really—and make a study of all the prophets, what they had to say. I bet a comparison of all their prophesies related to these next few decades would be an amazing thing. You'd think there'd be someone somewhere who'd jump at the chance to fund a thing like that. I mean, that'd be worth something. But then there'd be many wouldn't know how to use it. Maybe they'd get more passive instead of more active. Like

I've been saying all along, most people get confused between foresight and fate."

We arrived at the airport and pulled up to my entrance and he got out to shake my hand. "You didn't say when you're coming back. Or, I guess you did, as best you could. I sure wonder when we can get started. I wish I'd be flyin' out with you now."

"But I'm just flying back to New York City right now and then, later, back home to California."

"Well, I wish we were going somewheres, anyways. There's so much to do. I'm gettin' pretty doggone restless, I can tell you that!"

CHAPTER SEVEN
Those Who Care

"It's not a matter of saving our own necks. It's a matter of being aware and being helpful."

◐ **I stayed in New York** through November and into December and flew back home to California in time to spend Christmas with our Japanese-community family. Ever since Hiro and Yoko—the young couple who had lived with me during the Rolling Thunder days—had returned home to Fukuoka City, I had shared my San Francisco Bay Area home with a never-ending chain of friends from Japan. It was like a revolving family. Some of them stayed only a few weeks or months and then returned to Japan or moved away. But many of them stayed on while others arrived to add to our number. Friends told friends, and some left Japan headed directly for our address. It was a place to be with peers, to learn English, and to find help and support for their new affairs. Thus our number had grown and we had

spread out to several apartments, becoming a family of
neighbors.

I spent most of the holiday season working on our cross-
tribal American Indian communication project. I recalled
Mad Bear's urging. Time was short, he had insisted, and he
was "restless," as he had put it, and anxious to "hit the road."
My job was to outline a plan and a budget for the cross-tribal
survey of records and prophesies with which he wanted to initiate the project and to attempt to raise the necessary funds.

But I needed details. I understood the goals, essentially—
the purpose and the plans as Mad Bear had delineated
them—but to develop the budget I needed a more precise itinerary—and that had to come from him. For several weeks I
tried unsuccessfully to reach him by phone. I began to believe
that perhaps his restlessness had gotten the best of him and
he had already started off on some adventure. I continued
as best I could, going over the foundation materials I had
brought back from New York and outlining some hypothetical
treks and approximating their associated costs. This budget, I
knew, would have to stop far short of Mad Bear's imagined
caravan of dark green Jeeps. I was beginning to realize that
my assignment would not be an easy one. It would not be as
simple for me to communicate this cause to potential funders
as it had been for Mad Bear to communicate it to me, to the
traditional chiefs, or to his colleagues at the convention.

As I continued my deliberations in the absence of Mad
Bear, I needed someone with whom to talk over my thoughts,
and Masayuki Watanabe, a new addition to our Japanese-
family community, offered an accommodating ear. He had recently completed a cross-country tour on an excursion bus
pass, and had moved in next door for a brief stay before returning to Japan. Masayuki was articulate and innovative,
and as we discussed the project his interest grew. He was at a
time of freedom and independence in his life and was available to any interesting adventure—and together we became
convinced that this project needed an in-field research assistant such as he. He would get along handsomely with the In-

dian people, it seemed to me, and with his long black hair, deep eyes, sculpted face, and dark skin, he appeared as likely to blend in on an Indian reservation as in downtown Tokyo. The prospectus provided an incentive for him to extend his stay in the United States—a justification he evidently had already been hoping to find. Our discussions turned to the issue of his visa.

One day in late January, Mad Bear phoned. "Doug, what's up?" he bellowed loudly.

I jerked the receiver away from my ear. Then I responded almost as loudly as he, hoping to sound equally exuberant. "Hey, Mad Bear! I was trying to get ahold of you some time ago!"

"I know," he said, "and here I am. You called, and here I am. How about that?"

Yeah, I thought to myself, three weeks later. I paused to reflect. What was it I had needed to go over with him?

"Doug, just where you at?"

"Oh, sorry," I said. "I'm right here."

"Well, I know that. I mean, how far am I from where you live?"

"What?"

"I've got your address written down right here. But I don't know the streets. We're driving, so we can get to your place on our own, but you're going to have to give me some instructions."

Mad Bear had driven out to me.

"Or, maybe if you're free, maybe you'd like to come on down here. I'm calling from the Indian Center right here in Oakland. I got this guy travelin' with me here, a young Sioux who's gonna help us out, and you can bring that Oriental friend there who's helpin' you so's we can meet him."

Masayuki and I drove across town to the Indian Center. I wanted to explain to Masayuki how Mad Bear was "tuned in" as he himself had put it, and how he had evidently picked up on our arrangement though I had not told him of anyone helping me. I had not even had a chance to talk with him since before I had met Masayuki. But I decided not to tell Masayuki too much too fast. When we met at the Indian Center and introductions were made, Mad Bear related to Masayuki as though he had been part of the picture all along; and neither explanations nor confirmations were ever needed—for Mad Bear or for Masayuki.

"Well, looks like we got a little two-car caravan here anyways." Mad Bear chuckled as they jumped in his Toyota Land Cruiser to follow us back to our place. The moment we arrived, Mad Bear was through the front door as though he knew the place. He settled himself into the largest chair with a sigh and looked very much at home. "Well, I figured I might as well hit the road," he said, settling back and looking pleased with himself, "and get away from the worst of the cold. Winter's pretty heavy back up home this year, and I've gotta chop my own wood, you know. Anyways, I was getting restless, didn't I tell you? I told you that back home, right? How soon do you guys think you'll actually be ready for us to get started?"

Mad Bear and the twenty-four-year-old Sioux Indian from Semu Huaute's ranch stayed with us for several days, and the four of us spent the whole time working out the details and plans for our project. But, how soon? My question was how much, and how could we get it? I personally would have been willing to set out without any itinerary at all. I would have felt all right just to go as the wind blows, as the medicine men would say—to simply follow Mad Bear around and trust to his spontaneous intuition. But in any case, we needed funds to get anywhere at all, and for that we needed a proposal. I knew that the standard procedure was to be as specific and as sure of both the plans and the outcome as if our purpose had already been accomplished. And I doubted that we could include anything about spontaneous intuition and going as the wind blows. Since Mad Bear had already made two preliminary "scouting trips" across the country and since he was now here, we felt we could come up with a thirty-day itinerary to make a competent-sounding presentation.

◑

I had a half dozen acquaintances in the Bay Area who knew more than I about the ins and outs of grant writing, and they had volunteered to help us work on our proposal and to help launch the fund-raising part of the project. They wanted to meet with Mad Bear because he might be helpful in supplying some of the specifics that were required. Together we prepared a biographical sketch and job description for each of the four of us and sketched out our first thirty-day itinerary. We began preparations for two grant proposals to be sent to foundations. One was to be for the full six-month project, and one was for the thirty-day field research phase, which we called the pilot study. Mad Bear appeared to feel uncomfortable with our use of words like "research" and "study," but I knew these words were useful in an application for funding—and he had seemed to approve of our new name: Cross-Cultural Studies Program. He had, in fact, been the one to suggest "something institutional sounding." Still, in all his elaboration about this work, he had always spoken of communication and sharing—an offering on the part of his people of their understanding of global events. He had never mentioned the word "research." There appeared to be a difference in the way some of us were viewing this project.

It seemed to me that this issue ought to be discussed, now that we were all sitting here with Mad Bear. Those who were working on the proposal needed to be able to present a true picture of our purpose and our process. "I think there's an important distinction," I said, "in our intended methodology here. I think we need to make it clear that this is not just another pedantic probing into some bizarre culture. This is not our culture sorting and selecting data in its usual habitual way. Rather, this is a process of simply listening and assimilating—of observing and recording what these people choose, among their various tribes and traditions, to communicate to us. It's like they have offered us some contribution—a way of understanding that is not a part of our own culture, and we're setting out to receive it."

But our friends here were thinking about credibility. Po-

tential supporters might think that what we could gather
regarding Indian records and prophesy would sound like un-
substantiated claims. Everyone would be interested in verification, and we had best try to make our reports believable
enough to attract further support. There are so many conflicting opinions, they pointed out, among so-called scholars
regarding the arrival of the first humans upon this continent—about who arrived from where and when and what
happened after that. Many so-called experts seem to think
that American Indians have little understanding of their own
history and culture, and need to be taught about themselves
by us. Even those facts regarding our American Indian heritage that have been well substantiated are seldom taught and
are little known. It seemed to our group here that there were
already so many conflicting and confusing opinions about the
Native people that evidence and validation ought to be at least
a part of our goal.

"Listen," Mad Bear said. "Just listen. Let me explain something, and I don't mean to sound disrespectful to any scholars
or experts or anyone else. The whole point of this project is
that this time, we are talking—I mean, we, our Indian people—and not all the students and scholars with all their opinions and judgments. This is the time for your people to hold
off on their compulsive judgments and keep them out of the
way—to forget about their verifications and their conclusions
until they have a chance to grow into some real firsthand understanding. We don't need these judgments. And we don't
need more students and scholars. In fact, neither do you.
We've had enough of them for a while. We're not specimens
here. We're not here to be studied and studied and put into
textbooks and museums. To be truthful, I couldn't care less
what the so-called experts think. We want to contact and
touch you people directly, not indirectly through your endless
studies and reports. We want direct encounter on a personal-
relationship and friendship level. Let us reach out to you for
once and tell you what we have in mind to say. Let us tell you
our own story for once, and let us tell it in our own way. This

◐

has never happened—not once in these hundreds of years of history since you people came over here.

"We once thought you people came to live with us. You still could have that chance. We're still here, and we live on this land. We don't live in your libraries in the pages of your books. This project is not for digging up our pottery—or for digging up our bones, for that matter. It's not even for digging up data and statistics about us. We have a long-surviving and sacred tradition and an experiential wisdom that's been passed on for more centuries than you people can imagine. This is your chance to benefit from that. All you have to do is be quiet and listen and quit worrying about proving and believing. I want this to happen because this is still our home here, and you are our guests here—and because you still do not understand our home and you are spoiling it."

No one responded. No one said anything. In the long silence that followed Mad Bear's words, people began to shuffle papers and to look through their notes. It was not that anyone had failed to understand what Mad Bear had said. There was the question of the implications and of how this might be expressed in grant-proposal terms. There was the question, "So, what do we do now?" But no one spoke it out loud. What I learned from Mad Bear's words were the implications for our new Cross-Cultural Studies Program (we retained the name) and its ongoing stance and strategy. Cross-cultural study was indeed a goal, but studies in a different sense than I had ever observed in my lifetime. We had always been saying, "Never judge the old Indian until you have walked one hundred miles in his moccasins." That was an Indian concept—not a concept I had witnessed among my own people. In Mad Bear's view one can understand another only from the perspective of the other and not from one's own. To properly study an eagle one must endeavor to know not how the eagle appears to the observer but how the observer appears to the eagle. So we set out to put ourselves in the place and in the position that we might receive some useful knowledge from this ancient culture and pass it on to our own.

◑

This idea was extremely uncomfortable—even threatening—to "charitable" endowments who felt their financial activities were under official scrutiny. This was not apparent to us at first. Dozens of foundations identifying themselves as American Indian philanthropies declined our applications saying simply that though ours was a noble cause, it did not fit within their contributing guidelines. As, over time, we became more closely acquainted with "contributors" involved in "Indian affairs," their communications became more revealing. There were those who questioned how we had come to our glamorous illusions regarding these backward and savage peoples. Others conceded to us that after so many years and so many millions had been spent in the effort to destroy the Native culture, they could not dare to openly assist in the support of the tradition. "The persistence of that culture threatens many powerful people because of land and resource issues," we were told. "Unless you can do so under some less candid pretext, you'll never be able to obtain funding." We learned that proselytization, acculturation, and subjection—what Indians called genocide and what might at least be called "culturecide"—remained an earnest and expensive effort. "Well, it's their money," one of our advisors said, "and they can do with it as they wish."

Weeks passed. Mad Bear and his young Sioux helper had returned to their respective homes, and Mad Bear continued to call to inquire when we might be able to get started. One day he phoned to report on a "vision" he had just been alerted to. "You know that place out there in Berkeley where we are expected to speak? That institute? Well, we better look in on that. Something has got to be done about that now, or it might not even be there. And that's coming up pretty quick now, right? These people up Canada way, a coupla Mohawks, they came down here and they had a vision about that place. They saw you and me sitting in front of a fireplace in a living room. The fire was going, and we were giving a talk to a group of people. They described you pretty good too, and they've never seen you. But we're not gonna be speaking in a house, right? I tried to tell them it was an institute."

"It is an institute," I acknowledged, "but it's in a house with a big living room and a fireplace." I had been somewhat involved with the Institute for the Study of Consciousness. It was the Berkeley branch of the Foundation for the Study of Consciousness created by Arthur Young, philosopher, engineer, and inventor of the Bell Helicopter. I had talked with him about Mad Bear, and the Youngs had contributed to the "Indian fund" for the event at the United Nations. The program staff had invited Mad Bear and me to speak at the institute in the spring, and Mad Bear had agreed. I had hoped to introduce them when Mad Bear was in the Bay Area, but the Youngs were at their center in Pennsylvania at the time, and Mad Bear had not seen the Berkeley Institute. "That's where we'd be," I told him. "There in the living room. The speakers sit up front near the fireplace, and they usually have a fire going."

"Well, so we're sitting there in front of the fire," Mad Bear said, "and all of a sudden there's this big rumble and the roof caves in and the walls and everything. It's an earthquake, and I don't know what happens after that 'cause then their vision expands and they see buildings falling apart all over the place, and bridges, and everything!"

I said nothing. I could think of no response. Our scheduled talk was nearly two months away. If Mad Bear decided to cancel, how would I possibly explain it?

"Well, listen to this," Mad Bear went on. "I figured I really gotta check that one out. So we got these dreamers down here—maybe I told you? Tuscarora. They're a mother and son—pretty old—both of 'em. Well, the way they do, they lie side by side when they're dreaming, and they both gotta share the same dream. So when they come into the same dream, they physically clasp hands, right there on the floor, and they simultaneously clasp hands in their dream. Then they have their look and they come back together and agree on what they saw." He waited for my reaction.

"What did they see?"

"Chinatown, first. Chinatown in an earthquake. It caved in—just like a cone-shaped sinkhole—sank right into the ground. I knew it was Chinatown because their description was so accurate. Anyways, they couldn't pin it down as to time. Those things, you can't pin down. Could happen any-time, it all depends on how long it can be held off. That's a job that some are given—holding things off. So I says, 'What about this institute the Mohawks saw—the place where we're speaking at? Wouldn't that put a time on it?' They went at it again, but they couldn't see it. They found the place, all right, seems like, by what you've said. They came in over the roof—dropped down right around the eaves—and right there they clasped hands. When they woke up they said they saw the fireplace in the living room. No one was in there when they were there. See, they were actually there. They said there's an L-shaped porch, and you can see into the living room from either side. That's another thing I wanted to check with you—'cause you know the place."

"That's right. There's a kind of deck with the roof over-hanging it. And it's L-shaped with a window on either side."

"Well, they went to the right place, sure enough. 'Course in that trip they didn't see the roof cave in. But then, they didn't see us in there either. It's a question of when it is. So, they went back yet again. They said they clasped hands and tried to push on up—way up above to get out of the time lock—but they couldn't get a view of the place with us in there. Maybe we're not going. What do you think we oughta do? Maybe we should hang out in the Sierras, this side of Sacramento. That place is safe from danger and you can watch over everything."

I tried to picture myself telling my friends at the institute that they were likely to be crushed by an earthquake and Mad Bear had decided not to take the chance. I felt myself become suddenly irritated. "You mean, cancel, I guess, to escape any risk. I guess it's every man for himself in a case like that." I regretted the way I'd put it.

"It's not a matter of saving our own necks," he responded. "It's a matter of being aware and being helpful. You get caught off guard and you lose your intentionality. I'll tell you what—you figure it out for yourself. I'm gonna take a little dream medicine, okay, and I'm gonna look into this. But this time, you're gonna to do it too. Whatever you do, in your own way, you do it! You come up with something so you're not left empty. Then you let me know, and we'll talk again. So I'll say so long for now." Abruptly, he hung up.

All right, I thought, I'll do it. I can do that. I don't have any dream medicine, I'll just dream. But, in spite of my bedtime resolve, I either received no pertinent dreams or I forgot them upon awakening. I decided that what I was looking for would not come in my sleep, and, over several days, I spent hours in a deliberate effort to inquire within. I was barraged with images. I pictured Mad Bear the first time I saw him—with his shiny Hawaiian shirt and his tipped cigar—sitting there with Rolling Thunder in the Berkeley Hills—talking about floods and earthquakes and natural disasters. I recalled how so many trees were bowed over and how Mad Bear had pointed them out to me, saying that they were bending toward the Earth in fear and despair. His words about transition echoed in my mind. I recalled him saying how some Indians, despite "knowing it's not right," as he had put it, now prayed for earthquakes and destruction that the transition might be hastened, the Earth cleansed, and a new world ushered in. But I supposed my thoughts were self-induced, and I learned nothing from myself about roofs and walls and bridges caving in or what we had best do.

After several days, I decided I'd let it go. Prophetic visions were not my work. Still, Mad Bear's words echoed in my memory: "It's a matter of being aware . . . you get caught off guard and you lose your intentionality." But that's exactly what Mad Bear wanted to lecture about, I thought, and now he wants to cancel? He hadn't said that, exactly, but I knew he would. I felt a rush of indignation. So what if a few dreamers could foresee enough to save their own skins? Most people will never know. If an earthquake comes they'll not know in advance and, afterwards, they'll never know what hit them.

◐

At least, they'll never understand. We've been told we've destroyed the natural balance. Some have said nature will fight
back—that natural disasters are inevitable. It will be like a
giant hand reaching down to crush people—and they'll never
have sufficient warning nor sufficient understanding why.

"*We do care,*" came the response. I had been pacing in agi-
tation, and was suddenly overcome by a feeling of solace. I
looked around. I was fully awake, and I had heard something
quite distinctly. "*We are those who care.*" It felt like a group
speaking in chorus and with very evident compassion. It was
as though some external scanner had found a frequency inside of me and had locked in on it. I simply listened:"*Those
Who Care care deeply and strongly, and blame is beside the
point with us. We do not define the work as the meting out of
just desserts. For those who would seek to find an adversary,
we long for a wider and more thorough view, and for those
who fear, we long for peace . . .*"

It went on, and it was not a deliberate pondering or
thought process. It was not I. It was like dictation, I thought,
and perhaps I ought to write it down. I took a pen and paper
and tried to write from memory, but other thoughts inter-
fered. For one thing, I began to wonder, how could those
words have anything to do with the revelation, or whatever,
that Mad Bear had expected me to come up with? Well, it was
what I got and, perhaps, all I was likely to get. This sort of
phenomenon was not a part of my own practice. So I sat down
at my typewriter and held my fingers on the keys. "If you
want me to get what you said," I spoke out loud, "say it
again!" It came again, just as before, and I typed it. I took
dictation. I read it over several times, and I decided that I appreciated having it—it was a helpful and reassuring response
to my state at the moment. But I still doubted it was the information Mad Bear had requested. The last sentence was rather
like advice and seemed relevant, in a sense. Jump, "They"
had said, jump free of the sense of peril and fear. "*Hold
hands together and jump up—up on to the level of the
Heart.*" But how, I wondered, would Mad Bear take it should

I decide to repeat those words to him? He would be on the phone again, and I would have to say something.

The next time Mad Bear phoned, I brought the matter up myself before he had a chance to question me. I briefly paraphrased the entire paragraph and concluded, "So that's about all."

"Great!" he said. "Maybe that's the important part. That's got to be included. We can't control how it's received by others—the same as we can't control what becomes of any knowledge. That's not up to us, though we have to gather it up and put it out. But that part about no blame, and about the heart level, we can't leave that out. That's the Fourth World." Then he changed the subject.

It seemed to me that he was perhaps intending to appear at the Institute in Berkeley after all. He and I had entitled our spring topic "The Emergence of the Fourth World."

Our endeavors to initiate our project continued. Throughout several weeks of correspondence, meetings, and telephone conversations, we heard things like "If only you were helping lead 'these people' to Christianity" or "You should be helping 'these people' take advantage of what modern life has to offer." One San Francisco foundation seemed intrigued with the idea of funding a cross-tribal communication from traditional Native peoples, but they opted instead to pay for an eighteen-wheeler for some organization thinking to distribute surplus food to pickup points along reservation roads. One of the foundation staff remarked to us: "If we can't see our way to help their culture survive, after all that's been done to stifle it, at least we can help feed them—but just between us, we could do better than simply keeping them on the dole."

After what Mad Bear convinced us was an unnecessary amount of time spent in futile endeavor, we finally set out to begin our pilot project with a bank loan cosigned by some of our colleagues. Masayuki and I flew to New York to meet Mad Bear. He wanted us to get together with representatives of several Southwest tribes and also to examine the rock writings in southern Arizona near the Mexican border. Mad Bear

needed to make the cross-country trip in his Toyota Land
Cruiser so that it would be available for our travels in the
Southwest. He also needed to find someone to replace the
young Sioux who had been unable to hang around while we
pursued our funding. So Masayuki and I flew out to Tucson to
wait for the next rendezvous.

As soon as we were settled in our temporary quarters, we
notified the Tucson Indian Center as instructed, and Mad
Bear had no problem finding us—though I suspected he could
have psyched us out in any case. He introduced us to his
young companion: "Here's our new assistant and copilot—
he's from way up north—Mohawk Nation." Then, as usual,
he marched right in, picked a chair, and made himself comfortable. "Why, this is just like uptown," he remarked.
"Pretty doggone snazzy!"

"Well, based on their weekly rates, this seemed about the
most reasonable place for the four of us," I explained.

"Well, we don't need it," Mad Bear replied. "One thing, I
found a place near the Indian Center, which is where we better be. It's cheap and yet they have a Jacuzzi too—now you
can't beat a deal like that. Another thing, if I'm going to be in
Tucson, it's going to be South Tucson. That's where the real
people are—Latinos, Indians, everybody. Anyways, we'll be
pretty quick heading down toward the border, on down to the
reservation, which is where we're really s'posed to be."

So we relocated to the place of Mad Bear's choice, and he
was in the Jacuzzi before the rest of us had finished unloading
his vehicle. "Better jump on in here and soak up some wet-
ness," he urged when we looked in on him, " 'cause in about
an hour or so we'll all be sittin' out under that desert sun."

In the heat of the late afternoon, we and more than a dozen
Papago Indians were gathered around picnic tables among
cacti and saguaros just east of Tucson. Mad Bear made sure
we were personally introduced to each and every one of them.
There was no way to remember all these names and who was
related to whom—but Mad Bear wanted to generate the impression that we were all supposed to become great friends.
Everyone was cheerful and playful—full of laughter and

kindness. Then Mad Bear made his speech and everyone became silent and stoic—except for the very young ones who
had no idea what he was talking about and soon jumped up to
run about again.

Mad Bear's speech sounded like a rally. He spoke of getting
back to the spiritual tradition and of the new, urgent responsibilities of the Native peoples. It is time for intertribal unity,
he claimed, time to stop quarreling and complaining, time to
regain the rightful role of spiritual leadership for the sake of
the land and the life—and time, therefore, to give up alcohol
completely, to give up that which has been holding the people
down.

There was no visible reaction. People accepted him as a
spokesman, it seemed to me, but there was no way to tell
whether they approved of his words. Perhaps, I thought,
some may have taken his words as critical of them.

Mad Bear seemed pleased, however, as we drove back to
the motel in the sunset. "They all agreed," he said, "and they
all agree with what we're doing. They even offered us the use
of a cabin down there on the reservation. Remember that old
white-haired lady with her two sons? She has a little cabin
away out there in the canyon near the Mexican border. It'll be
just right for us." He turned to look back at us from his driver's seat and gave Masayuki a wide grin. "I know you'd
rather be out in that canyon than hanging around here in this
motel," he said. "I know you've been waiting to get out on the
'res.' Well, you're gonna love it! Why, you can walk out in the
dark any night and suddenly throw a flashlight beam anywheres on the desert ground. And you can count two scorpi-
ons, two tarantulas, three black widows, and a rattlesnake
right there in your light beam."

"I don't really like snakes and spiders too much," Masayuki whispered to me.

Mad Bear laughed. " 'Course, we'll be keeping one of these
rooms here in town," he allowed, "so's we can alternate back
and forth between the snakes and the Jacuzzi!"

We spent most of the next day gathering supplies in town to
take out to the cabin. Mad Bear had invited everyone out on

our very first night for a great big pot of his famous menudo. As always, he was in the very best of humor as we went about the very wonderful business of shopping for food.

"I keep thinking about so many snakes and spiders," Masayuki confided in me, "and I don't like to eat that menudo very much. Maybe we're better to stay in the motel."

"There aren't really that many snakes and spiders," I assured him, "and we may not even see any. They don't chase people down, after all. The best way to eat that menudo is don't look at it and don't inhale. We'll be okay."

CHAPTER EIGHT

Connections to the Spirit World

"It requires offering. It requires a relationship."

◐ Fortunately, Mad Bear's menudo was easier to eat than most. All the extra herbs and lemon seemed to help and, with Mad Bear's obvious elation in his role as host and the refreshing evening breeze in the canyon, I managed to politely consume a second bowl.

Again, as soon as everyone had been sufficiently fed, Mad Bear made another speech. And again he spoke about getting "back on track" and about "stopping this drinking" in a manner that seemed almost like scolding.

That night in the cabin, Mad Bear spoke up in the darkness just as we were all about to fall asleep. "You guys might have been wondering how's come I got on about this drinking. Well, that was for some ears that were there among us in that group, and the others understood and appreciated that. For one or two of them, this is either not going to become any problem at all or it's going to be a big one. If it comes to be a

problem, it's a problem for the tribe and then a problem for
our traditional people. Of course, there's medicine for that—
our kind of medicine. Anyways, these particular people, we
need 'em. We really need 'em." No one responded, and soon
we could hear him snoring.

One of the men from the Indian Center came out early in
the morning, and with what he brought added to our supplies,
we had a hearty breakfast. Then the old Papago woman arrived with one of her sons. "Now, do you remember her?"
Mad Bear quizzed. "This is our landlady here. So we have
her to thank for all this hospitality. There may be no Jacuzzi
out here, but there's a roof over our heads and it's rent free at
that, and all we had to do is rustle up a kettle of menudo.
We may just do that again tonight." Masayuki and I looked
at each other, and Mad Bear laughed. "Well, maybe not
tonight," he conceded. "Tomorrow night, I guess. Two nights
in a row might be a little much—although these folks here do
love my menudo." That would be the night, Mad Bear knew,
that Masayuki and I would be at the motel back in town, as
previously planned, since I had paperwork and phone calls to
catch up with.

The old woman had brought her youngest son—probably
in his early twenties—out to be our guide. He was to lead us
down through the old dirt roads that went along the Mexican
border to examine and photograph the ancient pictographs
that told of the arrival and the history of these earliest humans. Mad Bear had wanted her to go along, he told us as we
made our way over the rough desert roads. With her many
years of learning and her long memory, she was the one with
the expertise sufficient to interpret the images for us. But
then, he acknowledged, it would be difficult for her to climb
around through the rocks and the cacti—too much to expect
of her at her age. "Well, it doesn't make no difference," the
son contended. "She knows all them rock pictures by heart.
It's like a reg'lar photograph right there in her brain." So we
would get a good look for ourselves and discuss them with her
when we returned.

There were many large hills of solid rock and many places among these that were abounding with both pictographs and petroglyphs. Many of these were etched into the rocks hundreds of years ago, our guide claimed, and much later, as they began to wear down, were painted to revive the impressions. We drove on as far as we could and hiked up to a secluded spot among the hills. There we found a long sequence of images, rather like a mural, that stretched across the face of a cliff. Some of the impressions were faint and barely visible.

"This is the beginning," Mad Bear explained. "You can see that it is the beginning because this first picture here, this shows the landing—the landing of the first people on the Earth. This was way back in prehistoric times. I can interpret this for you in my way because this is all in our records and the oral histories of all our tribes. And then we can talk about it more later." He advised Masayuki, who was our recorder and photographer, to take pictures and make tape recordings because all this would be more than we could hold in memory.

"You see this here?" It looked like a cylinder with legs and a triangular top. "Now if you wanted to get into this so-called verification, well, just think about this. There's ways to prove how many centuries ago this was carved into these rocks. And once you recognize it, there's no denying that this is a rocket ship. This was understood by our people and handed down through generations of our ancestors. That's why I told you we understood jet propulsion and antigravity way before the Europeans came to this continent. So this is the spaceship—at the beginning of this whole description here because this is where it starts—when our ancestors came purposely to this planet many thousands of years ago." We proceeded along the series of images. There were humans among what we were told were representations of prehistoric animals, and there were images of spirits and ceremonies representing the early instructions from the spirit world. Mad Bear pointed out an impression of two characters further along in the chronicle. It looked at first like a portrayal of two women, both in long dresses, one chasing the other. They appeared to be running, and the one pursuing was snatching the other's dress with one hand while holding up a cross with the other hand. "This is an Indian woman," Mad Bear said. "And this is a priest with his robes and his cross. You remember this and you can ask about it later." But I could already guess what this depiction represented.

"Hey Bear! Look at this!" our young Papago guide shouted, waving his hand in the air. He had started down the hill ahead of us and had apparently found something on the ground. As we approached him, he held it out toward Mad Bear in the palm of his hand. It was an arrowhead. It seemed symbolically significant in the context of these historical images and the visions they had induced. There could have been a hunt or a battle in this very spot, I imagined, or perhaps here was an ancient village where some young warrior sat to carve his arrows. "Do you want it, Bear?" he asked. "Or should I keep it?"

"You found it," Mad Bear answered. "There must be a reason."

He looked at it proudly and put it in his pocket.

"Wait, hold it!" Mad Bear warned. "You can't just claim it like that. You know better than that—you don't just find and take. Either you put it back where you found it or, if you think you're meant to keep it, you make some offering and some acknowledgment."

"Bear, I don't have anything on me. Maybe if I could come back . . ."

"You don't have anything? What do you mean by that? You have your strength and your spirit. If you don't have a material offering, you make a pledge."

The young man stared silently into his palm, then held up the arrowhead, and gazed long into the sky. Then he put it again in his pocket. "I made a pledge to quit drinkin'," he reported. "I promised the Great Spirit I'm never gonna touch another . . ."

"You don't have to tell it out loud like that," Mad Bear said. "That's for you. You and I can talk about that later, if you like." We walked back toward where we'd left the car.

Mad Bear looked pensive. "Yeah, you and I, we'll talk about that later," he enjoined our guide. "A thing like that, it becomes a sacred object. When you make a pledge, it becomes a sacred pledge. It's a serious thing. You've got to mean it."

The old Papago woman and her son left as soon as we returned to the cabin saying that if we wanted to talk it would have to wait until breakfast. They promised to come early and to bring supplies for a hearty breakfast, and Mad Bear offered to start another pot of menudo. "It's for tomorrow— tomorrow evening," Mad Bear hastened, looking at Masayuki. "You guys'll be back in town havin' supper in the coffee shop at the 'Jacuzzi Motel.' "

"Where do they go when they leave here?" I asked. "Isn't this where they live, or do they have another place?"

"No, no. They've got their regular house back there in that residential part of the reservation—back by the San Xavier Mission." He chuckled and looked teasingly again at Masayuki. "You don't think for a minute they'd be nuts enough to spend the whole night out here in this canyon with all these snakes and spiders running around."

The cabin had a main room for cooking, eating, sitting, and talking, and here we had placed three folding cots. Through a swinging door atop three rickety wooden stairs was a small bedroom with a bed. This is where Mad Bear slept and snored. I lay on my cot with my arms folded behind my head wondering about that spaceship and about the so-called prehistoric arrival of the humans. Fortunately, as Mad Bear had said, verification was not our work. There could be no verification, one way or the other, only conjecture. It made no difference anyway, it seemed to me, just how many millennia the humans had been living here. The records and prophesies served the general argument. It was a fact that humans had lived on this land for unknown eras of time. And only very recently, through our very recent "progress," have we so adulterated our environment that we have placed our continued survival in question. That, I supposed, was what Mad Bear expected to be the Native people's message.

The director of the Indian Center drove up with our hostess in good time to put together an ample breakfast, and driving up behind them was a middle-aged Indian couple from Tucson who also brought supplies. Our young Papago guide had not wanted to come back. "Well, I can git him on up here," his mother offered, "whenever'n yer ready to go snoop around ag'in. He'll come if I tell 'im."

"Too bad," Mad Bear said. "I was going to have a little talk with him. Anyways, we did have a pretty good look at lots of rock writings yesterday, and you're the one we wanted to talk with about that."

She shrugged her shoulders slightly and managed to look typically indifferent. "I don't know nothing about it," she said, causing Mad Bear to laugh out loud.

In fact, she knew. She had a vivid mental picture of everything we had seen. She went on shrugging her shoulders, nevertheless, with every description and explanation, as though she had no idea whether she was right or whether it mattered. Occasionally she was forced to smile because Mad Bear was also appearing totally ignorant in order to induce her to speak. He asked her about the age of the carvings, the dates of the events, and about that "ship from outer space" and just when that might have been.

"That's the first people which we came down from. Our ancestors, I guess you'd say. The dates, I never heard nobody tell no dates. They musta had their dates, but it wouldn't mean nothin' to me. All's I know is January, February, like that, and the different years we count by. That was brought over and put on us later, I guess, but that's all I know now."

"Yeah, as far as the calendar's concerned," Mad Bear said, "but I don't mean the date exactly like that. About how many years ago did the first people come here?"

"How should I know? Give or take a few thousand years, it don't make no differ'nce. That's the beginning of the records, that's what we know. Then after that the records tell the order—they don't give no dates. But that's our ancestors, sure enough, and the white folks, they still don't understand. Some say Adam and Eve and different things, and then the rest of 'em says monkeys or gorillas or somethin' like that. That's because they didn't know about those ships yet. Those Europeans, when they came over here, they didn't have no idea of such a thing. We didn't have it either by that time— them kinda ships—but we had our records so that's what we kept telling—even way back then. They had some sailing ships, that's about all, and they had horses and wagons. So they denied it. You know why? They said there ain't no such of a thing. Spaceship is not possible. So they stick by that even now. Stubborn. But the day's comin' around they'll be doin' it theirself. Then they'll see others doin' it. Space travel. And then they'll say, 'Yep, it coulda been.' Well, 'course it was, that's just the way it was."

"Where do the records say they came from, those first people?"

"Where you see them seven stars, that's about it. That's the area, the way it's told to us. Bear, you know that. You'd say the same thing, same as I'm saying. You don't need to talk to me."

"Well, you're the one here who's been given these interpretations as they've been passed along. The oral history has remained unbroken." Mad Bear looked at us for our reaction. "But isn't that something? You could have come here hundreds of years ago and asked any member of any tribe. Those who had the records, they'd all tell you the same thing. And these rock writings, they were made long before your exalted Columbus—the spaceships, the whole bit!"

She shook an admonishing finger at us. "But it was still from the records the way our people had been told. Don't you kids go tellin' no one those pitchers was put there by the sky people. Our people done them pitchers long, long after that. Only thing, if you want to tell your people something, you tell them we were knowing about space travel way back in the covered wagon days. And we were predictin' it agin, and they said we was loco. Now comes the time to get the record straight. After all these long years. 'Course, it'll take time. I'll be dead."

That last comment stopped her. She sat back and fell silent as though there were no point in going on after that. The rest of the questions and answers would be up to us. Mad Bear only watched her quietly. Then after a moment she sat up again and went on.

"But anyway, Bear, that boy of mine, guess he took these fellers to the right pitchers. But now, those seven stars, you didn't see those, maybe. But you can see those right in the sky, most any night, just by lookin'. That's another thing. There's only six you can see, they sez. They kept on saying us people must be crazy 'cause you can't see seven. Since my gramma's day they were goin' on like that. Some years back, they put them telescopes up here on our mountain. Kit Peak. That's our mountain—my land up there. We never sold that, 'cause we don't sell our sacred mountains. You can ask 'em, they'll tell you it's ours. They says, 'Well, we'll just share the place, we wanna put some telescopes.' First we says nothin' doin' 'cause every time we've seen how the white folks mess up everything. Cuttin' down trees. Never talkin' to the trees. White folks, they never been taught about that. No natural manners. Killin' the little four-legged peoples. Up there on that mountain they can't do that. They promised, and we keep checkin' up on it. That's our land, and we come and go as we please—and we don't need no appointments. That's the best place in the world to see the stars. We always knew seven stars—seven sisters. And behind that there's a bunch of 'em—same group—stars and planets—where us humans was—still are. Hundreds of years we been knowin' that.

"Long, long ago, we named that mountain 'Place to Look at Heaven.' That's why we finally agreed when these scientists came along. Then their telescopes got developed real good and they learned a lot about the place our people came from. Well, how did we know them things all along? We were taught them things. You don't even have to look and strain. You could just close your eyes and listen. Anybody could do it. Used to, anyhow. Listen is what our people did, listen and look, and they could learn all about the stars—and about this

Earth, too. There's such a thing as them who knows." She looked at me as though to see whether she'd gone too far for a white man.

"That's right," I said. But then I supposed she was wondering how I would know. "I mean, that's what Mad Bear's been telling us."

"He told you them things yesterday, did he?"

"Well, no, he's talked about it before."

"You might coulda picked up somethin' from those writin's. There's the people and the animals and there's the different Earth bein's. Then there's the sky world and the different peoples. And there's the spirits. See, it's all one big house, and it all works together. But now it's closed off, mostly, so we can't say much about it. Well, it's all in the records, and it'll all come around agin." She had been looking at me, and then she pointed at Mad Bear. "That's what you oughta be puttin' out to the white folks, Bear. We usta get instructions from the spirit world. We oughta open that up agin. Nowadays, with all the diggin' and cuttin' and choppin' up the Earth, seems like the lines get cut. Broke connections to the spirit world. Just when we need it, too. We better get that back!"

She looked up. The couple from Tucson had come in from outside and stood watching us as though they had been waiting. "I ain't goin' yet," she piped. "I'm settin' up here t'day an' I'm havin' some o' Bear's menudo later."

"We're going back," Masayuki hastened.

"But I thought Bear and me were s'posed to have a little game of chess," said the man from Tucson. "That's what I'm hangin' up here for."

"That's right, we were," Mad Bear remembered, slapping his knee. "But hold up. Come in and listen to Grandmother here for a minute. She's giving us some pretty interesting information—things to think about."

"No, I ain't," she said. "I already done it."

Mad Bear wanted her to comment on one particular depiction he had pointed out to us, but she did not want to talk about it. "But that's clearly a Papago woman running from a priest," he said. "And we know why."

"So why ask me?"

"What isn't clear is whether they actually did that to the women or they just tried to or threatened to."

She frowned at Mad Bear. "You know, Bear. We all know. Everyone knows. It don't need to be repeated."

"Repeated?" Mad Bear questioned. "It was carved in stone!"

"Because there's more meanin' behind it," she said. "It was for others. Like a whatcha call warnin'. It was for the inside meanin'. All that writin'—the whole thing—it's all put there for teachin's. That was the reason." She got up, excused herself, and turned to busy herself in the kitchen.

The rest of us went outside, and Mad Bear removed his traveling chess set and folding board from the back of his Toyota. Masayuki and the young Mohawk carried a small table and some chairs from the cabin, and the three of us sat down to watch the game. Mad Bear rubbed his hands together, slapped his forehead, bounced in his chair, and kept up a witty commentary. Masayuki was amused. Mad Bear was far different from any player he had ever seen. I had become used to watching him at his game, and at times I had wished that I was skilled enough to engage him at it.

"Look behind you!" Mad Bear suddenly shouted, pointing over his opponent's shoulder.

"Hey, come on Bear. Don't be pullin' . . ."

"No, no. It's got nothing to do with the game. Somebody's up there. They might be up to something. Doug, can you see them?"

He was pointing to the mountain in the distance beyond the cabin. We could see nothing but the bare, rocky hillside, and Mad Bear's competitor continued to watch him suspiciously.

"No, look, there's a Jeep—a light brown Jeep—it blends in with the side of the mountain. Guess I've got the only good eyes here."

We could all make out the Jeep, once we knew what and

where it was, but it was much more difficult, even with Mad Bear's description, to see the two men among the rocks just above it. They were two tiny forms that seemed to be moving. He insisted they had pickaxes and were chopping into the rocks—and by that he could tell they were not Indian.

"Prob'ly rock collectin', Bear," the man said, turning back to the game. "Just a coupla rock hounds from Tucson or somethin'. It's your move."

But Mad Bear did not want to let it go. "They shouldn't be up there cutting rocks. From now on, these things have to be done in the right way. That's just what we've been talking about. Besides, this is the reservation. They're supposed to get permission." He went to get the man from the Indian Center who had been napping in the bedroom, and the three men stood peering at the mountain with their hands cupped over their eyes.

"We oughta drive up there and tell 'em they're arrested and bring 'em back here for a talking to," Mad Bear said. They decided to defer their chess game, and they piled into Mad Bear's Toyota Land Cruiser. "These guys better stay here," he told his Mohawk helper. "So you wait here with 'em. They gotta see only Indians, and there's no room for you guys anyways. In fact, you three better wait in the cabin—in the bedroom so they don't see you when we bring 'em back here." Then he added with a chuckle, "We oughta put some paint on, is what we oughta do, and scare those guys right outa their boots!"

Masayuki and I and Mad Bear's young assistant watched from below. They did "arrest" the strangers, and as we saw the two Jeeps heading down the mountain, we concealed ourselves in the bedroom. They brought the two strangers into the cabin and sat them down with the old Papago matriarch, and we listened by the door trying to make out what they were saying.

But then we heard laughter and we decided it had become a friendly chat. Mad Bear put his head through the door and whispered. "These are okay guys—well meaning. They just didn't know. They got a shop in Tucson where they polish these rocks and sell some kinda jewelry or something. You guys oughta come out and join us so's they'll see we got all kinda different friends up here." But the two men left just as we came out, and headed back to Tucson.

The chess game was resumed, but Mad Bear had his mind on what had just occurred, and he was moved to talk about it, even as he scrutinized the board. "Those guys were given permission as far as the reservation is concerned," he informed us. "She can do that. And they were told something about the right way to go about these things. Anyways, that was interesting timing." He cupped his chin in his hands and stared at the pieces on the board. "Just what we'd been talking about. That's the meaning of that carving on the rock. That's what the old lady meant by instructions—because it's symbolic of a lot of things. What it referred to really was rape, but it was recorded as a warning. There's more than one kind of rape. There's ideological rape and there's rape of the Earth. Anytime you take anything sacred without permission, it's rape— whether it's some woman's person or someone's tradition or Mother Earth herself. Rape of the Mother, that's what was warned against, way before even the so-called explorers."

The other player, who had at first appeared annoyed at Mad Bear's inattentiveness, sat back and looked at him with interest. "That's right, Bear," he contributed. "That's what those guys were doin' up there. But I don't think they realized it. White people, they don't know no better." He glanced at me. "Most of 'em, anyway, unless they've learned better from us." Then he looked at Masayuki. "I don't know about your people. I've never been to your . . ."

"Our people too," Mad Bear interrupted. "Our people aren't exempt. We have our so-called progressives. Look right here in Arizona. How many of our own people are raping the Mother? No one has the right to take anything from another person or from the Earth. Neither for profit nor for pleasure—I don't care who they are. No one has the right to simply take—not a single tree or a bird, or even a hunk of rock."

"Except they get permission, Bear. We're taught to get permission."

"It needs more than permission to make it right. It requires offering. It requires a relationship. You don't take but that you give. You don't take from your woman, you give. And you don't take from the Mother, you give—and with consent at that. It's a mutual thing—mutual consent and mutual exchange. Anything other than that is rape."

CHAPTER NINE
So Many Contests

"There's choices behind choices—a reason for everything."

◑ Masayuki and I sat in the motel coffee shop back in Tucson and talked about plans. It was only a little more than a week before Mad Bear and I were scheduled to speak at the Institute for the Study of Consciousness in Berkeley. I was arranging appointments for both of us in Los Angeles and San Francisco, and Mad Bear had wanted to spend a few days in Los Angeles looking up his own contacts before heading up to the Bay Area. He would be driving in for breakfast in the morning and, after taking care of some business in town, we'd be heading back out to the reservation.

Our guess was that we would be leaving Arizona before the end of the week and driving to Los Angeles. We would all be in Mad Bear's vehicle as Masayuki and I had flown in. We'd have several drivers and could perhaps drive straight through. After our presentation in Berkeley, we supposed, we'd be heading southwest again, back to the Sonora Desert.

Actually, it would all be up to Mad Bear and, as such, it would all remain indefinite and spontaneous. We'd have to play it as we went. I had become accustomed, if not adept, at playing by ear, remaining flexible and spontaneous, always being ready to go with the flow—the flow, at least, of whomever I was following around at the moment. But it was a challenge, always, considering I was responsible for making appointments, reservations, and travel arrangements and had to work within a confining budget.

It appeared that Hiro and Yoko were returning from Japan, and I was hoping to have a few extra days in the Bay Area—or at least to know what to plan for and when. As willing as he was to travel, Mad Bear remained adverse, I knew, to spending any more than a minimum amount of time in California. We talked about Hiro and Yoko as we sat in the coffee shop. They had been my first Japanese houseguests, and had left for home long before I met Masayuki. I had received some photos from Japan just as we were about to leave, and Masayuki had seen these. Among them was a picture of a Japanese monk. He did not look like a monk, though he wore robes and clogs. He had long black hair, intense-looking eyes, and a dramatically sculpted face, and he looked like an actor. They had called him a new teacher in their letter and had proposed that they bring him to the United States so he could meet me and, through me, some American Indians, yogis, doctors, scientists, and others who, they supposed, would "be having same mind just like teacher." I'd had time to respond, before we'd left California, to suggest they wait until I could be in touch again to discuss it, since we would be traveling for an unknown time.

Masayuki and I had called home from our room, just before coming to eat, and we had learned that Hiro and Yoko had telephoned from Japan. Our housemates had told them that we'd soon be back for a scheduled talk in Berkeley and had gotten the impression that, this being the case, they would hasten to be on their way from Japan. What, I wondered, could I be expected to do to make their trip worthwhile? I could not be sure whether, if they had arrived, I would even be able to see them.

Masayuki insisted I should not feel responsible, or even much concerned, whatever should unfold. "To come all the way from Japan without exact arrangement, they have to take their chance," he said. "Maybe I can help with them. Anyway, we can't arrange it now. Our job is to Mad Bear, and we can't control anything."

In the morning, Mad Bear arrived at the motel much earlier than planned. When I was awakened by the insistent knock at the door, I supposed that someone had come to the wrong room. I opened the door a few inches and saw his face through my blurry eyes. It was barely light out. He did not have his usual smile nor his usual: "C'mon up! Things are poppin' already!" He just stood there waiting for me to open the door wide enough for him to get through.

"We were still asleep," I pleaded. "Seems like we barely . . ."

"You guys get up and come over to the coffee shop. I'll be waiting over there. Hurry up. I gotta tell you something." But as soon as I had closed the door he knocked again. "I'd better tell you in here. There's a couple others from the Indian Center sitting with us over there—not that they don't know it anyways—but you better hear it before you go over there. Is Mas awake? He should hear it too." Masayuki sat up in his bed and Mad Bear turned on every light in the room.

"What happened?" I asked, realizing he had brought bad news.

"That young Papago that took us out the other day to the rocks—the old lady's son—he's dead." He looked at us for our reaction. Masayuki rubbed his eyes. "Killed," he went on. "Stabbed to death with a knife. Someone found him dead, just a couple hours back, and came to get them. Some of them went out there, some of the relatives, and they left the mother waiting home. He was leaning against some old shack along the path. Bled to death. He'd bled to death through the night. They don't know how it happened yet.

There was no knife around. But there was a six-pack there beside him. Beer. Apparently he'd gone to buy some beer. You guys get ready, and we'll go on over to the coffee shop. I'll just wait here."

Mad Bear stopped us just outside the coffee shop. "Lemme tell you two things before we go in there. We might have a little change in our schedule. We won't be going back out to the cabin today, and then we'll see. I'm going to their house to be with the mother. I'm gonna do a little ceremony tonight—I guess just for us Indians. I mean, I'm all right with it, you know, but for the family in a case like this, I guess it's better you two stay here at the motel. One more thing. He was on the path coming from the liquor store. The guy that found him said he'd seen him in there last evening buying beer, and there was that six-pack beside him. I have a feeling he had that arrowhead still on him." We joined the others for breakfast and Masayuki and I only listened as we ate. They talked about the police and the arrangements for the funeral and, after breakfast, they all left.

We did not see Mad Bear until late that night. This time he knocked softly on the door as though hesitant to awaken us. He stood outside and talked in a whisper. "I got my room back, same one as before—right on the other side of your door again. I just sent our Mohawk buddy back up home an' I'm staying here in town. Listen, you unlock the door from your side, and I'll go around and open it in my room. Then we can talk." We opened the double doors between our rooms. "And your window too," he said. "Let's crack these windows and get a little air through here. I oughta smoke these rooms too, but I guess we can do that later."

I carried a chair from our room to his and we sat down. "I'm kinda beat, I'll hit the hay here pretty quick. I guess we'll be staying right here a couple more days. I thought tomorrow we might go pick up something—some flowers, maybe—to send for the funeral, but we won't stay for that. We might as well head on West. No point in going back out to the canyon for these few days, and then it's getting time to head out to the coast anyways. You guys hungry or no? I guess I woke you up, isn't it?"

"That's okay, but we did have supper—we don't need anything now."

"Me too, I ate over there. The ceremony went pretty good. I got ahold of the young man and he recognized me. I didn't feel too much from him—not too much fear or confusion. 'Course he was still kind of detached. I got him to follow me around. I walked him around his house, his bedroom, everything, talking all the time. I told him this is where he used to sleep—but not anymore. I told him this is where he used to eat when he had his body. I told him this is where he used to live before he decided to go. So he got a lot of explanation and encouragement. And then came the instructions to help him on his way. Everyone was there, the family, you know, so he could take a good look at everyone. See, you got to get everything closed out—that's the purpose in it—a ceremony like that. Then there's nothing left open, nothing to struggle over trying to figure it out. That can hold you trapped something terrible. It can go on for years. Time was, everyone in the world had ceremonies for that. Now it's mostly lost—'specially where there's no traditional medicine people left. Well, we found out what happened, anyways—how the thing happened. The whole story got put together. And that's good too—I mean, that understanding is important."

He leaned back and yawned and put his face in his hands. I thought he looked exhausted. I wanted to ask how it happened, but it seemed best not to make him talk more now.

"Yeah," he said, looking up, "you're right. Like I said I'm pretty wiped out. But we can sleep in, get a good breakfast, and take a look at our situation. Not much more we can do out here just now—but we'll come back. There's just the three of us now to drive out." Mad Bear shook his head slowly. "He put that arrowhead right in his pocket, and that's where it was, right where he got stabbed. Made that pledge like that—you saw it, right? And in no time at all he broke it. Imagine that, he went and bought himself some beer—arrowhead in one pocket, beer money in the other. Well, that was his choice. Choice is a funny thing. In one way he forgot his pledge—let himself forget. In another way, he made an unconscious choice. There's choices behind choices—a reason for everything—however it might look to us. But I'll tell you one thing. If you are going to die—I mean get killed, a young guy like that, right outa the blue—that's the best way to go. There's no better way. It might sound funny to say it but, the way he went, it's a lot better than being shot or blown up or something. It's a lot easier. You don't get jolted into a confusion that you can't get out of by yourself. Bleeding to death is slow and easy, and you can watch yourself go. You're right there. You know what's going on." He stood up and stretched.

It seemed reasonable, since he'd said that much, to question him. "But how did he get stabbed?"

"With another guy's knife. Now they've talked to everybody, including some who saw it. None of them actually realized what had happened. That's why the guy took off. He didn't know. It was an accident, anyways, and he didn't know. Guess our young friend didn't know either—till it was too late. This guy's dog went after him—big dog. The guy said he didn't know why—said it wasn't like his dog. The dog went after him, bitin' at him as he was walking out of the liquor store with his six-pack. I guess to defend himself he kicked the dog in the mouth or something, but the dog stayed on him. That's what the guy said—said when he ran up to get his dog, his dog was still getting kicked—so he showed his knife just to stop it. The guy claimed he never made a swipe with the knife—never made a lunge at him. They think now the way he got stabbed was he kicked the knife—either on purpose or not—and the blade caught him. Musta hit some vein or artery or something. Caught him right through the front pocket— right by that arrowhead—that broken pledge. Certain things have power, that's for sure. But some things, we don't know all the inside details why they happen."

The next day over breakfast, we turned our attention to our California trip. I proposed that we consider driving first to San Francisco so we could spend a few days in the Bay Area and then drive from there to Los Angeles. Through a contact in California, I had arranged an interview for Mad Bear with a woman from the *Los Angeles Times*, and I was working on a similar arrangement in San Francisco. I had also arranged several meetings with funding prospects in both San Francisco and Los Angeles.

Mad Bear seemed increasingly apprehensive about being on the West Coast. I recalled the dream descriptions he had related to me many weeks earlier, but I did not want to bring up the matter of earthquakes. For the sake of our project, we needed for him to be available for several days. In any case, I could not but agree to his resolve, at least for the moment. He insisted on waiting in Tucson until only a couple days before our talk at the institute in Berkeley and then driving directly into Los Angeles. We would leave the car there, and fly up to San Francisco. It seemed like an inefficient and costly arrangement. "We'll make our appearance at that institute," he said, "and then fly right back down to L.A. We'll give our talk, fly back down, pick up the car, take care of business, and hightail it out of there." I could only hope that once there he would become involved, as he usually did, and change his mind.

On our way out of town, we selected a flower arrangement. We prepared a handwritten note, and the three of us signed it. Mad Bear left instructions for delivery, and we headed West. "We can drive straight on through," Mad Bear declared. "This thing rides as smooth as a boat in the water. Guess that's why they call it 'Land Cruiser.' And these seats—that's why I picked it—I never get tired. 'Course with the three of us and all our luggage, we're a little tight. But we can cruise straight on in—snug as a bug in a rug." He was eating as he talked and tossing orange peels out the window. Masayuki looked at him, and he chuckled. "I pick up your thoughts, you know. You know that, don't you? Well, these are biodegradable. I never litter—never. But I always throw food on the ground in appropriate places. Doug can tell you that."

◗

Masayuki drove while Mad Bear nodded off in the passenger seat. Some time in the middle of the night, we checked into a hotel right in the center of Los Angeles—another "cheap" place that Mad Bear had picked out. "I know most all the cheap places," he said. "Hotels, cafés, everything. Much as I've traveled, I've learned these things. So you can count on me for holdin' that budget down. Just don't expect a Jacuzzi every place we go. This place I know on account of the Greyhound bein' right over there. Some of our Indian people used to come in by Greyhound and we'd stay here. Indian Center's near here too. We'd go over there when an earthquake was looking near at hand. That's where we'd call everybody—Indian people, I mean, so's they'd have time to prepare. I can't get back into that now, but I'll tell you this, and you know it already, I can't stay out here on the coast but a few days at the outside. Quick as we've done our thing, we're out of here."

The next day we were on the plane for San Francisco. Mad Bear seemed his jolly self again, even as he squeezed himself into the seat beside me and fumbled with his seat-belt extension. His cheerfulness somehow eased my own discontent. In spite of my own wishes, I had purchased return tickets for the following day and rebooked our rooms for the following night. Since his own plans had been cut short, Masayuki stayed behind to visit friends in L.A., seeing little point in going home for only one night. I could at least feel thankful that Mad Bear had not opted out of our scheduled lecture.

Someone slapped me on the back as we came out of the jetway at the airport. I turned to face a man about my height with dark hair and glasses, and I stepped back to see more clearly. It was Hiro. One of our housemates had come to meet us as arranged, and had let Hiro step up first to surprise me. I was more confounded than surprised. I had been looking forward to seeing Hiro and Yoko again, but I was hoping they would return when I could spend some time with them.

"It's okay," Hiro insisted with a smile, "really okay. We are so free. We know you are busy. We stay in motel in San Francisco—just in the city. Sen Sei doesn't want we are disturbing

you. Just now I came for only saying hello. Really we are understand. We'll just waiting you and follow you anyway."

It wasn't reassuring. I now had two problematic projects
and wasn't sure I could manage either. I could only think to
get the number and promise to phone the motel. I introduced
Mad Bear and Hiro briefly, and we were on our way to Oakland leaving Hiro to return to San Francisco. Hiro and Yoko
had arrived days earlier, I learned during the drive home.
They had come with Yoko's mother and the monk named Jison, and the four of them had checked into a motel in San
Francisco. Hiro had called our place many times and had
learned of our arrival just in time to make it on his own to the
airport. In any case, I needed to turn my thoughts to that
evening—to make sure we got settled at home and were prepared for our talk and on time for dinner.

Once again, Mad Bear pulled from his little carry-on bag
his complete traditional regalia. He put on his large, blousy
shirt of purple—the sacred Iroquois color—his buckskin
vest, and the wide sash with its various symbols and emblems
that crossed his front from left to right. He wore his bear-claw
necklace with its heavy metal medallion and carried his feathered Tuscarora hat. He looked splendid as we sat with Ruth
and Arthur Young in the Chinese restaurant on College Avenue—but he was a spectacle in the dining room as many
faces turned to watch him eat. No one looks weird to anyone
in Berkeley, I knew, only various shades of interesting.

Mad Bear was never without his medicine bag on its leather
thong around his neck, but it was very rarely visible. On this
night he wore it outside his shirt, and it was clearly noticeable
against the purple cloth of his shirt. I never asked him by
what criteria he determined to wear it out. In fact, I never referred to or looked too closely at his medicine bag. At one
point during the meal, Arthur reached to touch it. Instantly,
Mad Bear's hand flew up to block his. No one ever touched
Mad Bear's medicine bag. Arthur was startled, but he quickly
realized his infraction. Mad Bear, on the other hand, well
understood the intent and was not offended, and both men

apologized at once. Mad Bear laughed. He was in his usual excellent humor, smiling constantly and commenting with delight at everything from the sound of the sizzling rice soup to the challenge of the chopsticks.

Everyone was enjoying this time and, since the restaurant was only a few blocks from the institute, we waited until starting time to walk down the street and make our grand entrance. There again, unannounced and unexpected, sat Hiro in the audience—and beside him sat Jison. I knew him from his photograph and our eyes met briefly in recognition as I entered the room. We walked through the audience to the two chairs beside the fireplace. It was a modest fire but, as Mad Bear was dressed rather elaborately, we pushed our chairs a little farther to the side. This was precisely the scene that was perceived in the dream, but I believe neither of us gave it more than a passing thought. The crowded room was still with anticipation, and Mad Bear was obviously elated. He told our hosts he was thirsty and would really appreciate a cold drink for his throat. The word was passed, and someone brought him a cola in a bottle.

My job was to introduce our topic and to present Mad Bear in a sufficient manner. We had not planned our talk, nor even discussed it, but I knew that Mad Bear was never at a loss to make his point. Fortunately, he had a talent for making people feel cheerful and comfortable and an ability to speak of atrocities in an impersonal and nonaccusing manner. He spoke first, as he always did, of the catastrophic assaults against Earth and nature that, in his view, had already assured the end of contemporary civilization and brought about the initiation of a new arrangement. For Mad Bear, the inevitable wrath of nature was not the ultimate issue. He was interested only in circumstances—in the unfolding of events and in what lay beyond the transition. Mad Bear recognized that the destruction of wilderness and the decline of society were apparent and undeniable facts—but to him these circumstances only confirmed the beginning of transition and the inevitability of a new world. So he talked about the ancient records and prophesies of the Hopi, the Ojibwa, the Iroquois, and other Native peoples—records and prophesies that, after all these long years, could finally be shared and might at last be heard. Ancient records attested to centuries of "living in balance" with the natural world, and the prophesies told of the abandoning of this relationship for the pursuit of dominion. But the prophesies also forecast the coming purification and rebalancing, he told us, and they predicted a transition beyond which waited "a beautiful golden age."

When he finished his presentation, he stopped and asked for questions—and for another cold drink. Mad Bear had invoked intense interest, as well as curiosity—for he had presented a picture and a prospectus that was more exciting than ominous—and there was much discussion. People asked about this "transition," about how to predict natural disasters and how to prepare for them, and they wanted to know about this "new world" and how it would be different and "beautiful." During the discussion, he began to appear distracted and, suddenly, in the midst of a response, he stopped himself and stared into the audience. "Let me just interrupt this a moment to acknowledge someone here. There is a medicine person sitting right here—or one we would refer to as a medicine person. I don't know this man but, in our way, if we're speaking in the presence of another medicine man, we are supposed to acknowledge him."

I realized he was referring to Jison. I had never had a chance to mention him to Mad Bear and there had not been time even to explain who Hiro was when he had met him briefly at the airport. I was seeing Jison for the first time myself and had certainly not expected to see him this evening. He did look impressive, and he was wearing his robes, but no doubt Mad Bear saw something in him beyond his appearance.

"I should have done this earlier but . . . I'm sorry I don't know your name . . ." He looked directly at Jison, but Jison only looked back with a detached expression. "If you don't mind, would you stand up and introduce yourself?" Jison re-

mained expressionless and motionless and continued only to
look back with unblinking eyes. "It's not right to point at such
a person," Mad Bear went on, extending an open palm in Jison's direction, "but I'm referring to this gentleman here."

Hiro tapped Jison's shoulder and told him to stand, and Jison came to his feet and stood calmly with an open expression. We waited. Jison looked totally at ease, and it appeared
as though he would stand there until told to sit down again.
Hiro spoke up shyly, sounding as though he were asking for-
giveness. "He doesn't understand even a little bit English and
so he cannot speak something." He tapped Jison again, but
Jison reached for Hiro's arm and pulled him up. "Anyway, I
met him in Japan and now he is my teacher, but only short
time and so I cannot explain well his teaching. Just he has
small temple in Japan mountainside and he is helping for people so many kinds of things. Now we come to United States for
meeting Mr. Doug and Mr. Mad Bear." He sat down and
pulled Jison down with him.

Jison and Hiro waited in their seats until most of the crowd
had left. While Mad Bear was still talking with a small group
who had come forward, they took me aside so that Jison could
speak to me through Hiro. I had explained our one-day
schedule to Hiro at the airport, and Jison wanted to know
whether, in spite of our limited time, we would be able to meet
for a brief conversation sometime before our return flight. I
told them where they could meet us in San Francisco the following morning. Mad Bear had agreed to one interview with a
San Francisco newspaper if it could be completed within the
few hours we had in town. It had been arranged by one of our
associates who had worked with us when Mad Bear was here
before, and it was scheduled to take place in his house in San
Francisco. This would be the only way, I told Hiro, that we
could possibly get together. Jison readily agreed to the brief
and not-so-private meeting saying that we could spend more
time in the future. He wanted me to tell Mad Bear something
that he would not have the chance to tell him.

Mad Bear's diabetes was very serious, Jison was saying,

and Mad Bear was in considerable danger. He needed to be
told that he must control his thirst and, particularly, his urge
to drink sodas. I was not sure how I could relate this to Mad
Bear. Certainly, with all his concerns, it would have to wait
until an easier time. I had no idea that Mad Bear had diabetes. If it were true, perhaps even Mad Bear was unaware of
it. He had made no sign or mention of it. And how could Jison
possibly know? Perhaps he was wrong?

Mad Bear was pleased with the evening and he retained his
elated mood—and I held out some hope that he might yet
change his mind and allow us to extend our stay. On the way
back home that night, he spoke of Jison with such great interest that I found myself relaying Jison's warning about the diabetes. Mad Bear looked uncomfortable and I almost wanted
to apologize for having mentioned it.

"Well, he happened to pick it up," Mad Bear said softly.
"See, that's what I mean about him. Medicine people can pick
these things up. Most people would never know. And he's
right that I shouldn't be drinkin' that pop. Sometimes we give
in for other reasons. Anyways, maybe one of these days we'll
get together with that man."

The following morning, a group gathered at the house in
San Francisco. Mad Bear and Jison had their chance to talk.
They talked before, during, and after the interview. Hiro was
hard pressed to translate. His English was beginning to warm
up again after a long period of disuse, but the subject matter
was strange to him and difficult for him to understand much
less to restate in two very different languages. "I cannot explaining so well in translation each other," he begged. "Anyway, I'm just beginning for this." What little help he was able
to offer was more than sufficient for both Mad Bear and Jison. They were both enjoying their contact beyond their ver-
bal communication.

Mad Bear seemed now to regret leaving—and yet he remained determined. He kept reminding me to watch the time
so we would not be late in leaving for the airport. I was still
hoping you would consider extending for one more day, I said

◑

silently to myself, as though testing whether to say it to Mad Bear. As much time as we had spent together, I continued to forget that he listened to my thoughts.

"Why don't you stay?" he responded. "I'm telling you, I can't or I would. There's no reason you can't extend one more day, seeing as these folks are here and the wife and mother are waiting at the motel. I can go back by myself and we can meet tomorrow night. That way you might arrange how we can all get together down the road. Anyways, it'll be cheaper than the both of us changing our tickets."

I phoned to confirm whether I could change my ticket. There was only a late flight available on the following day. "Oh good," Hiro exclaimed, "you'll have more time." We saw Mad Bear to his gate and returned to the city. I spent the afternoon and evening with Hiro and Yoko, Yoko's mother, and "Sen Sei," as they referred to Jison, and I met them again for breakfast the following day. There was no way, in this limited time, to work out plans for assisting Jison; but in the time we had together, I was able to learn something about him and his objectives and to propose some possibilities.

It was through Yoko's mother, I learned, that Hiro and Yoko had met Jison soon after they returned to Japan. And it was Yoko's mother who was financing their trip, according to Jison's wishes. "We think him as our teacher," Hiro explained, "but she is not his student. Only she respect him so much and she is helping his temple and helping him for everything." I had met Yoko's mother when she had first come to the United States to visit Hiro and Yoko, and I knew about her situation. She was a modest, young housewife when her husband was killed. He had been on business in Nagasaki on the day that the atom bomb was dropped, and she had been left with two little children to raise by herself. In her middle age, she had become a wealthy and well-known entrepreneur in Fukuoka City. They explained to me that while they were living with me here in California, the mother had taken a sick and dying friend to see Jison and that Jison had healed this woman and saved her life. As the mother was financially well off, she was helping him out of gratitude. They were prepared to stay in the motel, they assured me, to wait until I could be free to spend some time with them.

Mad Bear and I would be attending the Council Grove Conference in Kansas in April, and I offered to explore whether Jison might be invited. I had first been to this conference years earlier when Rolling Thunder was there as a guest speaker, and had attended many years since. The Council Grove Conference was so called because it took place at an isolated site a few miles from the small town of Council Grove, Kansas. It was an annual conference on the voluntary control of psychophysiological states and states of consciousness and was attended by physicians, therapists, and researchers by invitation only. Accommodations were limited, I explained, and the conference had already been filled. It was doubtful they could be accommodated at this late date or that they could all attend even if Jison were to be admitted.

"Yes," Hiro translated. "Of course he will go. He says thank-you to you for your good idea."

"But it has to be arranged first," I said. "I can only try."

•   •   •

It was past midnight when I landed in Los Angeles, and by the time I got the bus into town and checked into the hotel, it was nearly morning. Masayuki was still with his friends, and Mad Bear, I was sure, was sound asleep in his room down the hall. There was some hope that we might have one day for catching up on sleep. But Mad Bear rang my room at five A.M.

"Hey! It took you a long time to answer the phone!"

"Mad Bear, I just got to bed a couple hours ago," I urged. "Let me at least try to get a little more . . ."

"Well, come down here and have a cup of coffee! I'm down here in the coffee shop. I'll wait for you down here."

Reluctantly, I told Mad Bear that I would be down as soon as I could, and I had barely gotten dressed when the phone rang again.

◖

"How come you're still up there? I thought you were coming down."

"Mad Bear, it's only been a few . . ."

"But your coffee's getting cold! I've got your coffee sittin'
here. C'mon down and have your coffee. I was wantin' to talk
to you, and I'm kind of in a hurry."

He's in a hurry at five in the morning, I complained to myself as I rode down the elevator. Sometimes the man is pro-
foundly insightful and sometimes he makes no sense at all.

He sat hunched over his cup and did not lift his face until I
was sitting across the table from him. He did not appear restless and eager as I had expected—he looked groggy and exhausted, and I wondered whether he had been up all night. I
was not sure what was happening. I sipped my lukewarm coffee and waited for him to speak first. "I have to leave," he
said. "I mean pretty quick, too. I was thinking of heading
back to Arizona."

"Well, I assumed we'd be heading back to Arizona quite
soon," I said, trying to find some delicate way to hold him to
our commitments. "Masayuki and I were already figuring on
that anyway. But, you know, there's that interview with the
paper tomorrow, that's one thing that's pretty much set. I
could make a few phone . . ."

"I can't stay here," he interrupted. "I can't stay for anything. You can stay, but I have to leave right now."

Perhaps he was not feeling well. Perhaps he was just being
stubborn about minimizing the time. There was no way to dis-
pute him—I had to be subtle and try for some compromise.
"Of course we're not sure where Masayuki is at the moment. I
do have his friend's number, but I know he'll show up here
this morning, anyway. Maybe you and he could drive out and
I could catch up with you in a couple days. I'd have to check
if they'd do the interview with only me." I wished that he
could be more forbearing. We needed at least this one day.
There were too many complications. I lifted my cup. "What
time is it now?"

He grabbed my wrist, nearly spilling my coffee. "Doug, you

don't get it! I'm dying here, can you understand that? I've only got a few hours to live! I was trying to handle this without scaring you. Either I leave or I die. You've got to call Mas and get him over here now. I could pass out any minute, and if I pass out you've got to drive me away from this area as fast as you can. I'm trying to hang on here. I think I can stay conscious for another hour or so—and as soon as I'm headed away from here with my back to the coast, I'll start to revive. I wanna just drive out of here and I'll be okay. But if I slip much more, I can't drive."

We rushed up to Mad Bear's room and began to prepare his things. I believed that he was slowly dying. He could have, I realized—and perhaps should have—simply jumped in his car and left in the night. He had tried to be accommodating by waiting for me and inviting me down to discuss it over coffee, but now we were racing against time. I reached Masayuki at his friend's place and he came within minutes. We gave Mad Bear all the cash on hand and the record book for his gas and mileage, but Mad Bear was fading fast, and could only plead, "Get me to the car, get me to the car." He seemed to perk up a bit the moment he slid in behind the wheel—and it was a relief to see because we were worried whether he could safely drive alone. "You guys go back up home," he said, managing to sound somewhat alive, "and take it easy for a coupla days. That way I can phone you from Arizona, and we can take it from there." Within only forty-five minutes from our hasty meeting in the coffee shop, Mad Bear was heading as fast as he could away from the coast.

Masayuki had helped without questioning to get Mad Bear on his way. By now both of us were accustomed to his unpredictable and often whimsical behavior. But usually he was sanguine, even jolly, in his willfulness; this time he was different. "Something is really serious with him!" Masayuki exclaimed as soon as his Toyota was out of sight. "He looked really not so good. He thinks he's dying or what? Why he just drove away by himself?"

"He just couldn't stay here any longer and it was getting

◗

him down," I said, trying to offer an explanation that might sound reasonable. "He didn't see any reason why we should leave—we would have delayed him, anyway. He just wanted to escape as fast as he could, and he thought he would be okay once he got away from here."

"It's too strange," Masayuki retorted. "He shouldn't go away. He should stay and rest. If he's getting sick, it doesn't help anything to go to another place."

"Well, this place just doesn't agree with him. It never has. Remember, he told us that. I guess it just got worse than he expected." I hoped Masayuki would be satisfied with attributing Mad Bear's actions to his willfulness. I hoped, in fact, to satisfy myself with that explanation—at least for the moment. All the visions and predictions notwithstanding, we had made it safely through our evening beside that fireplace at the institute in Berkeley. Apparently, Mad Bear was simply holding on to his apprehensions—and I saw no point in discussing those with Masayuki or in dwelling on them myself. I described our encounter with Jison and told Masayuki what he had said about Mad Bear having diabetes. "That might explain things a little bit," I offered. "If he really does have diabetes, it might be affecting his mood. It wouldn't help that problem just to get out of the area, but you know how Mad Bear is."

"So what should we do now?"

That was a good question. Our agenda had been uncertain from one day to the next ever since we had left home. Now we were suddenly free to make our own plans. Fortunately, since Mad Bear had been so noncommittal all along, all of our tentative appointments had been left open. This was the day I had planned to confirm them. "In a day or two we'll go back," I answered. "We'll just go home and wait like Mad Bear said. I have to make some calls. I might have to keep a couple appointments, and I might do the interview by myself."

"Let's go now," Masayuki pleaded. "I just want to go back home. Anyway, for me, I have nothing more to do here now."

So Masayuki left by himself and I kept my room in the hotel and made an appointment for the following day. I had a couple of friends who had recently moved down from the Bay Area. They had wanted to meet Mad Bear and to help with some contacts, and they suggested I should meet with them myself since I was still in town. Since the woman with the newspaper was a close friend of theirs, they proposed that the interview should still happen.

As I sat alone in my dreary hotel room, I began to wish that I had invited myself to stay with these friends. For some reason—the whole Mad Bear episode, most likely—I felt extremely morbid. Then I decided it was best that I was here by myself, for I realized I was feeling ill. For more than an hour, I paced the floor, unable to remain still. Then I got sick. It was as though I had food poisoning. I spent the entire night in the bathroom wondering whether or not it was I who was now about to die. At some point in the middle of the night or in the early morning, I either passed out or fell asleep, and I awoke, perhaps hours later, to find myself lying on the bathroom floor. My neck was stiff and my bones ached, but I discovered, to my amazement, as soon as I had stood up and stretched and walked around a bit, that I felt great—more rested and refreshed than I had felt for many days. I was also extremely hungry. I got dressed and headed for the coffee shop. I would be absolutely fine for my afternoon appointment. It would be a great day.

I decided to walk out and find some really excellent place to eat. Then I saw the headlines. There had been an earthquake during the night. I had not felt anything at all, though it had been serious and there had been damage. No doubt I had been too sick to feel anything. The article described the earthquake. Apparently it had happened in the early morning about the time I must have passed out. There was a companion item on the front page. It said: SEISMOLOGISTS PREDICT DEVASTATION OF SOUTHLAND. It could have been a coincidence that this article appeared following an earthquake. It could have been that there was no longer any point in keeping it a secret. In any case, this was the first published report I had seen on the conclusion of the studies and the position of the researchers. It was rumored that scientists had been warning of the destruction of cities along the San Andreas Fault, but that business interests had managed to keep this information suppressed. It was published now, and it meant that the scientists and the medicine people were in agreement on at least this issue. I wondered whether Mad Bear had heard about the earthquake. No doubt he already knew.

The newspaper reporter and several others had gathered at the home of my friends, and I spent the afternoon with them and stayed for dinner. Partly by way of an explanation for his absence, I told them about Mad Bear's growing discomfort, his deteriorating condition, and his sudden leaving—making it clear that this information was not part of the interview. My account evoked an unexpected response from one of the group.

"They draw on him!" she said. "You know that. Just think how they draw—and for so many things. Do you have any idea how many people they have to draw on at times like this? Or how many people are living here just for that?"

I thought of asking, "Who are 'they'?" but then I thought better of it. What difference could it make how "they" might be defined or described. Several reflections flashed through my mind at once. I recalled Ram Dass sitting in our living room talking about the "high beings" who were dwelling on the West Coast to assist in forestalling earthquakes—and later Rolling Thunder explaining how medicine people dreamed of "mushroomlike" places that threatening forces were trying to topple while spirits and shamans barely managed to hold them up. I recalled Swami Kaivalyananda in India telling me that nothing can happen by chance—that nothing can move but that it is moved.

"He's a volunteer for that because he's long ago made himself involved," she went on. "But he's involved in so many contests. He is not prepared, not physically able, to offer so much energy in so many areas."

I believed that she had never met Mad Bear or seen him—

or even heard of him. She could have arrived at her theory from what I had told and her own views of how "they" and this energy work. Perhaps she was psychic, or believed she was. In any case, she spoke as though she knew—and not as though she were trying to be impressive but only informative. I simply nodded. I could only go on with my images and could not find either a question or a comment to speak out loud.

"So, he had to leave. He was trying to close that channel. What happened to you was such a small taste of what he would have gone through—a sort of empathetic response, maybe. Except for your association with him, you'd have probably felt very little. We all feel something—usually for hours in advance—most of us just don't recognize it. But I fear Mad Bear may have lost a great deal of energy. I hope he'll be able to recuperate. He's so busy in so many areas."

CHAPTER TEN

Sen Sei and
Mr. Bear

"Let us put our minds together as one."

❶ The following day, I was back in the Bay Area, but where Mad Bear was—or how he was—I had no idea. I tried to reach him through the motel with the Jacuzzi, through the Indian Center, and through everywhere I could think of.

Finally, he called collect, from somewhere on the road. "Yes, I have a collect call for anyone," the operator told me, "from—would you please say your name?"

"Mad Bear!" he said.

"Mad Bear!" I repeated. "Yes, I'll accept. Where are you?"

"Well, I'm halfway home. I'm drivin' up home. I thought I'd reach you there. How you doing?"

"Fine," I answered. "For a while there I was pretty . . ."

"What?"

"No, nothing. I'm fine. How are you? Are you okay?"

"I'm okay to drive home, but I'm gonna hafta rest up a bit."

I had nearly mentioned the earthquake, but decided it was best not to. The Council Grove Conference was only a week away, and Mad Bear was to be a guest speaker. Again, I was concerned whether he might cancel. Had circumstances been as I had originally envisioned, I would still be with Mad Bear, and we would have traveled together to the conference in Kansas. I had just spoken on the phone with Larry Davis, conference chairman for that year, and reported I was uncertain whether I could confirm Mad Bear's presence. Attempting to explain things as best I could, I had told him about Mad Bear's diabetes. Larry had suggested that if Mad Bear would still come, they could perhaps take care of him.

"Are you there?" Mad Bear asked, picking up on my silence. "Are you thinking about Council Grove? Look, I'll go, I'm still planning on it. But I'm gonna hafta take it easy."

"That's fine," I responded, trying to sound more encouraging than relieved. "Jison will be there too. They've invited him and his people, so we'll be going out together. You know Larry the chairman and his brother Jim are both physicians. I was told to ask you what type of insulin you need, because they offered to have it on hand and to look after you."

"Insulin? Why insulin?"

"Well, Jison told me you had diabetes and it was pretty serious. And then I mentioned that to you and you . . ." I felt awkward. I was not sure what to say.

"No, I don't use it. You know I would not insert such a substance into my body. Hey, but tell them I said thank-you anyways. That was nice of them. No, I'll be okay—I'll just take it easy. But I'm gonna hafta fly out. I can't do all this driving by myself. You'll need to arrange it. Maybe we can rendezvous somewheres out around that place."

"We'll be able to meet right there," I told him. "There's a bus that picks up everyone at the Kansas City airport and drives right out to the site. We'll all be driving out from here. We'll arrange your flight to arrive at the right time and send you your ticket and instructions. And I'll have someone meet you at the airport."

"Great!" he said. "I'll call you again soon's I get back up home."

Yoko's mother, in her role as Jison's "sponsor," provided our rented vehicle, and the six of us headed out in a large station wagon with three seats and a luggage rack on top. We spent Easter weekend on the freeway, starting out early Friday morning while most of our Japanese community and other friends stood on the sidewalk to see us off. We drove straight through to Reno and there we stopped for the night. It was a good place to stop, in a way: All the big, fancy hotels were casinos, and thus the rates were more than reasonable. To Yoko's mother, it was a delightful place to stop. She loved the games and considered herself possessed of remarkable luck and skill. (I had to wonder what Mad Bear would have done in a place like this.) Yoko's mother generously provided five rooms for the six of us, so that, except for Hiro and Yoko, we each had personal accommodations. As soon as we had checked in, she started for the casino, and we had to retrieve her so that she could join us for the evening meal.

Yoko's mother was a fascinating woman—an amazing combination of strong will and Oriental graciousness. She was wealthy—the owner of some very successful restaurants and a resort in Fukuoka Prefecture—and she was generous with her money.

I was the one, it seemed, who had to spoil the fun. I was driving, and I got a ticket for speeding. In such a huge and heavy car, there was no way to discern one's speed except by watching the needle, and I had allowed myself to get distracted on one of those long, gradual, and almost unnoticeable slopes. When the cop pulled me over, I was so surprised and disbelieving that I invoked everyone's sympathy—including the cop's who seemed genuinely sorry and Yoko's mother's, who paid the ticket immediately. "I wish I could help it, but I can't," the patrolman said. "I shot you from across the freeway. The speed's displayed here on my radar gun. It's recorded in the computer, and it can't be deleted. The fine recorded has to match this record."

Jison made a comment in Japanese.

"What did he say?" the cop asked.

"He said that camera looks like his," Hiro translated, "except he doesn't make such money with it."

"Tell him the money doesn't go to me. It doesn't go to me— I'm not going to touch it."

The Colorado Highway Patrol is set up for such instant payment. There is a little fold-down desk in the patrol car for the convenience of the offenders, and the officers watch— only watch—while the money is sealed along with the ticket in a ready-and-waiting envelope. Then the culprits are escorted to the nearest letter drop and allowed to go on their way. Yoko's mother apologized so earnestly for my misfortune that I could barely communicate my regret at having cost her a ticket. But the happy mood quickly resumed, and everyone was laughing again.

"He feels bad still, I can see," Yoko's mother claimed, as we sat in the restaurant where we had stopped for lunch.

"No, that's not it," I explained, when Yoko translated her mother's concern. "It's just that I have a really fierce headache. It's purely physical—behind my eyes. It happens to me sometimes from the glare of the sun—even with sunglasses. Maybe someone else can take over the driving—and if I just had a couple aspirin . . ."

"No, no!" Jison exclaimed, jumping up. Those were the first words I heard him utter in English. "Aspirin," I realized, is understood in Japanese. "No aspirin, no aspirin!"

He walked around behind my chair and held his fingertips over my eyelids and my temples with such a feather-light touch, I wanted to turn my head to see what he was doing. I barely opened my eyes to peek at his hands, and I could see that nearly everyone in the restaurant was watching. Jison was always an impressive sight in his long gray and black robes with his striking eyes and long black hair, and this little performance was attracting much attention. I closed my eyes

◐

again, not wanting to be distracted. The effect came so intensely that it surprised me and I nearly turned around again. There was a sudden change in my entire muscular and skeletal structure, it seemed, as though my head, neck, and shoulders had been making a tight fist and then, in an instant, let go. I believed I let out a sigh, and I hoped it was not audible to the observers. I kept my eyes closed for a moment as though to confirm my condition, and when I opened them again, Jison was back in his seat.

"Tell Jison the headache's gone," I requested. "Tell him I feel really different."

"No, he knows," Hiro replied. "He could feel it exactly, same as you. At that time he becomes just you, there is no different. We don't have to tell him anything."

"Well, tell him thank-you," I suggested.

"Thank-you," Jison said.

"Anyway," Hiro offered, "from now I can drive next."

I learned more about Jison from Hiro. Jison had spent days, weeks, and even months in meditation without eating or sleeping or even lying down, they told me, and had written lengthy manuscripts in his meditative state. They had met him through Yoko's mother and had spent much time with him after their return to Japan, and they had learned a great deal about him from his students. He had once disappeared for some time and then been found near his mountain temple, they said, sitting in the snow where he had been nearly completely buried for days. Even as they brought him inside and placed him on his mat, he remained undisturbed in his meditation.

"Anyway, he is very strong, I think," Yoko concluded. "To take such a different food and everything for the first time. And we never see any change in him. He is always so healthy, so happy. He never changed his condition."

As we had nearly an entire day to drive through Kansas, we enjoyed a late sleep, another morning tea ceremony, and a casual breakfast. I accepted the "leftovers" that Jison and Yoko's mother offered me without comment. We paused several times along the road to walk about and stretch our legs and to allow Jison the chance to get some unobstructed photographs of the wide open spaces of the Kansas prairie. Once at a rest stop, while Yoko's mother was climbing into the backseat, the heavy car door slammed hard against her hip, causing her to cry out. She held her hand over her mouth, either in embarrassment or pain. Jison tried to assist her, but she hastened out of the car and back into the ladies' room. Yoko went in with her and came back to report that her mother had a horrible bruise on her hip.

"She always get such a thing more badly than other people," Yoko told us, "and it takes so long time to get away."

At length, she returned to the car, trying to look as dignified as possible; to her considerable chagrin, Jison insisted that she show her bruise, not only to him, but to all of us as well. She got back inside the car so that no passerby could see and, kneeling on the car seat, she managed, with her typical Japanese gesture of shyness, to manipulate her dress so that only the bruise was revealed and nothing more. It was a huge, nasty-looking contusion, and it was nearly black. Hiro let out an exaggerated groan, forcing both Yoko and Masayuki to stifle a snicker. I kept my silence.

"Okay!" Jison said in English. Then, in Japanese, he told her to get out of the car and stand up. Jison stepped back and regarded her from a distance, and he casually waved his fingers at her hip. Then he moved closer and, without touching her, swept the palm of his hand up and down over the area. He spoke to her in Japanese, and she had once again to go through her demonstration. Kneeling on the seat, she carefully arranged her dress just as she had done before. Since she could not see behind her, she asked for confirmation. There was not even the slightest sign of discoloration, and as soon as she had learned that fact, she slapped her thigh in acknowledgment right where the bruise had been. Then she turned around and plunked down on the seat with a look of satisfaction, thanked Jison, and said, "Let's go." Though she seemed sincerely grateful, there was something in her manner

◖

that suggested she was becoming accustomed to having a healer around.

We drove directly into the little town of Council Grove. (Council Grove itself had acquired its name from the historic American Indian intertribal councils that took place in the area—according to the tourist literature from the little town and also to what Rolling Thunder had told us when he was here for the conference several years earlier.) Perhaps the actual Indian gathering site had been closer to the White Memorial Camp a few miles from town where the Council Grove Conference was always held. Though the shared bunkhouse accommodations at the camp were fairly comfortable, we had decided to book rooms in the motel in town—partly for the convenience of Jison and Yoko's mother, and mostly for Mad Bear who had informed us he would need to have a place where he could get away from people.

By the time we got to the conference site, the bus from Kansas City International Airport had just arrived and discharged its passengers. Mad Bear's huge, smiling face was the first one we saw as we walked up. He was sitting on a bench in front of the main building with his satchel on the table as though waiting for us to appear. The last time I had seen him he had looked dreadful, but now he looked himself again.

"Hey! I've been sittin' here all day wondering where you people were," he joked. "I was about ready to give up and go back home." He jumped to his feet and shook hands with all of us.

"Right," I responded. "About ten or fifteen minutes, at least. We saw the empty bus heading back as we were coming in."

"Mi-su-ta Bear!" Jison said happily.

"Boy, this place is really out in the boonies!" Mad Bear continued. "All this way on that rugged dirt road. I've often heard about the so-called middle of nowhere, but this is the first time I've been here. I gotta say I rather like it—fresh air, open spaces, plenty of birds—long as you got room in that car for me to get back and forth with you. You got rooms in town already, isn't it? Or no?"

"We did, that's where we came from. Otherwise, we would have been here ahead of you."

"Well, I'm kinda lookin' forward to washing up and kickin' back a bit. But not till after supper. That's comin' up here pretty quick, I hear, and we sure don't wanna miss the main event. Those airline snacks make a halfway decent appetizer, and now I'm ready for some food. Here we go through and serve ourself, I understand, help ourself to however much we want. This is gonna be a pleasant few days. You people eaten, or no?"

"No," I said. "We're all pretty hungry." Mad Bear always wanted everyone to be hungry.

"Oh, Jison, by the way . . ." Mad Bear started, and everyone laughed. "There's people here already waiting for you. I hope I wasn't too quick to let the cat out of the bag. I told 'em they were gonna get to meet a first-class Japanese medicine man. How come you're laughing?"

"It's the way you pronounce his name," I told him. He continually pronounced Jison's name with a soft "O" though I had tried to get him to say it as in the word "Sony." It often sounded to everyone as though Mad Bear were calling him "oji-san," which meant "grandfather," and it made them laugh.

All seven of us sat around one of the large, round tables in the dining room, leaving room at our table for only a few others—and several hurried to crowd in. The participants were encouraged to mix during mealtimes so as to meet as many others as they could, but none of our group wanted to separate. One of the young men at our table asked Mad Bear if it would be all right to approach Jison during supper.

"No, you have to go through this man," Mad Bear told him, patting Hiro on the shoulder. "Jison doesn't understand English, anyways, but even if he did, you'd hafta go through his assistant. That's the way these things are done—and you oughta wait till after supper." Mad Bear turned to me and spoke softly: "Isn't that right? For a healer like him, they ought to observe the proper way—just as we do in our tradition."

"Why?" I asked. "Do you think he wants a healing or some-thing?"

"I know he does," Mad Bear said. "But just wait. We'll talk about it later."

"I can tell to Sen Sei anything you want," Hiro offered. "Really, he's okay. He never disturb about anything."

"No, let it wait," Mad Bear repeated. "I'll tell you about it later."

I supposed Mad Bear could pick up what the young man was concerned about just by looking, but he could not attend to it himself and wanted Jison to have his meal in peace. I looked at Jison. He was quietly eating, and Yoko and her mother were talking in their own language. Apparently, only Hiro and Masayuki had been aware of our conversation. I was glad that this time none of them tried to donate their food to me.

After supper, many people came around to talk with Mad Bear and with Jison. Mad Bear seemed in excellent spirits. He was warm and outgoing and talked cheerfully with everyone who approached. As more people gathered, Hiro took my arm. "Sen Sei is telling we should get Mad Bear. We should go back. He is okay himself, but Mad Bear, we have to help him."

I looked at Jison. "Mi-su-ta Bear," he said, motioning to-ward me and then toward the car.

"This is quite the dirt road," Mad Bear remarked when we were on our way. "Good thing we're makin' it through now before it starts to rain."

"I don't think it'll rain," I commented.

"Well, it ought to," Mad Bear replied. "I gave that some at-tention while I was waiting for you. This is just the kind of event that's s'posed to open with a rain and close with a rain every time. These people don't know about that, probably. Even among our own people, it's pretty much lost now. People forget to attend to those things, though it was a part of our instruction."

Jison said he wanted to do something with "Mi-su-ta Bear," so as soon as Mad Bear had unpacked and showered, he let us

know he was ready and we all gathered in his room. Mad Bear
lay face down on his bed and Jison stood over him, passing his
open hands over his body, most of the time barely touching
him. Mad Bear lay quietly, saying nothing, except that one
time he remarked that he could feel "warmth and energy"
from Jison's hands. Jison spoke softly as he worked, and Hiro
interpreted. He directed his remarks to me as though he did
not wish to appear to give advice to Mad Bear.

"Mr. Mad Bear is so strong," Hiro translated, "but we have
to help him. He suppose to care more himself. He is working
for everything but he takes care all the people more than himself. We cannot see it what he is working—it is like in a different place, many happenings. It is like not this world, maybe
another world. So he is divided his mind and his heart for
many things, but we cannot see it. I cannot translate exactly,
but it is very danger, Sen Sei is saying that way. But he said
this decision belong to Mad Bear, but still he supposed to be
careful himself."

I had never discussed with Mad Bear what I knew about his
less-visible projects, and I had never felt it appropriate for
me to caution him, though I was happy to have others do it. It
was a curious situation: I believed that Mad Bear could use
some encouragement when it came to caring for himself, but I
also believed that he was very much in accord with his own
will. In any case, as in the advent of the Los Angeles earthquake, he seemed to know when it was necessary to take steps
to save his life.

For a time we were silent. We were all in the room, and all
our eyes were on Mad Bear and Jison. Suddenly Mad Bear sat
up as though he had determined that the session had reached
a satisfactory conclusion. "Great!" he said. "Now let's open
up that door and take a sniff of that air." Masayuki opened
the door, and Mad Bear moved himself to a chair so that he
could look out. "Smell anything?" he asked. "Give it another,
let's say, ten minutes. Well, I feel better, I sure appreciate it.
See, this man he's really something! I hope it was okay to put
the others onto him. One thing he's right about, I gotta lay off

doing any medicine for others at this time. Let's say I've been
pretty strictly instructed. This man picks things up, I told
you. I was really cautioned before I came out here, so I gotta
be careful. And I may not be able to stay the whole time." He
interrupted himself and poked his head through the doorway.
"Can't you smell that? It's the rain coming. Really. About ten
minutes away. I bet Jison can tell it. Ask him."

Jison allowed that if Mad Bear said it was going to rain, it
was going to rain.

"I don't know why some of these people picked up on me
like they did. Right on the bus, two or three of 'em asked me
if I could help 'em out. I could pick up their problems, but I
couldn't offer to help. I thought there's a lot of doctors out
here for this conference. How come they jumped on me?
Maybe they're curious about my medicine. Who put out the
word on me, anyhow?"

"Quite a few of these people know about you," I told him.
"That's why you were invited and, after all, you're on the
program. As for the others, the word got around, I guess—
even on that bus."

"That's where they talked to me. On that bus, and even
when we were waiting for it at the airport. I didn't want to put
anybody off. You can't really refuse, you know, once you're
asked. So I told them they were gonna have a chance to meet
one of the most powerful healers they'd ever see, just as soon
as they got off the bus. Like I said, I sure hope I didn't jump
the gun here. I mighta been a little outa place without Jison's
permission."

"No, it's not problem," Yoko assured him. "Hiro can explain to Sen Sei, but he is always okay for anything."

Hiro nodded his head in agreement. "He knows. He knows
already."

"All right, here it is!" Mad Bear exclaimed. The steady,
soft rain patted on the rooftop and on the walkway in front of
the door. "Here it is—just perfect. It'll last a short while and
then let up. This is the proper way a council should open—
every time, just like this!" He jumped up, stood in the door-

way, and took a deep breath. "By golly! A soft female rain! It's an opening rain, and it works like a purification and a blessing for the council."

Jison laughed out loud. He was amused at Mad Bear's exuberant delight. "Mr. Bear has a best combination," Hiro translated. "Old like our ancestor and plays like a boy."

"No, but this is perfect," Mad Bear said with a chuckle. "I wanted this this way. I was just so tickled the way it was arranged. It's s'posed to happen soon as everyone has gathered—it's a blessing for the whole bunch. Then at the close, after everything's wound up, then the male rain comes. That comes when the people have departed. Puts the right wrap-up on the whole thing."

Early in the morning we drove out to the conference site and pulled onto the grounds just in time for breakfast. Mad Bear trotted right up to the food line, and several people who had apparently been waiting for him followed up behind him. I saw him flick his wrist and wave a thumb in Jison's direction, and as I approached I could hear him say: "I can't really help out much right now. I'm working on some other things. But that man there might be willing, and he's fantastic—I can vouch for that myself." He looked at me as I walked up to him. "Well what can I do? That's all I can do. They told me Jison doesn't mind."

I glanced at Jison. A group had already gathered around him, and both Hiro and Masayuki were trying to translate as they spoke to him in English. Hiro came to where we were standing in the food line. "What should I do?" he asked. "They want to take him to that cabin down there. Then I should go too. Sen Sei is okay for everything, but I was going to take breakfast."

"No, no," Mad Bear said. "They can wait. They shouldn't rush him like that—there'll be plenty of time."

We all had breakfast together while the would-be patients waited. As soon as they had finished eating, Jison left with Hiro so that he could begin his treatments, and they did not reappear until nearly lunchtime. Jison and Hiro missed hear-

ing the first of the speakers and missed several other presentations over the days that followed as they repeatedly left with
people who wanted to be worked on. It was intriguing to see
him walking across the grounds in his robes and his clogs with
some physician, psychiatrist, or therapist who needed his
help. From time to time I listened as someone approached Jison with, "I've had this chronic pain in my lower back for
years now . . ." or, "Sometimes I get these horrible cramps for
no apparent reason and it hit me again just this morning . . ."

One day after lunch, Hiro drove Jison all the way back to
the motel so that he could have a rest and meditation. "We
can find a bed for him here if he wants to take a nap," I had
suggested. But Hiro felt that he needed his room with its in-
cense and altar. "It's like his temporary temple," Hiro told
us. "I will wait for him and when he is ready we drive back.
Maybe only few hours."

Mad Bear and I stood outside and watched the car head
down the dirt road. "It's kinda rough for him," he said, "not
understanding English and all, and yet they've sure been
keeping him busy. It's sort of my fault, too. Maybe I wouldn't
have said anything if I'd have known it would come to this."

"But I think he's okay with it, though. I mean, he could decline if he really wanted to."

"I think that's what he's doing. I think he's makin' a little
getaway here. But it seems kinda funny. I thought most of
these people are doctors and the like. That's what gets me."

"Yes," I said, "but even they could use some help sometimes. They probably figure it can't hurt anything. It's not
like surgery or something where there's a risk involved."

"What I wonder is, did anybody think to offer him any tobacco or anything? It's bad if they don't—that's the way it's
supposed to happen. There's supposed to be an exchange. Or
has anybody even bothered to say thanks?"

"I'm sure they have," I said. "I think people are trying to
experience him and what he does. That's one kind of exchange. In a way, it's like thanks in itself—it's like reaching
out to him. They can't communicate with Jison verbally as

most of us are doing with each other. People come here to have a meeting of minds, to experience each other. In this way, even though they can't talk with him, they can have direct contact with him—in a totally experiential way."

"Well, I guess that's what I've done too—I've experienced him. But we do have our exchange at that. Anyways, that thanks has always got to be there—for each other and our food and shelter, everything—even the ground we walk on. That has to be brought out more."

That idea became the heart of Mad Bear's presentation. When we were talking about Jison, I had been thinking, and had suggested to Mad Bear, that communication and contact could be a means of exchange and thus a way of giving thanks. His message was that giving thanks is a communication exchange that provides the way for direct contact and experience. What is important is to walk upon the soil and the grass with thanks and thus to experience the Earth—to give thanks for every breath and thus to experience life.

So he opened his talk with a prayer of thanks, and he opened his prayer with a comment about the rain. "You may have noticed," he said, and he described the female rain and its significant role in the opening of a conference. "And I might just mention, though it might not look it at the moment, that at the close of this conference it's gonna rain what you people call 'cats and dogs.' That'll be the male rain, just as it's supposed to be—but most of you may not see it. A rain like that is good for the closing, but it comes hard and heavy so it'll wait until you people have left. Especially with this long dirt road out to the highway, I suggest you leave before the closing rain comes. But it's good, it puts a cap on the whole thing.

"Our people look at everything natural and we recognize it and we say 'it is good.' We acknowledge the sun when it rises in the morning, and we give thanks to Grandfather Sun and we say, 'Today is another day, and it is good.' And whenever our people get together, we put our minds together as one, and we give thanks." He paused and looked over his audi-

ence. About one hundred people sat before him—mostly helping professionals who, in one way or another, spent their lives
in caring for others. "Now you say 'Yo!' " he told us.

A few people uttered "Yo."

"No, everyone, all together, loud and clear—you shout
'Yo!' "

"Yo!" everyone shouted, and some repeated it twice.

"You do it all together, as one voice," Mad Bear instructed."Every time I give thanks I say, 'Let us put our
minds together as one and give thanks,' and all together you
come in with 'Yo!' Now we give thanks for all the rocks and
minerals because they make up the Earth and the ground on
which we build our homes and on which we walk and they
make the soil and even give us medicine. So, let us put our
minds together as one and give thanks for the rocks and the
minerals." He gestured toward the group.

"Yo!" everyone exclaimed in unison.

"And then, let us give thanks for the soil, for it is the soil
that feeds the trees and the roots of all the foods that give us
life. It is the soil that is the breast of the Earth Mother who
nourishes us all. So, let us put our minds together as one and
give thanks for the soil."

"Yo!"

And he went on. His prayer of thanks used up more than
half of his allotted speaking time. He went through the grass
and the plants and the trees. He covered fruits and vegetables, streams, ponds, rivers, and oceans. He had us say "Yo!"
and "Yo!" again for all the living creatures: the six leggeds,
the eight leggeds, the four leggeds—and he acknowledged
their place in the world, their function, their purpose, each
and every one of them, and their contribution to the whole of
life. He acknowledged all our brothers and sisters—including
the winged and the finned—and he went on to acknowledge
all the races, and all the planets, the sun, the moon, the stars
in the heavens . . .

After the first five or so minutes, people became restless
and they wiggled in their seats. Some turned their heads in an

obvious manner to look at the clock on the wall behind them. But Mad Bear went on and on, and we had to follow. Then, somehow, the restlessness faded and everyone seemed to melt into the process. What for a brief time had threatened to become monotonous became spellbinding—a magnificent meditation that grew increasingly powerful. It was as though with every repetition of the words, "minds together as one," the illusory wall of separation between our individual selves faded, and with every "Yo!" we reached to embrace an expanding realm of consciousness.

In the midst of all this the birds came, and people noticed. They began to tap one another and point at the windows. Birds kept flying up to the windows in such numbers that eventually the sunlight in the room was diminished, and their collective chirping made such a sound that it surrounded our chorus of "Yo's."

Then Mad Bear shared something of himself, and it surprised me. I and a few others and, no doubt, his own people had heard him talk this way—but only in more private settings. Perhaps it was because of the group participation or because of something he saw in the coming of the birds. Perhaps it was because, owing to his "strict instructions," people here had not had a chance to experience him directly. He talked about his childhood initiation. When Mad Bear was only a child, his father had been killed when his car rolled off a reservation mountain road. His mother had been a clan mother in their tribe and his grandmother had been a medicine woman. It was this grandmother who "recognized" him. She initiated him and gave him his name and his "medicine" when he was only nine years old. Even as a youth, he was able, with his "medicine," to help feed and look after the welfare of his mother and his brothers and sisters. Mad Bear knew that this was a protective and supportive setting where there was no recording and people's sharings were held in confidence, and he described in some detail the process and the experience of that initiation. Then he spoke about his tradition and his work, and about the struggle among opposing forces and the eventual emergence of the new world. I believed that perhaps people might be able to recognize to some degree his function as a medicine man—as a mediator and a mitigator.

By the time Mad Bear had completed his prayer and his subsequent talk, he had taken us well into the lunch hour. Though people needed to get up and stretch, to take a break, and have their meal, it was apparent that most everyone would be happy to hear much more from him. Many eyes were on him as he came through the lunch line, and people hurried to get a place at his table. This time he did not beckon to me, and others were able to have a chance to sit beside him. In fact, at this meal, I noticed, every one of our group sat apart—even Jison and Yoko's mother—and everyone was able to make new friends.

Mad Bear left before the conference was over, and the moment came suddenly. Donald Keys of Planetary Citizens had to leave a day early for another commitment and he made arrangements to take a little commuter plane from a nearby town to Kansas City International Airport. Mad Bear hurriedly found me. "I got a chance to head back now," he said, "and I think I better jump on that little plane while I got the chance to get to the airport. My New York ticket's an open return, you know, and I can maybe fly all the way back East with Donald."

"When would you be leaving?"

"Right now! I mean, pretty quick here. Talk to Donald and them, I gotta get ready. Maybe we can jump in the station wagon and drive up to where this little bitty plane takes off." He slapped his hand over his mouth. "By golly, I hope I can squeeze into the doggone thing!"

Hiro quickly drove Mad Bear into town to get his things together and check out of his room, and they pulled back just in time for Donald and the rest of us to head for the plane.

"Wait!" Mad Bear said. "I gotta do something here!" He jumped out, hurried into the building, and stepped in through the door of the main conference room. The next presenter was just about to begin. "Hey!" he shouted, and everyone turned to look. "I'm leaving you all now—I don't want to, but I have to—and we're headin' out in a hurry here to catch this little plane. I just can't leave without saying my very best wishes to each and every one of you. Stay in balance, go in peace, an' all that, an' my heart will be with you the whole time until we meet up again somewheres, and I'm pretty sure that'll happen!"

"Oh, no!" many voices said, and it was as I expected. Everyone flocked around him for a phone number, a request, directions to his place, or some last-minute question or comment.

"There's no time, talk to Doug here," he said.

"There's no time," I repeated. "Talk with me later; you can be in touch through me."

Hiro and Masayuki and I got in to take Mad Bear and Donald to the little airport in Manhattan, Kansas. Jison appeared and jumped in just as we were pulling out. He felt it his place, as well, to see Mad Bear off. Most everyone tried to talk on the way. There was a sense of insufficient time and the need for communication. I knew I would be in touch with Mad Bear again, within a matter of days, most likely, but I was not sure whether Mad Bear and Jison would ever see or hear from one another again. They both appeared more content than the rest of us, however, simply to ride in silence.

We just made it to the plane, and there was barely time for a hasty good-bye. Both Mad Bear and Jison seemed convinced that they would meet again, but they conveyed their hearty farewells—each in his own language—and there was no time for translation. It was the first I had seen either of them hug anyone.

As we were heading back down the highway, we heard the sound of the engines overhead, and we stopped and got out to look.

"You think that's his plane?"

"I know it is," I said, watching the little plane on its upward climb. "Look how that tail end is hanging low."

"I know what you're going to say," Masayuki piped up.

◑

"They must have put Mad Bear back there in the rear of the plane."

Jison asked for the translation. He smiled slightly, but he put his palms together, and raised his arms toward the plane in a gesture of respect. Just then a car slowed down as it went by, and its passengers looked at Jison and then looked skyward.

"What do people think when they see Jison?" Hiro asked.

"I wonder too," I answered. "These Kansas folks have probably never seen anything like him. Maybe those people thought he was some alien from some past era who was worshiping a plane."

Jison became busy again from the moment we were back at the conference site. I knew it was valuable for these people to experience him so directly and to be really helped, perhaps, in the process; but I wondered whether this experience was what Jison himself had wished for. His presence here at this conference had been arranged in order that he could encounter others "of like mind," as he had put it. I supposed that this was happening, in a way, and with the language problem it may have been the best way. Still, he was, for the first time, thousands of miles from home, at great expense, and with a real sense of purpose, and I wanted to be sure that we were doing our best for him.

As this was the last evening of the conference, we stayed until long after supper and returned late to our motel in town. This time we all gathered in Jison's room. "Now we can feel something different with no Mad Bear," Hiro told me. "Sen Sei is missing him already. He cannot meet again soon. But next chance he will come back to United States."

"How do you think he feels about this trip?" I asked. "You know, I've arranged a couple introductions for him in the Bay Area before you go back, but that's not long off now. I'm not sure whether things are going the way he had hoped. I mean, he's doing an awful lot of giving, but I'm not sure whether he's getting what he wants. I talked with the chairman and a couple other doctors and they thought about having a little panel in the morning, if Jison is agreeable, so that they and others could ask him some questions. But that's still a kind of giving on his part."

"But we know he is okay for anything. Anyway, this trip is practice one, I think. In the first time, he just have to become accustom for everything."

"I think it's all good for him," Masayuki offered. "It's all helpful because he can find out what the people are like. He just wants to try everything, whatever happens. I think he is satisfied."

They asked him about the following morning and he agreed to speak briefly and to try to answer some questions. "You'll have to translate for him," I said. "And it'll have to go rather quickly because there won't be much time. The last day is only a half day—people leave right after lunch, and there's a lot to do."

Jison's brief interaction with the group was quite interesting, people told me as we lined up at lunchtime for our final meal, but certainly less than satisfying. Most of the questions had been fascinating, but the responses always fell short on the translation side. Masayuki and Hiro and Yoko had all tried their best, but Jison had been too much for them. They had had to explain that even Jison's everyday Japanese was often difficult for them to understand. When he talked on these subjects, it was virtually impossible, for he used an extremely archaic vocabulary that would challenge even aged Japanese philosophers.

"He is using old-style words," Hiro had explained apologetically, "and we don't know nowadays. Maybe only best scholars. Also, we don't have knowledge enough this subject, so we are studying now. Even what we understand, we don't know the English words for it. So it's only the problem."

"But you know, he seemed to be focused on the blood," someone commented as we sat at the table. "Did you hear how many times they used the word 'blood'? I wonder if that was actually his word."

"I think blood was what he meant," another said, "though I'm not sure just how he meant it, because they translated 'blood' and also 'bloodstream.' They said he claims that he himself enters directly into the bloodstream. But if that's what he means, he can't mean it literally, of course."

"Why not?" questioned the first. "It wouldn't have to be physical."

"But the bloodstream is physical."

"That wouldn't matter."

"You know, I was talking with him when he worked on me," said another. "I think of it sort of like adding fuel to your tank—or adding something to the fuel. So maybe 'blood' is one word but maybe 'energy' would be a good word also—giving energy so you can do your own healing. It's a kind of empowerment."

"Right. It's like once you know where you're going, and you've got the will, he can add the fuel."

"I think those are all good words," I suggested. "I haven't had a lot of chance to talk with him myself. I don't understand Japanese either, so there's the same translation problem, and my focus has been on all the arrangements. But from what I have gathered, he believes that healers are people who empower others, as you put it, to do their own healing. What he wants to do is to meet other healers wherever he can so that eventually they can work together on an international level. I believe he thinks that healers working together can help empower the entire population. It would be like adding fuel to the collective will."

"Ya, but he's going to have to have a lot of help—with translation and everything else. You know who should have been here this morning? Mad Bear should have been here. He may not understand Japanese, but I bet he really understands Jison."

As we had only a couple hours' drive ahead, we lingered until everyone had left, and headed out behind the few cars that were headed east to Topeka. Thus, we had barely made it to the end of the five-mile dirt road when the heavy downpour started, and we drove in the rain all the way to Topeka. It was that strong male rain that Mad Bear had wanted for the consummation of the event.

◗

CHAPTER ELEVEN

The Ring

"All this about sin and evil and fear and everything doomed to hell. . . . They use this image as a doom image—invoking doom."

◖ "'Chautauqua' is the name of the lake," explained our driver. "You'll see it when we get there. It borders the property. Actually, the word is Seneca for 'bag tied in the middle,' or so we're told. It's hard to think how one word could mean all that, but it is obviously an Indian word and this is Seneca territory. The lake's shaped like a kidney bean or a peanut or something, and they say it reminded the Senecas of this type of bag that they used to carry that was tied in the middle. So they named the lake after the bag, I guess, and then the place got its name from the lake."

I was on my way to spend a week as a guest speaker at this New York resort accompanied by a student from Hong Kong named Victor Lamb. *Rolling Thunder* had been selected as a "book of the year" by the Chautauqua book club, and I had been engaged for a series of talks for the adult education summer program. As part of the arrangement, accommodations, meals, and complimentary admission to all the seminars and performances had been offered for me and my "assistant." Since Masayuki was returning to Japan, a Berkeley friend had introduced me to Victor Lamb, suggesting that this would be an ideal opportunity for an exchange student such as he. Victor was free for the summer, and he gladly came along as volunteer "assistant."

Our driver was a member of the staff at the Chautauqua resort, and she had come to pick us up at the airport. "Have you been here before?" she asked.

"I'd never even heard of Chautauqua," I admitted, "until just some weeks ago. Actually, I had heard the word as a child. My mom traveled for years as a stage actress long before I was born, and she used to talk about traveling 'on Chautauqua,' but I guess that's something different."

"No, it's related," she alleged, "but I'm not sure just how. Chautauqua dates back more than a hundred years, I think. Once it was a nationwide society with tent camps and performances all across the country. It was named after this place here, which was originally a training center for Sunday-school teachers. They say it was really strict, almost like a prison. Well, it's certainly different now. It's a fantastic educational and cultural resort. There are movies and live plays and musicals going on all the time—and concerts and performances by top entertainers. But the main emphasis is still educational—classes and lectures in art and music mostly."

"Victor here is originally from Hong Kong," I interjected, "but currently he's an art major at the California College of Arts and Crafts. We've been told there'll be a number of exhibits and demonstrations that he'll be able to attend."

"Oh, definitely," she affirmed. "There'll be lectures and demonstrations by lots of famous painters and sculptors. He'll be welcome to attend anything he wants. You're both guests here, so everything is open to you whenever you're free. You'll be surprised if you've never been here before. I don't know how much you've been told, but there's an unbelievable amount of activity all summer long. People come from all over. All through the summer, there are no less than ten thousand patrons on the grounds here."

We were taken to the guest house where the speakers and performers were accommodated, and introduced to the hostess of the house. As soon as we had been shown our rooms, we were escorted with the other guests to the formal and fancy dining room in the hotel across the street. Here we had three abundant meals a day—in the same assigned seats at the same table with the same group. Each evening at suppertime, everyone at our table was allowed to select two desserts from a long list of exotic choices and, since some people, especially the dancers, were avoiding desserts altogether, Victor and I always had several.

Chautauqua was like an entire village of hotels, restaurants, theaters, and auditoriums. The theaters, shops, and lodges, including our guest house, looked quaintly old-fashioned, as though they were as old as Chautauqua's long history. There were so many exhibits, shows, and concerts going on all day and evening that when we found ourselves free to attend an event, it was difficult to decide what to do—or what not to do. Victor brought his camera to almost all my talks and meetings as he was studying photography in college and wanted to consider himself my official documenter, but I managed to persuade him to attend a few lectures and art exhibits on his own. We became acquainted with our hostess's son who was a student about Victor's age. He and his college friends were on summer break and were spending nearly every evening hanging out in the family quarters downstairs.

One evening, after we had finished our own supper, our hostess invited us to join them in the recreation room in the basement. Her son and four of his friends were sitting around a table having milk and cookies, and we sat on the basement stairs to talk with them. One of them noticed my ring and asked to look at it. I had become so accustomed to wearing it, both day and night, that I had virtually forgotten about it. I slipped it off and held it in the palm of my hand, and I began to tell them the story of how it had one day simply appeared in my drawer. Since they seemed interested, I supposed it would be all right to tell them the truth.

Our hostess, who was sitting beside me on the step, took the ring from my hand and held it up to the light. With her other hand, she reached to flick the ashes from her cigarette and knocked the ashtray off the banister into her lap. As she stood up to brush off the ashes, she set the ring on the table. One of the students reached across the table to pick it up and his arm bumped the pitcher of milk. The pitcher tipped over and the milk spread across the table and dripped onto the floor. The son brought a roll of paper towels from the other room and everyone got busy wiping up milk. Another student picked up my ring as he was returning to his seat. With his eyes on the ring he sat on the corner of his chair, and both he and the chair fell to the floor. Everyone laughed and one student exclaimed, "You had better give that ring back!" The fallen one stood up and handed me the ring and I slipped it back on my finger.

Later I told Victor about the filmmaker with The Rolling Thunder Revue and what he had said about the ring. I wondered out loud whether I should take off the ring and put it out of sight. "I've heard about something like that," Victor said. "All Chinese people are hearing about such things. But still, I don't like to believe in it."

The following afternoon our hostess questioned me as we relaxed in the sitting room after my morning talk. Someone had provided her with a copy of *Rolling Thunder* in case she wanted to read it before I arrived, and thus she had questions about the medicine people. She wanted to know if indeed Mad Bear would be coming to visit and, if so, when. When Mad Bear learned of my Chautauqua agenda, he had suggested he might "drop by," as he had put it. Since he was within driving distance, he could easily come for a day or two if I would phone him to confirm arrangements. Our hostess had assured us he would be welcome to stay at the guest house, and now she was looking forward to meeting him. She was sure that he had something to do with my ring and its curious effect on people. But I was certain that the ring had no connection with Mad Bear. As far as I knew, Mad Bear was not even aware that I was wearing it. If he had noticed it, he had never mentioned it. The only thing strange about it was the way I came by it, I told her, and I had never before known it to have any effect on any one.

"Well," she said, "when Mad Bear comes I'm going to ask him about it. I can't understand why you haven't discussed it with him. I believe in things like this and these are the type of people that know about things like this. I'll bet you never let anyone hold it before, right? So naturally you wouldn't have seen any effects like that."

Mad Bear and I talked by phone every day during my week at Chautauqua. He always asked me how the talks were going and said, "Well, give my greetings to everyone"—and I almost always did. He was uncertain about coming to Chautauqua. He had received some sort of communication from India and was expecting visitors, but he was not sure when they would appear. They arrived at Mad Bear's place on our fifth day at Chautauqua. "I won't be able to make it down there now," he said. "They'll be here three or four days for sure, and you've only got a couple more days down there, right? We'll have to make it next time. Just give my best regards to everyone."

His visitors were a group of Tibetan monks and lamas. They had been sent from Dharmsala by the Dalai Lama with whom Mad Bear maintained an ongoing association. "In fact, I wish you were up here," Mad Bear went on. "Then you could see these people. But by the time you get to New York City and on up here, they'll have left already. Too bad. Such high-spirited people and yet so humble—just like the 'real people.' And have they got a sense of humor! Boy, I'm telling you—just like the Dalai Lama himself! Well, like me too, as far as that goes. And they sit right down on the floor—right here in my funny little room. And they get to laughin'! You know me—with my weight I can't sit on the floor. I get down,

and I can't get up. They'd have to lift me up. Wouldn't that
be something? But I'm telling you, they talk so warmhearted
and get to laughin' so beautifully I just wanna be right down
there on the floor with them. So anyways, when you coming?"

"We're leaving here this weekend," I told him. "We'll be
up there some time next weekend—Sunday, I guess. I'll
phone you from New York."

"Listen, one thing I want to tell you. We've been comparing
notes up here—mostly on our ancient prophesies. We can talk
about that when you're up here. And we're in agreement on
our predictions on China. There's gonna be a lot of changes in
China, but the problems are going to go on. And the situation
with Tibet is going to get even worse—except they'll get more
support—more awareness, I guess you'd say. There's one
nearby thing that's comin' right up. That's what I wanted to
tell you. You watch the news. You'll be in New York City, I
guess. Right around Friday or Saturday next week, there's
going to be an earthquake in China. I mean major. It'll be in
the news, I'm sure. Between us here, we've pinned it down
pretty good as to the timing."

"Do you think I should mention anything about that here?"

"You mean in your talk? Just to a couple friends, maybe.
You can use your judgment. Such things when they're close to
home, we don't do it, you know. Your people, they just don't
want to hear it. They don't deal with things that way. They're
not used to it, so it doesn't do any good. A distant thing like
this, they don't have to deal with it personally, so they don't
have to argue about it. They can just let it go—wait and see.
They might be a little amazed for a while that someone told
them in advance and then it came out on the news. But they
won't learn anything from it—we've seen how that works.
They don't learn how to foresee things, you know, they just
don't want to learn it, so they'll never know."

"I don't know," I said. "One young guy here came up from
the audience after my session the other day and handed me a
note. He was so angry or disturbed that he was actually shaking. He said, 'You promised to share the Indians' prophesies

and give us the predictions on the natural disasters.' His note said the same thing. It said: 'That's what we came to hear and it's not yours to keep to yourself.' I don't know where he got that idea. I didn't claim to know any predictions or promise to reveal anything. In fact, I've been really careful here—just talking about culture, traditions, and the planet without getting into anything ominous. I think most of the people here are the type who'd say, 'You mustn't talk about anything negative.' "

"See, that's what gets me," Mad Bear rejoined. "People are hard to figure! They either declare you don't know what you're talking about, or that they don't want to hear it anyway, or else they expect you to give them the whole upcoming scenario, as though it's all been written down in detail somewhere. In the first place, if it was all determined, there'd be no point in working on it. We'd just close our eyes and let it happen. There's those that want to know, but they don't want to work on it—and the others, they don't even want to know! It's not what you can see coming, it's what you can see yourself doing about it. Otherwise, it's best not to know. You just get scared and add to the predicament. That was my point in bringing up those dreams about California. My only question was what we oughta do about it. Even this thing in China, it wouldn't have to be—but we sure don't see anybody doing anything about it. I'll tell you one thing—there are precious few people holdin' back earthquakes and floods and such these days. It makes it pretty rough. That's gonna hafta change pretty darn fast."

In my last talk at Chautauqua, I paraphrased as much of those words of Mad Bear's as I thought most important and most appropriate. For those who were expecting others to share their prophesies, I thought it would be useful to know that those others were expecting them to share responsibility. To members of the staff who were disappointed in not being able to meet Mad Bear, I suggested they consider inviting him on his own sometime. And, of course, I'd be pleased to come with him. The week at Chautauqua had been a pleasure. It was an exciting place—absolutely rich with images, ideas, and inspiration. I did tell everyone I hoped to return, and I meant it.

Before leaving for the airport, we walked around to say good-bye to whomever we could find in the guest house. One of the college students we had talked to was in the kitchen in the basement standing with another friend. "Show this guy your ring," he piped up as soon as he saw me. "He wasn't here the other day." I hesitated, but I thought it would look strange to refuse. I was hoping it might be hard to remove, thus providing an excuse. But it slipped instantly off my finger the moment I touched it, and I handed it over. The young man turned to hold the ring under the light above the stove and backed into a large glass dish on the edge of the counter. There was hot casserole and broken glass all over the floor, and he was horrified. His friend seemed delighted. "That's what I thought," he exclaimed. "That proves exactly what I thought!"

I took the ring back and put it in my pocket. They wanted to talk about it but, fortunately, our ride was waiting and we had to leave. Also fortunately, our hostess had not been there to see that, and I did not have to discuss it. I did think about it several times, but I put the ring in my toilet kit and did not look at it again. Perhaps I would discuss it with Mad Bear.

We got our usual reduced weekly rate at the Lexington Hotel in New York City. I had become a familiar sight at the Lexington. I had been here several times, by now, most recently with Masayuki before we had flown out to Arizona. No doubt there were many who stayed there more frequently than I— certainly the airline personnel who were contract regulars. But I had made myself conspicuous when I had nearly filled the place with Indians who had walked about the halls and the lobby in their traditional regalia.

"Where are all the Indians?" asked one of the employees as I stepped up to the cashier's window.

"They're all home," I answered.

"Well, you never change," he said. "You look the same every time I see you."

"You never change either," I told him.

"We can't change. We have to keep the pace here."

The earthquake in China happened on Saturday—Saturday our time, at any rate, and Victor and I saw it on the news in our room. I told Mad Bear on the phone that he was right about the earthquake.

"I know," he acknowledged. "When you heading up here?"

"Tomorrow. We'll be staying at the Ramada in Niagara Falls."

"That's good," he said. "Easy to get to from my place. And they've got a really good restaurant in there—I mean, for you guys, you know. Look, we can meet on Monday. We're having a get-together, a bunch of our people in the park there in Niagara Falls. I'll pick you guys up. We can have a little bite to eat there in the restaurant—although we'll be having a picnic and there'll be plenty for you guys. Well, we won't be going hungry, anyways!"

The following morning we flew into Buffalo and took the shuttle bus to the hotel in Niagara Falls. Since we had the rest of Sunday to ourselves, I suggested we walk across the Rainbow Bridge to the Canada side of the falls. Victor carried his camera, and we stopped on the bridge to watch the little boats that took raincoat-clad tourists close enough to be splashed by the falls.

"We can get good pictures from here," Victor said. "I think if we were in that boat the lens would get wet and we couldn't get clear pictures."

"Wait till we get to the other side," I told him. "You can get the best pictures of the falls from over there." But Victor was stopped at the Canada end of the bridge and not allowed to pass. I was surprised. It had never happened before. "We'll just be a couple hours," I explained. "We're just going right over here to take pictures."

"Not from Hong Kong he doesn't get in," insisted the man in the uniform. "You can go to Buffalo and try to get a visa, if you want. But with that Hong Kong passport, I doubt it."

"Why is that?" I questioned. "I've brought friends from

Japan and everywhere. What's wrong with from Hong Kong?"

He frowned at me. "That's the rules," he said, with a tone of finality. "That's the way it is."

Victor looked uncomfortable. "Never mind," he said. "Let's go back."

The next day I told Mad Bear what had happened, and it became a topic of discussion at the picnic. Apparently, these traditionals, like Mad Bear, made it a point to be indignant at the very idea of a border. "If you don't mind knowin' somethin' about the history of this land," one of them told Victor, "and you'll never learn it from the white folks, they come along and made that split right through our own land where we're already livin'. That's a artificial border, as far as we're concerned, and we don't even like to recanize it."

"Ever' border's artificial," submitted another. "It's a un-natural notion and don't have no recognition in the natural world. The animals and birds, and the wind and water, they don't pay no attention to these so-called borders. We're the ones it oughta be up to, far as that goes, and we say you're welcome anywheres in the whole Six Nations. We'd give you our own stamp in your passport, 'cept we don't even use such a thing—don't need it."

"Tell you what you do," offered an elderly woman who had been listening and nodding. "You come on over with us. We'll tell them you're one of us, one of our relations, and that wouldn't be lyin', neither."

"Hey," said Mad Bear, "wait a minute. By golly, that's not a bad idea. We'll bring him with us on the crossing! How long you guys going to be here?"

Every year members of the Iroquois Confederacy and, per-haps, many others, marched en masse north over the bridge across the Canadian border. I was not certain whether they considered the annual event a powwow, a celebration, or a protest march. In a way, I suppose, it was all of these things. In any case, as far as I knew, it had always been allowed, even though at other times many Indians had been either held or harassed at the border.

"Victor's going back tomorrow," I told him. "He has to get ready for school. He just wanted to come meet you while he was up this way—since you didn't make it down to Chatauqua. Canada was just an incidental idea. We just wanted to look at the falls—it's better from over there."

"I know, but I wish he could stay for the crossing."

"You know, I'm planning on staying for a few more days, but not that long. I can't stay up till the crossing."

"Well, that wasn't the point. You can cross any time you want. Tomorrow he's going back? Best thing we can do for him in a case like this is go ahead and have one heck of a picnic here!"

We did. There was an abundance of food, and Victor must have eaten at least a little bit more than he had actually wanted. "It's the Indian way," Mad Bear had urged him. "Whenever someone offers you something, it's kinda the best thing to just go ahead and accept it. Everyone wants you to remember your time with us, brief as it is." They all went on talking about how they wished Victor could stay for the crossing and how good it would feel to be able to host their own visitors on their own land—and not be interdicted by this imaginary border through their own homeland—a border that in their reckoning ought not even to exist.

After the picnic, Mad Bear offered to take us back to the Ramada and also to drive us to the airport in the morning so that I would not need to take the shuttle back and forth. Victor thanked everyone for inviting him to their picnic.

"This here's a confederacy where you're at right now," one of them declared, pointing a finger at him. "And we don't recanize no lines drawn or barriers put up nowheres among these Six Nations—not for us or anyone. So you just know you're welcome here anytime, anytime at all—you and any of your people—and these folks'll back me up on that."

We checked out of the Ramada Hotel in the morning and, after we saw Victor off at the airport, I returned with Mad Bear to his place. He had a little teardrop trailer parked in back of his house, where I could sleep for the next couple of

◑

days. It was old and mostly gutted, but it had a somewhat comfortable bed. "Well, I got it for a song," Mad Bear explained, "or a song and a half, anyways. I got 'lecricity hooked up, and I plugged in a little radio for you. You'll be snug as a bug at night—your own bedroom. Rest of the time, you don't need to hang out in there anyways. First thing we gotta do here, we gotta try to rustle up something tasty. That's not gonna be too hard."

"You shoulda been here to see these lamas," Mad Bear said, as we sat at the table. "I told you about them. They've sure got a sense of humor, you would've liked 'em. They gave me gifts too—rugs and stuff—I'll show you later, after we eat. Main thing, we talked some pretty important stuff. We always compare the records and the prophesies when we get together with Tibetans. They're pretty much the same because we're the same people—you know, from the same original roots. And we talked about China and some various events upcoming. I told you all that."

"Right," I said. Just then there was a knock at the door. Mad Bear seemed not to notice. "Someone's knocking on the door," I told him.

"I know," he said, "I'm pickin' up who it is." Then he grinned and stood up. "You'll excuse us for a bit? It's nothing important, but he's come from a ways. I'll try to cut it off pretty quick."

It was one of his friends from another reservation, and I waited for what felt like several hours while they played many games of chess. I could only sit and watch and contemplate whether I ought to practice and improve enough to be able to play with Mad Bear. Perhaps I might take a brief nap out in the trailer. Mad Bear looked up from his game as though hearing my thoughts. "You going out to the trailer?" he asked.

"Why?"

"No, I was just wondering—where is your ring at? You're not wearing it. I thought maybe it was with your things out in the trailer."

Good grief, I thought to myself. I was planning on saying

something about that ring when the time was right. I didn't know Mad Bear had ever noticed it.

"I think your ring's out there in the trailer. Why don't you go out and get it and put it on. We're about to wind up here—soon's I whip him just one more time."

"No, Bear," said his friend. "Bet I'll whup you, then it's a draw, and then you'll wanna go 'round again."

I went out to the trailer to get my ring. It was in my toilet kit where I had intended to keep it. I held it a moment and looked at it, and then I put it on. It seemed that's what Mad Bear had suggested, so perhaps it was all right. I had wanted to bring it up. As I went back to the house Mad Bear and his friend were just coming out. "So I got one up on ya," Mad Bear said. "What'd I tell ya?"

"Just one, Bear," replied his friend. "Just one, then you sez, 'We better quit.' That's the way ya are, Bear."

Mad Bear walked him to his car and watched as he pulled out of the driveway, raising his arm high over his head to wave as he always did. He looked at my hand as we walked back in the house. "So you got it on again," he remarked. "Well, whatd'ya know? S'pose I oughta get me one like it? I know how to get one. I could get one to show up here, and then we'd both have one. We could say we belong to the same outfit. Only you don't belong to it yourself, so, the question is, what are you doing with it?"

"I was going to talk with you about this," I said. "But what is it? I mean, what outfit?"

"Can't you see what this is? Here, give it to me."

I handed him the ring and he sat down behind his "trading post" desk and glared at it with a frown. "This is Adam and Eve here. This is the tree here, and the snake and this little apple. This is not my thing. Not my thing, at all. All this about sin and evil and fear and everything doomed to hell. This is a cult ring, is what it is. They use this image as a doom image—invoking doom. But it's nothing to you—nothing one way or the other. I mean you can wear it if you want to, it won't do you a thing."

◑

I realized he was holding the ring and I had not yet had a chance to tell him about the others. I started to tell him, but he stopped me.

"No, I know," he said. "I don't care about that. You're going to tell me all this stuff, and then you're going to want me to deactivate it."

"Well, I wasn't think—"

"But then why talk about it? Anyways, I can deactivate it, but then it won't look for the birds, and you might not want to wear it. You want to look good, don't you? Don't you want to look nice?"

I had learned to tell when Mad Bear was holding back a laugh, even when his face seemed serious.

He looked at me as though he were waiting for me to say something. "Well? It's up to you."

"What?" I asked.

"Okay, we'll show you. It works like this." He held up the ring in one hand and he stuck out the index finger of his other hand in my direction. Then, with a flick of his wrist, he touched the fingertip to the tip of his nose and gave the ring a quick tap as though it were hot and let it drop upon the desk. "Now just look at the poor thing!" he said, picking it up to hand it to me.

It was a foggy, smokey brownish-black. It was indeed ugly to see—almost nauseating. Mad Bear let go his laughter. "It's neutralized," he said. "Pathetic as anything and one heck of an eyesore. Not only that, but it doesn't look too good either. It oughta be ashamed of itself. You better hide it."

I put the ring in my pocket and, as soon as I was out in the trailer for the night, it went back into my toilet kit, wrapped in a tissue—but I had to look at it closely, first, under the light, to confirm that it was still ugly.

In my sleep I heard someone singing in a strange, almost forlorn, tone of voice. For a moment, it blended with my dream, although I wasn't sure what I was dreaming. I seemed to ask myself, What is this? and then I woke up. It was a clock radio near my head and it was playing that song I had been hearing, almost too often, recently: "Someone's knocking at the door . . . Open the door and let 'im in . . ." Mad Bear had no doubt used this radio for himself and had set it to awaken him early. It was earlier than I would ordinarily choose to awaken. But I was at his place, and he was probably already up and about—preparing some huge breakfast, most likely. I got up and got dressed. For some reason, before I went inside, I took the ring out, looked at it again, and set it on top of the radio.

During breakfast, I went on repeating to myself, "Someone's knocking at the door . . . Open the door and let . . ." I tried to stop it. That song that had awakened me kept going through my mind.

"You know what I was hearing?" Mad Bear piped up. "Just like an echo floating through my head. Remember yesterday, when Freddie dropped by for chess? You said, 'Someone's knocking at the door.' That was going through my mind just now, just like an echo!"

"I was hearing that song in my . . ." I started. "Mad Bear, you keep telling me what I'm thinking! I'll be thinking to myself, and then you always . . ."

"No, not always. I'm just tuned in to you in a way, I told you that. You can prevent it, don't you know that? Anytime somethin' feels private to you, I can't get to it. It's not that I'm trying. I'm not peekin' into your head, you know. Anyways, it's not always. If it was always, we wouldn't have to sit here and talk out loud."

"Well, I'd probably still have to."

"Me too. I hafta ask you questions. Don't I ask you questions? And you can pick up on me, maybe. Whatd'ya s'pose I was thinking here just a moment ago? Who was I thinkin' about?"

"Jison," I said. Then I wondered why I'd said that. I had faintly pictured a man with serpents about his head.

"See, there you are! That's exactly right. I was thinking about Jison."

"It was a guess," I told him. "You said 'who' so I said 'Jison.' "

"Well, you were right, all the same. I was sittin' here thinking about Jison and why he came to the States here—wanting
to get with healers and all, workin' on the bigger picture. And
I was relating it—tying that in with that Shinto priest. You
know, the one with the serpents?"

"I know."

"You remember what he said? And we were all thinking the
same thing. Have been for a long time. Maybe the time is getting close. He said we've got to join together—travel in person
and actually meet up together so's we can make a powerful
force. Those of us in physical form—that's how he put it—the
spirit guides give us this duty. To get together in physical
form. But it's got to be the medicine people and the leaders of
the sacred ways and not the politicians or the big business
bosses. They can't do it, 'cause we're not talking about buying and selling here, we're talking about healing. We're talking about those who follow the sacred paths, not those who
just play monopoly with each other. 'It's not to the point to
communicate technologically,' that's what he said. I remember that, I made a note of that."

"I remember," I acknowledged.

"You know why that is? There's got to be the contact.
There's got to be the ceremony. You have to generate spirit
power. You can't make medicine over the wires. Even when
they get to where you send the voice and the picture all the
time, it's still not enough. You can't do enough with it. Now
there's some of us, and I think you realize it, who travel in
other ways and don't always transport the physical part. But
this is still gettin' together. That's different. Communication
includes communion and community—it's not just passin' information around. Technological communication could get to
be a problem, make things even worse, if it cuts back on the
actual travel. People have to push for the actual physical contact. The electronics could be just to set it up, open the door,
and that's all."

He paused and looked thoughtful and, in his thoughtfulness, he picked up a huge glazed doughnut and bit off at least
half of it. "You know, we could do something on this," he went

on, swallowing hard. "We could make this a kind of a project. Let's give it some thought. I'm gonna jot some notes on this so's we can think about it."

We thought about it and talked about it, off and on, over the time that I had left. "We could call a meeting," he kept saying. "One day I think we'll do that. We could host it really good. All different people on their different paths, gathering from all directions to talk about what we can do together." It seemed that when we talked we were usually sitting at the table and, almost always, eating or munching on something. At least Mad Bear was. When I could not keep up with him, I tried to make it look as though I was. But with this sort of talk he got restless, and he could not stay at the table. When he thought about travel, he always got restless, so he kept getting up and down, and we kept going in and out, sitting on the metal bench on his porch or walking around in the yard.

As we walked through the ankle-high grass, I wondered when Mad Bear was planning on cutting it. I considered asking whether I could cut it for him, but it was a lot of lawn and it was getting late, and I was leaving in the morning.

"I was just thinking about the little people," he said. "Maybe you were kinda picking that up."

"No, I was just thinking about the long grass," I told him.

"You might have gotten a glimpse of some little nature spirits or something. The little people rarely run through here but you can pretty near always see them when they come around. The little elementals, on the other hand, they're always around, but they're darn hard to catch a glimpse of. Now the little people, they're different—that's a similar line of evolution about like us—and we actually have a bit of contact with them from time to time. That came into my head, so I thought maybe it came from you. The little people. I'll show you something when we get back in the house. But you're right. I do have to call this kid about the grass, 'cause I don't want to have to mow it myself. Funny he hasn't come around."

We were standing in the driveway about where he was waving to his friend after he'd won the final game of chess, and

●

again he looked at my hand as he had done before. "Looks like that ring is still put aside, and I guess this time it's my fault. You're just not going to feel like wearing it the way it looks now, isn't it?"

"Yeah, but I don't mind. I don't need to wear it."

"Well, but you could. Anyways, why don't you get it and bring it in the house again. We ought to straighten it out and not leave it like that."

I brought the ring into the house and handed it to him again.

"It looks awful like this," he said. "Might as well throw it away if it's going to look like this. We can clear it up now, and it'll stay okay. Then you can wear it or not. But I'm telling you, I'm still not going to get me one. I could, but I'm not." He held up the ring so that I could see that it had resumed its original appearance, but he took a cloth and rubbed it. "We'll just shine it up a bit more. Too bad it's not silver, that'd be impressive, in case you wanted to look really sharp. You can wear it now, though, if you like. It won't hurt anything, one way or the other."

I took the ring and put it on.

He looked at me and grinned. "Now I'm thinking about something. You try to pick up what I'm thinking." But he pointedly glanced around the kitchen, giving it away.

"Eating," I said.

"Well, but say suppertime."

"Suppertime."

In the morning, I packed my suitcase and brought it in the house. Mad Bear was going to drive again to the airport in Buffalo, though I'd insisted I was willing to jump on the bus.

"You want anything more before we head out?"

"No, no, I'm fine. I don't need a thing."

"Well, you'll get something on the plane, I guess. Oh! Here, before you go—I almost forgot—I was going to show you something here." He sat down behind his desk and slid open a drawer. "This thing is for real," he said, taking a key and unlocking a small case, "but you can't tell that for sure just by touching it. There are ways, however, to confirm this chemically, if anyone doubts it. Our people know from direct experience. This is a human skull. I'm going to let you hold it. But I'm going to ask you not to go spreading this around. Most people wouldn't believe you in the first place but, as far as an interest in investigating it, that means reporters and everything else."

Without waiting for me to reply, he handed me the object. It was a tiny skull. It did look like a human skull, teeth and all, and it did look like bone—except, as he had said, I could not be sure by touching it. But it was only about as large as a Ping-Pong ball.

"These little people are about nine inches tall. They live here the same as we do, and many of our people have seen them. We don't go digging up graves and collecting bones, like the white people do to us. I wouldn't have this if they didn't want me to. It's a privilege to have it—something like a memento—a tangible token testimony of their presence. But we don't talk about them much, and I guess you can figure why."

CHAPTER TWELVE

Empathy

"Main thing is, you gotta stay lighthearted if you wanna be good-hearted."

◐ Joel Friedman reached me in Topeka and introduced himself on the phone. "I hope you don't mind my calling you. You never answered my letter."

"I was expecting your call," I told him. "I heard you were trying to reach me through The Menninger Foundation, so I asked them to have you call here."

"Anyway, what I wanted to talk about now was the possibility of contacting Rolling Thunder. I'm taking the summer to drive around the country, and I was thinking it might work out for me to stop by his place while I'm out that way."

"Do you think you'll be coming anywhere near here on this trip?" I asked. "If so, maybe you and I could meet first—before you meet Rolling Thunder."

Joel and I arranged that he would phone me again from somewhere on the road when his schedule was more definite,

and we might then make plans to meet in Topeka. I had allowed a somewhat hasty commitment, I realized, as soon as I
had hung up the phone; but Joel had made a good impression
and I had felt sorry that I had either missed or forgotten his
letter. He was attending medical school in Florida, he had told
me, and he was planning to use the summer for some broad-
ening exploration and experience. It was a purposeful as well
as interesting plan, I thought.

When I heard from him again, several weeks had passed,
and he was already in Colorado. "I came the southern route,"
he explained. "But it doesn't matter. Like I told you, my
schedule is pretty much open. At the moment I'm right near
Denver." Two days after that, he called me again from a
restaurant a couple blocks from where I was staying in
Topeka, and I walked down the road to find him sitting at the
counter with a cup of herb tea.

I said, "If you drove out here from Denver with a plan to
visit Rolling Thunder in Nevada, you've sort of come out of
your way."

We sat in my living room—on the floor, as was his habit—
and talked for hours. By the time he carried his sleeping bag
in from the van, we had arranged a whole new set of plans. He
was indeed free, as he had said, at least for the rest of the
summer, but he did have a purpose in mind and an ideological
direction he intended to pursue.

For my part, however, I was going East and not West. I had
a commitment at Slippery Rock State College in Slippery
Rock, Pennsylvania, to do a series of seminars for the health
science department. It was part of their summer program.
From there, I was heading up to Mad Bear's. Joel decided he
would like to make that trip and was willing to be the transportation.

This arrangement was an advantage to me, in terms of both
economics and convenience. Having our own transportation
would allow more options than a complicated schedule of
short flights. Over the hours that we sat on my living room
floor, we came up with some ideas for what he was trying to do

that could fit comfortably into my own schedule—so we planned an itinerary to accommodate both our agendas.

Joel was hoping to find an alternative approach to the art of healing, and he wanted to explore Indian medicine as a possibility for his own practice. "I don't know how familiar you are with med school or med students," he said. "It's totally institutionalized, like commerce and industry. Believe me, you can hardly find any soul or compassion anywhere. I could really relate to these ideas you wrote about. I haven't done much reading in this area, but there's nothing in our texts or lectures or discussions or even among my classmates or friends that relates to the most basic and essential values— at least not to mine. I mean, I feel like I left my soul on a shelf and years later, when I go back to get it, it's not going to be there. Or worse, after years of med school, I won't even want it anymore."

"Maybe it doesn't have to be that way," I suggested. I thought about the physicians and health care professionals I had come to know at places like the Council Grove Conference and The Menninger Foundation—and the Menningers themselves. I thought about Jim and Larry Davis, who had invited Mad Bear and Jison to Council Grove. They lived and worked in Indianapolis—more or less on the way to Slippery Rock—so we added them to our itinerary. Within a couple days, it was all arranged, and we were packed and on our way—from Topeka to Toronto to the Tuscarora Reservation—with stops along the way.

At the Himalayan Institute near Chicago, we sat in a doctor's office and heard a medical opinion that was intended to encourage Joel in his medical pursuits. Rudy Ballentine, M.D., was not only a practicing physician but also a homeopath and a recognized expert in diet and nutrition and was accomplished in such ancient Eastern disciplines as yoga and ayurvedic medicine. I had met Rudy Ballentine first at Swami Rama's ashram near Rishikesh, India, and had come to know him over the years through my contact with the Himalayan Institute. Since Chicago was an easy first stop on our Northeast

trek, I had thought it worth our while to visit the training
classes and the clinic at the Himalayan Institute. But if Joel
was looking for justification to leave medical school in favor of
some alternative pursuit, he could not expect to find it from a
practicing physician—not even this holistically oriented physician who also practiced homeopathy, yoga, and meditation.

"People of all kinds and descriptions parade through here
every day," the doctor told us. "They take off their clothes
and bare their very hearts and souls to me. I am privileged to
be able to witness the depth and breadth of human makeup
and experience. Every day is a wonderful and fascinating
learning opportunity for me. Every day provides an opportunity to serve—to help people. And it's my 'M.D.' that allows
me this opportunity—that legitimizes it. Within the limits of
law, ethics, and good taste, I can do as I see fit, as my best
judgment tells me. I have the whole spectrum of alternatives
at my disposal—from the conventional to the most ancient or
most modern alternatives. Being a physician doesn't subtract
from my options. On the contrary, it adds. I do some things in
the course of my practice that don't require a medical degree,
but these procedures are still more effective—more substantiated and supported—by the fact that I'm a physician. I can
reach people in ways that only a doctor can."

Jim and Larry Davis endorsed and expanded upon what
Rudy Ballentine had expressed. We sat for hours in their living room in Indianapolis. They were physicians and psychia-
trists with the Community Hospital Mental Health Center and
ran the Davis Psychiatric clinics. I had last seen them only
months earlier at the Council Grove Conference. Joel listened
as they recalled their encounter with Mad Bear at that conference and hoped aloud that Mad Bear might offer him a different sort of encouragement.

It seemed to me, as we continued on our way, that Joel was
looking forward more than ever to talking with Mad Bear.
The doctors had made sense and had tried to be encouraging.
But Joel had not heard enough. He needed to learn something
about "what else is there." If he were to remain in his contem-

porary setting, he needed at least something to anticipate—
something to look forward to to sustain him in his efforts. I
was curious myself what Mad Bear might have to say to a non-
Indian medical student. I knew he would not suggest that Joel
drop out of school and take up Indian medicine. But, unlike
the doctors with whom we had just spoken, Mad Bear could
easily volunteer some comments that could serve to make the
years ahead even less tolerable for Joel.

In any case, that meeting would come later. We were on our
way to spend nearly a week at the state college in Slippery
Rock, Pennsylvania, and from there to visit Dorothy
MacLean and others in Toronto. "It's been good to go along
the road, for a change, and not through the air, and still to
have time enough to make these extra stops," I told Joel. "But
I have no idea what these next days are going to be like.
You're welcome to sit in on the talks and the seminars, if you
want, but you should feel free to go on your own and do whatever you want."

"Well, we'll see," Joel replied. "I'll feel it out. To tell you
the truth, I'm curious what you're going to do with a topic
like 'Witchcraft' or, even more, what a topic like that's doing
at a state college school of nursing."

"Me too," I said. "But, like I told you, it wasn't my idea.
That was the topic they had chosen for these summer sessions, so that was the topic they gave me when they invited me
to participate."

"Yeah, but I bet they're not expecting the way you're going
to handle it."

"Maybe not, but I gave them a pretty detailed outline, so
they shouldn't be surprised. I told them I'd never used a title
like that, but that I could offer what I had to offer and they
could call it whatever they wanted. Actually, it could well fit
under the heading of witchcraft in the fullest meaning of the
word. Witchcraft isn't what most people suppose at all."

"That's what I mean."

The talks in the auditorium each morning were required
for credit, and the afternoon workshops were optional for

whoever wished to attend. The program was open to both graduate and undergraduate students from all departments and to health professionals from the surrounding community.

Both Joel and I went to the auditorium on Monday morning to attend the opening session. There were announcements about schedules and about campus rules and policies and then the introduction of the morning speaker. A professor gave a lecture about the superstitious belief in witchcraft in early American history. He taught everyone the names of some people who had been accused of being witches and gave various details regarding their so-called trials. Then he revealed the names of those who were found guilty and dictated the dates of those who were executed for the participants to put down in their notes. People occasionally raised their hands to confirm the spelling of the more difficult names.

After the morning session, the professor who had invited me introduced me to the professor who had spoken. "I didn't want . . . I didn't think I'd meet . . . Well, I didn't know you were going to be here already this morning," was all he said, and he walked away.

"This is about what I expected," Joel commented as we walked across the campus to the cafeteria. "In other words, I don't think you're what they're expecting. That was all names and dates—probably dug out of some history book somewhere. There wasn't a single concept of any kind presented—one way or the other. But it didn't seem like anybody noticed. I think these people are here for credits, not for concepts."

"Who knows?" I said. "That guy won't be around for any of my stuff, I don't imagine. The people that I talked to know what I'm going to do because I sent them a description, and who knows what these participants are like? Maybe we'll reach beyond their expectations. They shouldn't mind, they'll still get their credits."

"Well, I'm going to sit in on it. There's nothing else I want to do here anyway, and I'm curious to see how it's going to go. See, this is exactly what I've been talking about. Education is so institutionalized. Most of it is just rote memorizing.

Where's the thoughtfulness? Where's the caring and the humanity?"

"You know, you might find the afternoon sessions relevant. That's what we'll be dealing with in a way. I was going to do some sort of mini-version of the 'Technique of Seeing' workshop—or at least that's what I'd thought. I started doing that as a weekend workshop about ten or twelve years ago, and I've been doing it ever since. I used to just do talks—stories, I guess—true stories about swamis, shamans, yogis, monks, and medicine people. I thought people might find them kind of inspiring. One day a group of us, teachers, mostly, got to talking about how people can come to resent being stirred or turned on as much as they resent being force-fed an endless stream of bare and empty facts. Whether it's a speech, TV, LSD, mushrooms, or whatever, people don't want simply to be fed impressions by some external influence. They want validation. They want to expand their own direct experience. And they want to know that it's really them, and not something else—not just something they ate. People have often responded to the stories with bewilderment or even with frustration. It was subtle and hard to pick up, and at first it was hard to understand. It wasn't a matter of suspicion or skepticism—which would be okay with me, anyway, because I'm not trying to convince anyone of anything. People felt excluded. They wanted to know how they could have an experience—how they could meet a teacher, or find a path. People long for direct encounter."

"Exactly. Me too."

"Do you realize that direct encounter has been almost entirely eliminated from our lives, especially from the learning process? Do you realize how much this has cost us? We become the passive receptacles of secondhand descriptions and simulated displays and depictions—something like computers except not quite so efficient. And we wonder what's happening to empathy."

"That's what I've been talking about. And I don't want it to be done to me. Not even a little bit."

"Direct encounter. This is one basic aspect of American In-

dian medicine—or Indian wisdom. Like Rolling Thunder
once said, 'You can't just sit down and talk about the truth.'
Truth is something you experience, it's not just something to
look at. To people like Mad Bear—you'll see—understanding
is very different from disinterested observation. It's not simply a matter of noting and committing to memory. Understanding is nothing less than a participatory experience. It's a
two-way rapport—a mutual relationship."

"That's exactly what I'm looking for," Joel said, as we
walked through the food line at the cafeteria. "That's why I
wrote to you. That's why I'm here."

"But it seems to me," I went on, "that we have a ways to go
before we can just start chasing after an experience—especially if it's to involve medicine people or some other culture.
We have to put aside our old mind-sets. We have to step out of
that mold you just called institutionalization and develop a
more realistic approach to observation and cognition. Anyway, that's how that workshop got started. It was supposed to
be a response to those who were looking for an 'experience'—
an attempt to explore the technique of observation—of really
seeing. We call it description-free perception. For example,
from what I've seen, when Native people are walking in the
woods or the fields, I don't think they're constantly giving descriptions to themselves like we do. I can't imagine them
thinking: 'This is a tree. It's a this or that kind of a tree. And
there's a bird. It's gray and white and it's got spots, so it's a
such and such bird—a member of the whatever family.' I
don't think they're constantly giving descriptions to themselves like we always do. It becomes a habit with us, but it's
not the natural way. It's not the Native people's way."

"What do they do?"

"Just listen. Let the tree or the bird introduce itself—in its
own way."

"I'll do that."

"Okay, let's try it. I don't know who we'll have to work
with, but let's try it."

"You mean, with these people? How?"

"I don't know, we'll just try it."

The morning talks were the usual storytelling format. But they were real stories about real people—just as historically accurate as the professor's opening lecture—yet with some implication, or "concept," as Joel had put it. I left it to the participants to consider the implications and draw their own conclusions. "Guest speakers have no responsibility for student evaluations or grades," I had been informed. I knew the students would have to write and turn in something based on these sessions—but I would be gone. As I stood on the platform, I could barely see the faces of my listeners. I had no way to know what they were getting other than their credits. The one thing I could tell—because I asked for a show of hands—was that nearly all of what I had proposed for their consideration was news to them. For the most part, these students were unaware of even the meaning of witchcraft. They did not know what shamans were—or even swamis. They did not know the meaning of yoga or meditation, and they had never heard of the Dalai Lama, Don Juan, the Aquarian Age, or *The Whole Earth Catalogue*.

Also, for the most part, these students did not come to the afternoon workshops: These were not for credit. Those who did come were not students. They were nurses, mostly, or teachers or parents, or all of these. Just outside the room where we met was a small meadowlike area with small trees and bushes and, across the road nearby, a larger field. It would not be like walking in the woods, exactly, but there were living things to talk to and listen to, and enough space that people could feel somewhat private.

"Part of the technique of seeing," I told them, "and I'm using 'seeing' in its deepest sense, is to reach out strongly, to extend yourself, and at the same time to be still enough and open enough to be really receptive. You have to refrain from internal chatter, from constantly giving yourself descriptions. You have to refrain from saying 'This is a tree,' or 'This is a bush,' so that you can listen. We can all admit we could be better listeners, but we're just thinking of our conversations with other people." Everyone agreed to experience, or at least experiment with, listening to plants. I knew this sort of "research" was far from the usual health science department curriculum and, though this was an optional activity, I would not have proposed it without unanimous agreement. I also knew that, as Joel had observed, everyone who had enrolled in this summer program, for credit or otherwise, had not expected anything like what we were about to do.

Not only the exercise itself but also the results were unexpected—and it was this fact, I believed, that made it work. None of the participants were "into" this sort of thing and, aside from agreeing to try it, no one had a chance to develop any anticipation or mind-set one way or the other. We jumped right into it, but we took it one step at a time. The first step was to go out, walk around, and choose a tree, a bush, or a plant. The next step was simply to sit and hang out with it. People came in and out, back and forth, for their step-by-step instructions, always returning, again and again, to the same plant. At first, they considered suggestions as to what to say to their plant. Eventually, they reported, they were able to speak freely to their plant, out loud, and without feeling self-conscious.

Over a period of several hours and many encounters, they began to feel that they were establishing a genuine rapport with their plant. Eventually, the plants responded. The final step was to do nothing at all but sit and wait—twenty or thirty minutes, if necessary, until the plant offered its own response in its own way. "It doesn't matter what happens," we reminded ourselves. "It's now up to the plant."

People drifted back into the room, one by one. Some were smiling, some were ecstatic, some were nearly weeping. "Nothing like that has ever happened to me," one woman said, but almost no one felt a need or desire to speak.

We repeated the exercise with different people several times over the week, and then we left town.

"I wonder what the college would think about that," Joel said, as we were back in his van and on our way. "I bet none of them will talk about it, except maybe to each other. It's a good thing they didn't have to turn in some report to get credit for that part."

"Right," I said. "Especially if the credit depended on some professor trying to evaluate what actually happened. Of course, we don't know for sure ourselves what happened. No one ever does. We could discuss forever whether people had been set up to imagine something that never really happened. But that could be said about virtually every perception. One thing is for sure—everyone experienced something, whatever it was. They all did something they had never done before and they were all moved by it. And they'll likely go on with it. They'll all have to determine the implications for themselves."

•   •   •

We drove north across the Canadian border and checked into a hotel in Toronto. I called Mad Bear and told him we would be with him in a couple of days. Then we phoned Dorothy MacLean and told her we had arrived. She was expecting us and had set aside the following day for us. Dorothy was, along with Eileen and Peter Caddy, a founder of what had become internationally known as "The Findhorn Gardens" and had written about her conversations with the "devas" including the devas of the unbelievably huge vegetables that had grown almost miraculously right out of the sand in their gardens. She was a native Canadian and had returned home after years in Scotland. I had originally met her at one of the Council Grove Conferences some years earlier and I and my family had subsequently spent some time with her in their home near Topeka.

Though Dorothy had only a day to spend with us, it was a fitting follow-up to our experience at Slippery Rock and provided an additional bit of that "something else" that Joel was looking for. We spent the morning on a guided tour of Toronto, one of the few planned—and well-planned, at that—cities on the planet. "After lunch we can walk around down in the ravine," she told us. During lunch in her home, we talked

about the devas. She was doing workshops in Toronto and
elsewhere in which people were working with the process of
contacting or perceiving the presence of the devas—for themselves or for some constructive purpose. It seemed as though
anything that could be called an entity of any sort had a deva
behind it, there was even the Deva of Toronto. In all our conversations, there was no concrete definition or description
given for the devas. The devas were, apparently, something
that you became aware of through some internal process. One
need not define them in order to have some exchange with
them. Dorothy explained that she had to give her own words
to their communications, but that the information and instruction was not her own. As it was with her work at The
Findhorn Gardens in Scotland, she and others continued to
learn from these communications.

In the afternoon, we drove through town, parked near a
ravine, and made our way through the trees down along the
path toward the river at the bottom. "A place like this is a
godsend in a city," she told us. "It's so quiet because it's below
the level of the streets. You would hardly know there's a busy
city right over our heads. People come here during their
lunch hours or just to get away on a busy day. A place like this
is so important. It's more than relaxing, it's nourishing." On
that day, we did not see one other person.

As we walked, mostly in silence, I thought about the devas,
though no one spoke of them. I wondered to myself how
Dorothy thought of these trees and all the growing things, the
birds, and the river and what the world was like for her.

"I can't really picture those devas, whatever they are,"
Joel reflected later that evening as we returned to our hotel.
"Not that I can't conceive of their existence, I just can't pic-
ture them."

"I can't either," I acknowledged. "Maybe they're not pic-
tureable. But I don't know that I've really tried to picture
them."

"I have, I think, but I just don't get any image or anything
at all describable."

"Yeah, but then we can't picture or describe a mind, an

idea or a thought, or even consciousness itself. Well, maybe you can describe a thought, but you can't really picture it."

"No, actually, I think you're right," Joel resolved. "You can't describe a thought—only its content. You can quote your thoughts, but you can't picture or describe what a thought is other than its content. So you can quote a deva, whatever that is, but you can't describe it. You just know it's some kind of consciousness."

We had made contact with Anyas, who was living some-where near Toronto, and we were expecting him to join us for dinner. I had not seen him since United Nations Day, when Mad Bear had brought him to New York. I had the telephone number of an acquaintance of his, and Anyas had phoned back when he received our message. But he was late, and we waited way past the dinner hour. When we could wait no longer, we left word where we would be and went to the dining room for a very late supper. Not long after we returned to our room, Anyas arrived.

"We gave up on you," we told him, "and we've just finished eating."

"It's okay," he said, "I didn't want to eat. I came to see you. I didn't come to eat." He held out his hand toward Joel and said something in his own language. Anyas seemed differ-ent from our last meeting. He seemed serious and spoke so quietly it was almost difficult to hear him.

"But how come you're so late?" I asked him. "It's been hours, it's almost the middle of the night."

"I'm carrying a pipe here," he said softly, "so I walked. It takes hours. It's a long way." Anyas prepared a ritual, and he did it in a sacred manner. Everything was properly laid out, the sage and sweetgrass were burned and the prayers were given, and we smoked the pipe there in the hotel room. Anyas hardly spoke the whole time, except for his "hello's" and "good-bye's," and he left not long before dawn for his long walk home.

The next morning we pulled in at Mad Bear's place on the Tuscarora Reservation.

"My God, it looks like a fort!" Joel exclaimed as soon as he saw the cinder-block house with its barred windows. "What is this, protection or something?"

Mad Bear's place had been shot at, but never through, and no one had ever succeeded in breaking in, though attempts had been made. As his own friends and relatives had often said, "It's impossible to tell if he's even in there. He could be dead and none of us would even know it!" That was the way Mad Bear wanted it.

"Well, like you said about me at Slippery Rock," I told Joel, "Mad Bear may not be what you expected."

"I haven't got any particular expectation," Joel said. But he did look surprised, or at least amazed, when Mad Bear came bouncing out and rushed up to the van with a grin that seemed almost as large as the windshield. Unless one knew him well, one could never guess that Mad Bear often preferred to be left alone. He always appeared so delighted at the sight of visitors one would think he had been holding his breath waiting for someone to arrive.

Mad Bear yanked open the door on my side, and Joel and I both got out to shake hands. "By golly!" he said. "It's good to see yous both!"

Perhaps uncertain of the best thing to say first, Joel immediately gave him the tobacco he had brought for him.

"So you're the doctor? I've heard a little something about you already."

"Well, I'm not a doctor . . ."

"Sure you're a doctor." Mad Bear gave me a mischievous look. "And, Doug, do you still belong to that weird cult, or no?"

"What? What cult?" I asked.

"Well, where's your ring? Don't you still have that ring?"

"I don't know," I answered, looking at my hand. "I guess it's somewhere. I don't really care, and I don't belong to anything, you know that."

"So you can wear it if you want. You got nothing to worry about."

"I'm not."

◑

"What ring?" Joel asked.

"Never mind, I'll tell you later."

We sat down on the long metal bench on Mad Bear's front porch and looked over the front yard, across the road, and across the field beyond. It was a beautiful late-summer afternoon. Every few moments a car went by along the road in front of us. Occasionally one would honk its horn, but Mad Bear always raised an arm and gave a high wave whether it honked or not. "Well, it's a nice day," he said. "We can just sit out here for a while and enjoy the birds singing."

Joel looked at me. There were no birds singing, we both realized. Perhaps, I thought, they'll come soon, at the approach of dusk, as I had sometimes seen happen here. But I had barely finished the thought when a large group of birds swept by and settled in the tops of nearby trees. It sounded cacophonous, much closer to clatter than to song—like people at a party, all talking at once, trying to be heard above everyone else. We three just sat and listened, as though their demanding tone had trapped our attention. They left in a mob, just as they had come, and then we did hear real birdsong, but softly, somewhere in the distance. We remained silent.

After a moment, I spoke. "We saw Anyas up in Toronto," I reported. "He seemed different."

"He is," Mad Bear replied. "He is different. He's quite a kid. He's got a lot to him—too much to him, maybe, someway. But he's somebody, that guy is. How was Toronto?"

"Good," I said. "We were only there a couple of days. Saw Dorothy MacLean and Anyas. Then we headed down here."

Mad Bear looked at Joel. "That's all part of our Six Nations Confederacy, you know, all Iroquois country."

"Mad Bear!" Joel suddenly exhorted. "What do you know about devas?"

It startled me a bit. I had come to be aware of how Mad Bear and his people tended to duck a direct frontal approach, and I had also become aware that Joel's manner was somewhat forward. But I had come to like that in him. Whatever he said, and however he said it, it came out of a genuine caring and there was always warmth in it. Mad Bear felt it. I could tell by the way he responded.

"Devas?" Mad Bear scratched his head contemplatively. "I can't remember if we've met." He allowed a very apparent grin. Joel looked at me as if to check whether he ought to grin as well. I hoped these two would get used to each other quickly. "No, I think I know what you mean," Mad Bear resumed. "But tell me how you mean it."

"I guess you might know about The Findhorn Garden? Dorothy was talking about devas up in Toronto. Maybe they're what I might have called guidance or guardian angels, or maybe they're the mind or soul of living things—except a city isn't exactly a living . . ."

Mad Bear held up his hand and silently gestured with a nod of his head to call our attention to a little bird that had landed on a flower almost directly in front of us. It was a furry-looking, thistlelike blossom, and the bird began picking at it vigorously, flicking its head to fling little bits of fuzz from its beak. "Look at that," he whispered, leaning back and folding his arms over his large stomach.

We watched.

"Whatd'ya think he's doing?" he questioned us.

"Picking at the flower."

"He's doing his duty. Everybody has his part to play, and he's doing his part. He gets his reward—gets helped himself in the process. But what is he helping out here?"

"Spreading seeds."

"Right. He wouldn't be doing that if there were no purpose in it. But what do you suppose he thinks? What's his incentive?"

"What?"

"Nectar. There's tasty nectar down there at the bottom, under all those seeds. He knows it's there, and he's attracted to it. It's all arranged, see? It's a really neat arrangement, and we just see a little part of the picture. I mean, what's that flower for in the first place? What's its role? That flower's gettin' picked apart, and it'll be gone pretty quick. One day the plant's gone, but its kind will be around. The ever-coming new generations! But for what? And who's behind all this?"

"Devas?"

"I got a real treat in here for us, by the way. Green tomatoes! I slice 'em up, and I got a way to bread those things and fry 'em just right—absolutely delicious! And not only that, but they taste good too. Doug, I don't think I've made these for you yet. Just wait'll you sink your teeth . . ." He turned his head and peered down the road, squinting. "Uh-oh," he said.

A car came slowly along the road, and Mad Bear stared at it. It pulled into the driveway, all the way up to the porch. Inside were two elderly ladies. "We'll here's an interruption. Brief, I hope. Now, whatever you do, don't breathe a word about the green tomatoes. We'll just postpone it a bit." He nodded at the ladies in the car, but they just sat there. "C'mon!" he said, under his breath. "Don't pretend you're hesitant. I know what you're here for. These two are my aunts. Wait'll you see what they're up to." Mad Bear beckoned and the ladies got out and took two large bags from the car. It looked as though they had been grocery shopping. Mad Bear laughed out loud and jumped to his feet. "Okay, okay. Let's bring the stuff in here, and I'll put on some hot water."

We went inside and the "aunts" emptied the contents of their bags onto the little kitchen table: homemade cookies and macaroni and cheese in a covered casserole dish, several china cups and a little box of tea leaves. Mad Bear picked up a cup and held it toward the window. "These'll work," he said.

"We bring our own cups," one of the ladies explained to us. "They have to be right, not like he's got. Not glass but you can see the light through so it shows up like he has to have it. He gives good readings—has he done it for you?"

"You know I don't do this for people," Mad Bear commented. "This is not our traditional way."

"But he does it so well. Mad Bear, let these gentlemen try it too. But we go first, though."

◗

"They can if they want," he answered, placing a pot of water on the stove. "But not now, later. And you'll have to leave one of your cups. I can't use what I've got here."

"Well, we can get it when we come back for the dish. We're leaving this macaroni for you and there's enough for these gentlemen. We always bring him something good whenever we come over for tea leaves."

Joel and I went back out on the porch so that the ladies could have their tea-leaf readings—just in case, as Mad Bear had put it, there was something confidential. "He gets a lot of visitors," I explained to Joel, as we sat down again on the metal bench. "They're usually sudden and unexpected, and sometimes it feels like an interruption to me—when I've come all the way and don't have all that long to hang out. And then I remind myself that he's not here for me, he's here for his people."

"But tea-leaf readings? I never would have guessed that people come to Mad Bear to have their tea leaves read."

"Actually this is the first time I've ever seen or even heard of him doing that. I have a feeling it's just something those ladies are into. Mad Bear's so accommodating, that's the thing. People come for advice, for 'medicine,' for help in networking—because he knows just about everyone in the Indian world, not to mention representatives and spokespersons from all kinds of cultures—and people come for mediation, for conflict resolution, and everything else. Anyway, I think he likes it. Sometimes it gets to be a bit much, I guess. I've seen him sit in there with the lights off and pretend he's not home. And of course you can't see in. Maybe once in a while it's been for me that he's done it, I don't know. But if someone he likes comes around, he can't resist the contact."

"I can believe it," Joel acknowledged. "He seems real personable and real outgoing—especially for an Indian. Of course, I don't know a whole lot of Indians."

"No, you're right—especially for an Indian. But, in fact, he's got to be one of the most outgoing persons I've ever seen. He makes jokes and engages people all the time—everywhere. Like when we were in New York City, he was forever coming up with some off-the-wall remark to make people laugh. We'd be going up and down on the elevators and he'd say things like, 'Good heavens! Would you look at my shoes! You sure wouldn't know I shined 'em just this morning!' And people would wiggle around to get a look at his feet and he'd be wearing sneakers. Or we'd get on a crowded elevator and he'd say, 'Twenty-third floor, please.' And everyone would look at him strangely and someone would say, 'It only goes up to the twelfth floor.' Then he'd politely suggest, 'Well, could you push the twelve and then the eleven? Wouldn't that make twenty-three?' Everyone would look embarrassed for a moment, and then they'd laugh. At first I thought maybe he just wanted attention. It took me a while to realize that it's part of his medicine."

"Medicine? How so?"

"Public social behavior in our culture comes close to being pathological. I've thought that before I met Mad Bear. When I was living in Asia, I got used to seeing people behave communally—like family—even in crowds. Little kids on crowded buses would crawl up into whatever laps were handy. People would hold one another's packages—or hold one another, literally, on bumpy roads or quick stops. There's great similarity in the way Indians are with one another—or the way all traditional people are, for that matter. In our society, we are swimming in a sea of public paranoia and Mad Bear picks that up. Did you ever notice how people act in places like elevators? They stiffen up, hoping on hope that no 'strangers' make the slightest body contact. We people are uncomfortable with one another. We don't like people, in general. If they're not our friends or in some given way associated, they're either scary or yucky. Remember we were talking before about empathy? That's Mad Bear's medicine. Empathy."

"And that's what I was saying. The way we use the term 'medicine' is totally different. Medicine has got to be something different from—or, at least, far beyond—what we deal with in med school. Medicine has got to be healing, I mean, really healing."

"You know, I've heard people say that the real traditional

medicine people are reclusive, even among their own tribe, usually. Some say that authentic medicine people wouldn't travel all over the place, meet people, give talks and organize, and all that. But that's his medicine. He's a bridge maker. I know he's occasionally attended to injuries and illness, but that's not his real work. His real work is relationships. He wants to break this ice, this false isolation that makes us all strangers to one another and makes us dangerous to one another. I think that the real medicine people from now on, I mean the real healer heavyweights, will be working on that level. Anything else will be working on the—what the Indians call—the tail end of the problem."

"But, still, what gets me is this place here. I mean, it does look like some kind of fort. It's not very Indian, you know."

"But then, the teepees and the wigwams or whatever, you just don't see them that much anymore."

"Well, I don't mean that. But you've got to admit, this place isn't much in keeping with his outgoing character."

"There's a reason for that, though, or several reasons. Like I said, sometimes he pretends he's not here. He has to in order to do what he does. And at times when he's really gone, people think he may be in there, and he wants it that way. You know, sometimes I think he's really a bear. I'm not saying I'm convinced, but again and again, I've had hints from things he's said, or little glimpses I've had, that he takes on a bear or bearlike form. Or maybe he uses an existing bear. In any case, I'm sure sometimes when he's gone for periods of times, his body is in here in his bed. He has ways to keep his body protected. He has a lot of special things for medicine—another kind of 'medicine.' These are things that are 'doctored,' as he puts it, that no one should be able to get to or touch. Also, he does have some historic items and some turquoise and other things that are extremely valuable. So he has his reasons. I guess I told you, people have tried to break in here, or even to shoot him, and it never works."

"But why? He doesn't seem as though he'd have an enemy in the world."

"He doesn't. But they do. He has no opponents, but many

people regard him as one. He's involved in a lot of issues and contests—here and, I think, on other levels. Some people may just want to rob him. Others want him gone. Once there was a guy who tried to shoot him through his bedroom wall one night. It was supposed to be a drive-by shooting, and the guy stuck his rifle out the passenger side, shot, missed, and tried again. I don't think a bullet will go through that wall anyway—for a couple of reasons. Anyway, the guy had his eyes too long off the road, lost control, hit a tree, flipped over, and wrecked his car and himself. So stories go around that there's no way anyone can mess with Mad Bear."

"So was that because of Mad Bear's medicine?"

"In a way, but only in a way. The way he deals with conflict is interesting. He doesn't ever try to put anything back on anyone. He just doesn't receive it. It's like in martial arts. You just step aside, and your attacker trips and falls. It's the only righteous thing to do, you know, to step aside. But Mad Bear's real medicine, I think, is what he calls, simply, 'friendship.' He talks about 'friendship warriors,' and 'the weapons of friendship.' He once told me about a time that a guy came at him with a knife and he threw open his arms in friendship and they hugged. He says he doesn't want anyone to try that until they've learned it. But that's the learning that he believes we have to get on with now."

"Man, I was only thinking of things like nutrition and herbs, and natural medicines—and there's so much. There is just so much."

It began to sprinkle lightly, and we became aware that the sun had gone down completely and it was dark. We went back inside. By the sound of the chatter coming from the kitchen, it appeared that the ladies had had their readings. Joel went directly into the kitchen, perhaps hoping to witness some remnant or result of the tea-leaf reading process. One of the ladies stepped out of the kitchen to urge me to join them and to have my "fortune told" while Mad Bear was in such good form.

"No, no, I've had enough for now," I heard Mad Bear say. "We can do it later, if they like. Right now I want to bring

down these lanterns I've got here somewhere. Joel, look up on
that shelf above the cupboard there. Do you see a couple
kerosene lanterns up there?" Then he suggested to his aunts
that they might want to get on their way over the road before
the rains built up.

"Mad Bear, it's barely drizzling," one of them insisted.
"It's just a little mist in the air." The ladies looked comfortable and hardly in the mood for leaving.

"It's coming," Mad Bear proclaimed confidently, "a good
hard rain. Can't you smell that?"

"Not really."

"Wonder why not. Must be the tea."

"Well, I just thought we'd have a little peace and quiet,"
Mad Bear commented as the ladies pulled out of the driveway.
"That's it for me for tonight."

"How is that done?" Joel inquired. "I've heard of tea-leaf
reading, but I've never seen it done."

"Well, it doesn't matter really. It's just how you read them.
They drink the tea and the leaves are settled and stick on the
bottom. Then you can hold up the cup and read right through
it. It's just how you look at it, it helps to look at something,
but it doesn't really matter. If you can't pick up anything, the
tea leaves aren't going to help you. But if you can, then it
looks like there's symbols in there. That's what these ladies
want, that's what they believe in, so it works for them. What
you're really reading is the people. It just provides a chance
to say a few things that might be helpful. And they accept it,
since they asked. You can't do that with people except that
they ask. Well, you can, maybe, but it's not a good idea. It's
not right."

"I wouldn't mind knowing a few things about my future,"
Joel intimated.

"Yeah, but it doesn't work just like that. Some things are
up to you, some things aren't. But there's always some amount
of choice. The only reason for predictions is to do something
about it. Maybe you can change it. Or, if you can't change it,
or decide not to, then you prepare for it, or handle it in some

way. Speaking of which, let's light these things." He stood up
and found a match with which to light the two lanterns on the
table. "You gotta be careful talking to people about the future.
Sometimes it helps them, sometimes it doesn't. It all depends
on how you tell it, and what they do with the information.
Sometimes you might think you're reading the future when
you're making your own image. So you might start to bring
something about which you just then made up yourself. Other
times, it can sure be convenient to see something coming before it hits." He placed one of the lanterns on the bench by the
sink. "Anyways, I guess you got your own future pretty much
in your hands."

"I don't know," Joel reflected. "Sometimes it doesn't seem
that way to me."

"Some things depend on a larger situation. Our instructions are to pass our knowledge and our medicine on down
through our own generations. We've been told that when the
time comes for all the healers to share, it'll be a really powerful, powerful medicine we'll have. And it'll be a medicine
that'll help everyone—from the tribes to the nations to the
planet—everything. But we're also told that can't happen for
profit. Healing's got to get out of the for-profit business. I'm
not talking about offerings and exchanges, I'm talking about
greed. No sharing can be for selfish reasons, so it can't be like
some kind of ambitious commercial venture. But I'll tell you,
when the profit struggle is put aside—and that's coming up—
the healing art is going to get really, really powerful, like it
was in the past."

"But it seems to me," Joel said, "that if there's a better way
than some of these drugs, like some natural herbs that really
work and don't have all the side effects I'm learning about, it
would sure help a lot of people to share it."

"It's already there," Mad Bear declared. "It's already accessible."

Just then there was a loud, startling crack and a flash. We
jumped, and the lights went out. Mad Bear stood up and
looked out the window. "Electricity went out all over the

area, looks like, but it'll come back on pretty soon. That's why we got the lanterns here anyways. But we'll want juice to cook our supper, and for this coffeepot here. Although I've been known to cook on that wood-burnin' space heater, and pretty good, too."

"The natural medicines and medicine ways are all around us," Mad Bear went on, sitting down again at the table, and talking in an epical tone of voice as though influenced by the alluring glow of the kerosene lamps. He proceeded to give a number of examples, beginning with the particular plant with which we had seen the bird interacting, and all the plants were personalized and given names and spoken of as beings in their own right. He described a list of diseases and their natural remedies or treatments, and I thought perhaps Joel was hoping to memorize these as one would the lists and tables in one's medical texts. But to Mad Bear, it was a matter of observation, communication, and acquaintance. "All these things are right out here, all around us. It's all available and nothing's blocking it, except, like I said, putting profit first as though that's the goal. That blocks so much. But then for our people too, it becomes hard to hang on to. There's a lot of influence against it—a lot of counterforce to our traditional ways."

It made him think about diabetes, which in modern times had become a major concern for the Native community, and he described the natural remedies with which he had endeavored to "doctor" his people. I recalled the conversation I had had with him before he went out to the Council Grove Conference. "Is that how you treat your own diabetes?" I asked. He looked at me strangely, and again I felt awkward and regretted having referred to his diabetes.

"My diabetes? What diabetes?"

"Well, we've talked about it in the past, but you . . . Remember, Jison first told me about it . . ."

"Oh that. That diabetes didn't belong to me. From time to time I've been doing that. I was only hanging on to that for somebody else."

Then the lights came on. "Whatd'ya say we heat up that

macaroni?" he suggested. "That oughta be delicious—that and a few things I can put together. We've got those green tomatoes, but we don't wanna merge those in with this other stuff. You'd lose some of the effect. They kinda stand on their own, you know, but they're not quite enough for supper. We'd best save those for tomorrow."

After macaroni and a few other "delicious" things that Mad Bear hastily put together by opening some cans, more visitors dropped by. "Here we go again. I get so I can tell when some-one's comin' around," he announced, just before we heard the knock on the door. "I guess it's 'cause the lights are on and I got the car parked out front there. These kids pass by and they see that I'm home. But they'll be okay. We're just kind of kicked back here anyway, and they'll leave when I tell them."

"Hey Bear! What's happening?" came a loud voice the moment Mad Bear opened the door.

"You guys come on in! I got visitors here from out of town, so you can't stay too long. But maybe they'd like to hear a coupla songs or whatever."

The three young Indians walked right into the kitchen, looking very much at home. They appeared to be about high school age.

"So you got anything good left, Bear? Doughnuts or any-thing?"

"Well, I'll put something out," he offered. "But we oughta sit out in the garage. There's not room enough in here."

We all carried chairs into the adjoining garage. With the bed hoisted up and the car out in the yard, this was a larger space than the three small rooms in the house. Mad Bear carried a bowl of chips and a plate of cookies from the kitchen. We arranged our chairs in a circle, and a large washtub was turned upside down in the center. It appeared as though these visitors were accustomed to this ritual: With the three of them pounding out the rhythm as they sang, we were treated to an assortment of "social songs," with Mad Bear joining in from time to time. "Oh, I almost didn't think of it!" he exclaimed,

snapping his fingers and jumping up from his chair. "I've got
just the thing for this occasion. I think you guys may not have
seen this—I had it put away, and I ran into it and dug it out
the other day."

When he returned, he was carrying a strange-looking con-
traption and an extension cord. "Lemme just set this up here.
This's something really exquisite here."

"Oh my God, save us!" groaned one of the kids.

Mad Bear placed the thing on the floor and turned it on. It
began to creak and clatter as the little electric motor churned
inside. It was an artificial "campfire" arrangement of plastic
"logs" with some red cellophane and tinsel rotating around a
lightbulb inside. Mad Bear watched it contemplatively, trying
to look serious.

"That's totally ridiculous!" another complained.

"This s'posed to be a fire pit, or what? Looks like something some white folks would dream up . . ." He looked at us.
"Oh, 'scuse me, sorry."

"Well, it's not exactly a sacred fire," Mad Bear conceded,
holding back a chuckle. "But then we're singing social songs
in the cement garage, anyways. You've got to admit, it's kinda
stunning in a way—if you look at it just right."

His three young friends were eventually able to ignore the
thing enough to resume their drumming and singing—though
the little grinding motor and the crinkling of the cellophane
produced an incongruous background. They had a lengthy
repertoire of songs, and they repeated a few of their favorites
more than once. We had sat for nearly two hours when Mad
Bear suggested it was time to retire.

"This fire thing is pretty silly at that," he remarked, when
they had gone. "You would have thought they were a little bit
put out—but, actually, I think they kinda got a kick out of it,
to tell you the truth. These reservation kids, it's sure not easy
for 'em. They're raised in a somewhat traditional way but,
with school and TV and all, they have to figure how to fit in
and how to deal with their identity. Well, it's pretty rugged for
everyone these days, I guess. Just how to be—it's not too clear

anymore. And there's not enough support for people. But you can't take yourself too serious, you know, no matter who you are or what you're going to be. Otherwise, it gets too heavy. Main thing is, you gotta stay lighthearted if you wanna be good-hearted."

"He's the one you kinda get a kick out of," Joel commented after Mad Bear had gone to bed. "He's not exactly what I had expected—you were right about that—but he's more than I expected, not less. The way he eats though, man, that's got to change! And I don't know if I'm going to be able to handle those deep-fried green tomatoes."

The time for green tomatoes came around the following afternoon, and Joel watched the preparation process with anxiety as Mad Bear lifted the sopping slices from the hot oil and blotted them on paper towels.

"Here, take a plate and help yourself right off of there," he prodded Joel, "and don't be shy. There's plenty more to go around. You're gonna think you died, like they say, and went to heaven."

"I'd love to try some," Joel said, helping himself to a couple of the smallest slices he could find. "But I can't eat too much today. I think I'm having a little problem with my stomach."

"Well, you'll be all right pretty quick," Mad Bear assured him. "We'll fix you up."

After his green tomatoes—Mad Bear insisted he try a second helping—Joel excused himself and left the kitchen. "He'll be okay," Mad Bear told me. "It's not so much the food, although it's partly that, 'cause he's not used to it. I think he's a little shocked and disappointed that I don't just eat organic health food. He might have developed his own ideas about how Indians are supposed to be. 'Course he's right in a way, him being a doctor and all. I've been told I don't have the best of diets. But then I do all right for living alone and on a budget and all. At least it's all delicious—you gotta give it that."

Later that day, when Mad Bear's chance presented itself, he talked about Indians and food, and I supposed it was partly in order that he might account for himself to Joel. "I

don't know how much you've learned about our Indian history," he started, "but whatever you know that's true came
from our people and not from your own schools."

"You know, speaking of schools," I interrupted, "I was going to tell you this a while back, and it slipped my mind. When
I was out at Chatauqua, one of the women who was attending
my sessions came up to me after a talk and asked me where
she could find some indigenous sources for information or educational materials about American Indians. She told me she
was a junior high teacher who refused to present to her class
the section of American Indians even though it was part of the
curriculum and included in the students' texts. She told me
that she refused to include any materials or reference to
American Indians in her classes and she purposely explained
to the students the reason they were to skip the part about
American Indians. She said she refuses to teach falsehoods in
a public school setting and that her principal and the parents
accept that."

"Well, good for her. Anyways, what I was going to point out
is that many of the fruits and most of the vegetables that the
white people know today came from American Indians. The
Native people of the Americas had potatoes, tomatoes, every
kind of bean, over three hundred varieties of corn—and the
list goes on. They had all these things for literally centuries
before the white people made their first contact with them. So
much of what you people enjoy today, here and in Europe
too, including the majority of your natural diet, is part of
your Indian heritage. And, by the way, a lot of your so-called
American heritage comes to you from the Iroquois Confederacy—including your form of government with its three
branches and two legislative houses, your Bill of Rights, that
eagle symbol just like you see it today, and the colors red,
white, and blue. Did you know all that?"

Joel responded, "No, I didn't know all that."

"Do you have any idea what the original people's diet was
like over most of the centuries, from thousands of years ago?"

"No, I guess not. Does anyone?"

"Well, you're right about one thing. I do eat too much oil
and butter and sweets, things like that. Most of our people do.
I guess it's pretty impossible for us to eat like our ancestors
did, even though our ancestors developed so much of the natural, healthy foods known today. Even some of your own his-
torians have acknowledged that our people were unbelievably
skillful botanists and horticulturists. But see, we knew these
things that you were asking about before. These things work
by direct communication. See, those things you were talking
about with that Dorothy up there, that's what it is, that's how
it works." He stood up and opened the refrigerator. "There's
a lot of knowledge directly available to us," he went on, glancing over the shelves. "That's why I say it's all available and
not blocked. The commercialism blocks it, that's the only
thing. This so-called industrial age brought along some
knowledge, but it blocked out just a whole lot. If the motiva-
tion is mainly money, it changes everything."

He suddenly caught himself and quickly closed the refrigerator door. "Speakin' of food, here I am looking for something
to eat. All this talking about food and diets makes us hungry
all over again." He sat back down at the table and looked at
his watch. "But then it's not too much longer till suppertime,
so we gotta be thinking about that pretty quick, anyways. But
it's not just the natural food, it's the natural medicines—the
natural medicines that have been discovered and developed
over so many centuries. Look at the accounts of all the doctors
that first came over here right after Columbus. These are still
in the archives, if you need verification. The Indians of those
days, and of long before, had penicillin and all kinds of an-
tibiotics, and natural herbs for all kinds of things. All that is
still here, too. Nothing's gone. All the medicine we need for
every healing, for every personal or social goal is right out
here, all around us. It's only blocked in the sense that some
people personally block it. Just like our natural history
threatened religion and politics over the years, our natural
medicine threatens the medical industry today. And yet, it's
right out here for the asking. So, in that sense, it's not blocked

at all, never can be. And it doesn't belong to Indians or anyone else exclusively. It belongs to nature and to life, that's all.
So you don't have to figure what kind of a doctor to be or how
to go about it. Just ask Nature and the Natural Way and,
when the time is right, it'll explain itself to you."

For a while, we just sat quietly and even Joel had no questions.

"So, are you guys hungry yet, or no?"

We had an early supper, went to bed early, and got up early
so that we could be on our way. Mad Bear was up even earlier,
and had our breakfast ready. "Now here, looky, I got scrambled eggs with tomatoes and onions and wheat cakes cooked
up—I got 'em keeping warm in here—so it's all good and natural for you this morning. And you're feelin' pretty all right
today—or no? However, at least a couple of us are gonna have
some coffee, though, so I got that goin' here."

Just before we left, he called to Joel. "Come in here for a
minute. I've got a little something for you." It was a beaded
necklace that he told Joel had something special about it because he'd "doctored" it up a bit. "And you should wear this
next to your skin for about three days, so it can get used to
you, and don't take it off. After that, you can wear it in or out
or have it on or off. But don't let anyone touch it."

Joel slipped it over his head and tucked it under his shirt.

"He seemed pretty sure I'd be seeing him again," Joel said,
as we pulled out onto the road. "I don't know, I hope so. But
look back there in the driveway. Man, you can see that grin
from a long ways away!"

CHAPTER THIRTEEN
The Longest Walk

"We may still have a chance to feel safe and easy again."

◑ **In early autumn** I returned to Topeka. Rolling Thunder's daughter and son-in-law had come to live with me for a time, and together we had rented a house in Topeka. I had thought I would leave soon after they did—perhaps move back West also and rejoin them—but then I went on the road with Joel for nearly a month, leaving an empty house behind. An acquaintance at The Menninger Foundation suggested I might take in some Washburn student to share the rent since my place was near the university. "Students are always looking for living situations like this," he claimed, "and it's a chance for you to meet some more like-minded people who are interested in the work." I agreed to let him post some notices around his alma mater just to see what might happen. That's how I met Jon Cates and began a longtime working association.

Jon came to the door with a copy of *Rolling Thunder* in his hand. "This is why I called you," he said. "I'm not really looking for a place. When I saw your notice it just seemed like the kind of thing one ought to follow up on."

Jon was an employee at the university library, I learned, and he had ample time for reading as he sat behind the desk. He was right in the middle of *Rolling Thunder* when he saw my name on the bulletin board.

"I almost never look at that board," he told me. "There are only ads and notices for students that don't concern me. But yesterday I was on my way down the hall on my coffee break, and I happened to glance up and see your name. I don't know why it caught my eye—I just happened to look up. And then I looked at your book. I had my fingers inside the pages, just like this, to keep my place. This was just a little too much, so I thought, 'I'm going to find out if this is the same guy.' "

"Now I see why you asked me about the book," I said, remembering that this was his first question when he had called me on the phone. "I never saw those ads, and I didn't know what they said. A friend of mine put them up. I didn't know he was going to include mention of the book."

"No, he didn't. The one I saw said something like: 'Wanted. Student to share house near campus. Preferably someone interested in other cultures.' And it had your name and number. Of course, I'm not a student and I don't need a place, but then I guess I really wouldn't mind moving out of where I am. I mean, I'm open. I'm certainly interested in other cultures. The only thing, I have a lot of plants."

So over the next few days, during several lunches and dinners and coffees, we explored why Jon had noticed the ad and why he had responded to it. In little more than a month after we had met, Jon and I moved into a still larger house even closer to the campus and opened the first office and drop-in center of the Cross-Cultural Studies Program. It was on College Avenue, just a few blocks down the street from Washburn University. We began to hold "open-house" gatherings and, within only a few weeks, we had met dozens of new friends and neighbors who came around to share discussion and refresh-

ments. Through the winter we continued our weekly meetings—we called them "winter raps"—and in the spring we began to hold project meetings and Sunday-night *pujas* for
chanting, meditation, or simply silence. Interestingly, many
busy people dropped in for the Sunday-night sessions. "There
aren't many places one can go just for silence," people told us.

One day Mad Bear telephoned to relay some of his own impressions about our space and our gatherings. He had not yet
had a chance to visit our College Avenue center, or even to
come to Topeka. "I thought I'd drop in and pay a visit," he
told me on the phone, "so I went ahead and took my dream
medicine. I thought I might catch sight of you. There were
people in that room there where you hold the meetings, but
you weren't in there. I figured if you were, you might sorta
pick up that I was lookin' in on you. I didn't want to snoop, so
I figured I'd come around on one of those open nights, and I
saw so many shoes, I knew a bunch of people were there. At
first I didn't know where the people were, so I checked the
dining room and kitchen. But then I went ahead and went upstairs. Then I felt like I had my shoes off, 'cause I could feel
that thick red carpet on my feet. When I do actually come out
there, I hope you've got a chair or something at the bottom of
those stairs, 'cause I can't take my shoes off standing up—or
get 'em back on again. Anyways, I was just looking at everybody who was sitting there but, like I said, you weren't in
there yet. And then I got a little glimpse of the future there.
Well, I just caught sight of a future possibility, but I don't
think you have to worry about it. I'll tell you, but you have to
take it as symbolic—that's the way these foresights are."

The image that he related was so bizarre that it was obvious
and fortunate, as well, that it was only symbolic. There was
significant connotation behind it, however, and I discussed it
with Jon. We agreed that, somehow or other, Mad Bear had
indeed paid a visit. He had described our place quite accu-
rately. The *puja* room was indeed upstairs—and I had never
told him that. We had been here only a short while, and there
had been little chance during that brief time to speak with

Mad Bear. He had "seen" where the shoes were and even seen and felt the red-carpeted stairway. Even his prophetic "glimpse" made sense in its symbolic way. We knew who and what he was referring to. The people he described were both "overdressed" and "underdressed," as he had put it, trying to look both sexy and glamorous—and they were trying to glamorize the *puja* room. "They had this thick black velvet draped all over the place," he had said, "and they were sprinklin' this stuff on it—like they were trying to hurry so if you disapproved, it'd be too late. Whatd'ya call those little shiny things like some women put in their hair? Little spangles or what? Anyways, they're real artificial-looking. Well, it would make quite a flashy spectacle—but really pretentious, you know, not at all genuine. And not toward the purpose you're supposed to be set up with."

"It's pretty accurate," Jon acknowledged. "Symbolic, yeah, but accurate. We should take it as a kind of confirmation of what we've been talking about, and keep on emphasizing the work and the projects and deemphasize all the far-out stuff—new-age goodies or whatever."

In the spring, Jon noticed a bulletin posted around the college buildings and grounds announcing the appearance on campus of representatives of AIM. AIM, the American Indian Movement, along with traditional spiritual leaders from many tribes had begun a cross-country march in response to newly proposed legislation intended to abrogate existing treaties and "terminate" the remaining Indian reservations. They called it "The Longest Walk." The speakers who were scheduled to appear were part of several advance teams who were traveling ahead to generate publicity and support for their cause.

Jon and I walked up to the campus to attend the gathering and listen to the speakers. Vincent Bellecourt and Bill Wapapa, well-known AIM leaders, were there, among others, and both of them spoke. Though there had been considerable publicity, only a handful of students and a few people from the local Indian community showed up. Still, the speakers gave energetic and impassioned talks, explaining the meaning

and implications of these new bills before Congress and urging people to write to their senators and representatives to ex-
press their opposition to the pending legislation. The few who
attended were interested and concerned, and there was much
lively discussion. After the gathering, Jon and I stayed to
meet the speakers.

"Listen, if you're interested in helpin' out," Vincent Bellecourt told us, "you ought to come on down and set in with us
tonight. A bunch of us are gettin' together down at the Indian
Center for a planning meeting. There's lots to do—lots of
needs. You might pick up on somethin'."

When Jon and I arrived at the Indian Center, more than a
dozen Indians were already there, sitting in a circle. They
stared at us as we came through the door, and I wondered if it
was appropriate for us to walk in on them. "Hey, Boyd!" Vincent piped up, slapping the chair beside him. "Set right over
here!" Jon and I joined the circle, but we were the only non-
Indians there, and we seemed to have created an awkward
pause.

There was much to be planned, we learned, and the needs
were many. The Indians expected their numbers to grow into
the thousands as the march proceeded across the United
States from Alcatraz Island to Washington, D.C. There would
be need for supplies like shoes and bandages and even tooth-
paste, not to mention food and money, and there would have
to be places for them to stop at night along the way. We invited
some representatives to talk at a gathering at our center so
that we could help promote support for this momentous undertaking. We gathered a group about as large as had gathered on the campus. Several representatives from both the
advance team and the local Indian Center came. One young
man introduced himself saying that he belonged to a once
proud and powerful tribe that had lost its language, most of
its culture and history, and all of its population but for seven
known remaining members. He told us that if the bills before
Congress should pass and the government should take away
the remaining reservations, rights, and recognition of the In-

dians, this would become the fate of all the tribes.

Another Indian spoke up in disagreement. "No," he said, "it'll never happen. That's what they like to think. That's what they're aiming for, but we can't even think like that—we can't buy into that vision."

"I think that's what we mean," said another. "That's what this whole thing is about—to counter that image and strengthen our own vision—the vision of our people."

Everyone who had gathered for the presentation and discussion wanted to support the cause, and volunteered to help collect some of the basic necessities. The solicitation project was launched and, by the time the march reached Kansas, many individuals, shops, and markets had contributed offerings of money, food, and supplies. We had even obtained the use of a large property near Lake Perry not far from the Topeka city limits where the marchers could camp. This was an important halfway stop for the Indians because the marchers who had come all the way from the West Coast were joined by runners from the North, and the two movements merged and joined forces. Their numbers grew to over one thousand and they remained at the Kansas campsite for over one week, resting, making further preparations, and gathering additional supplies. The Iroquois people and other Eastern tribes were organizing in their own areas to rendezvous with The Longest Walk at some point farther east. We had been in constant touch with Mad Bear and, with his help, had contacted traditional leaders of the Kickapoo, Potawatomi, and other Midwestern tribes. The new and expanded configuration of leaders and medicine people needed several days of meetings for reorganizing and decision making.

Jon and I and others made several trips between the campsite and our center in Topeka. One evening, we talked with some of the Indian organizers as we sat around the fire. I told them I had contacted the local chapter of the Red Cross as it had seemed to me that they would have on hand such things as soap and toothbrushes. I had been questioned at great length by the woman in the Red Cross office who was trying to deter-

mine the "nature of the emergency." I was informed that in
this circumstance the Indians would not qualify for assis-
tance. Unless there were some crisis or catastrophe, such as a
flood or fire at their campsite, the Red Cross could not respond. That was simply a Red Cross requirement, she had
told me, and I had told her that I understood.

"Well, I don't understand these protests," the woman had
remarked. "That's not the reason for this policy of course.
We're just set up to respond to disasters. But I don't understand why these Indians insist on hanging on to their difficulties. We have equal opportunity in this country. Why can't
these people come off these reservations and join the real
world? You'd think they'd want to take advantage of all the
wonderful things that modern life has to offer."

"And I suppose she thinks she meant well by that!" one of
the medicine men remarked, holding his chin and leaning
over the fire. "She just doesn't know. Well, I don't understand why people insist on hanging on to their ignorance."
The others nodded. "The difficulties of which she speaks have
nothing to do with our Indian identity or our way of life. Any
hardships we're experiencing are related to oppression. But
it's the difficulties all people face—all people and all our relations on the face of this Earth that concern us now. That's
what this is all about—this historical long walk—and it's not
the end of it, either."

"And this ain't no protest, neither, this thing ain't," the el-
dest added. "This here's a sacred ceremony we're doin' in
our own sacred way. We filled that pipe with our prayers in a
sacred manner like we've been instructed. We put our heart
and soul in there. And that pipe's been walked—on foot—
ever single step of the way, too. That's our prayers, and that's
our prayers for everone, not just ourselves. That ain't no
protest, but that's what they been callin' it, ever step along
the way, and I don't appreciate that neither!"

One morning we arrived at the campsite to find two live
pigs tied to a tree. A local farmer had brought them out in his
truck that morning, we learned, and offered them as a dona-

tion. The Indians had considered this a worthy gift and had accepted the pigs with gratitude, and it had become a topic of deliberation among the elders and leaders. There was no way to take them along on the march, and they would have to be butchered and eaten in the short time that remained before the march began again. It would have been inappropriate not to accept them, but it would be equally inappropriate not to deal with them properly. It was a significant affair, and those qualified to deal with it had to be carefully selected. It had to be determined that the pigs were meant to be used in this way. An appropriate acknowledgment and offering needed to be made. It was essential that the pigs be slain without pain or suffering and that they be shared by everyone and no part of them be wasted. When next we visited the site, the deed had been done. Whatever was edible had been incorporated into the food supply, and the rest put aside for some further use.

The Indians broke camp quickly and quietly and set out on their eastward journey at sunrise one morning and, though for many days hundreds of them—men, women, and children—had cooked, slept, and played on the land and held their many sweats and ceremonies, they left not one single sign that they had ever been there. Some of the young people who had been helping during their stay left with them. They had made friends among the Indians and had been taken with their cause and, when they had seen that there were several Japanese Buddhist monks among them who had come all the way from San Francisco, they had asked if they could be allowed to join the march. The organizers of the march had made it clear that The Longest Walk was for people of all colors and cultures and that anyone and everyone was welcome to join them in support of their cause.

A few weeks after they left Kansas, I and three coworkers drove east to rendezvous with the marchers. Bill Hale had just finished medical school when he moved in with us in our College Avenue center and became one of our incorporating members. He decided that he and I should take his car all the way to Washington, D.C., and back. Tim and Pam Balling-

ham, a couple who had first come to one of our workshops
and had become interested in our work, took time off from
their teaching schedule in the art department at the University of Utah to join us on the trip and follow along in their little Honda Civic. We planned to meet up with The Longest
Walk at the state prison at Marion, Indiana, and from there
to continue east, joining the marchers at intermittent stops all
the way to Washington, D.C. Since we had embarked upon a
several-week journey to Washington, D.C., and beyond, with
several side trips along the way, both going and coming back,
our two cars were needed for our separate trips. Besides, we
had all our luggage, so neither car was large enough for the
four of us.

Marion was a major stop for the marchers and their movement—and thus another several-day layover. Here Leonard
Pelletier was incarcerated in the state prison. The circumstances of his arrest were very controversial, but it was generally believed among Native Americans (as well as by several
independent journalists who investigated the story) that he
was a "political prisoner" incarcerated on contrived charges
to weaken the traditional leadership. His had become a famous case among all American Indians as well as those concerned with Indian affairs and civil rights.

We arrived at the Indian camp before sunrise to participate in the ceremony outside the prison. Hundreds of Indians
of many tribes—and the various non-Indians who had joined
them—were shuffling about in the dim, gray light of early
morning to locate their groups, prepare their banners and
posters, and receive their instructions and their place in the
ceremony. The various leaders came around with papers, instructions, transportation assignments, and LEONARD PEL-
LETIER buttons to be pinned on shirts and jackets. It was
amazing to see the degree of preparation and organization
that had been established among so many tribes and groups of
people even as they had walked these hundreds of miles from
the West Coast. Everyone piled into cars, trucks, and buses
for the ride to the prison, and the four of us followed in our

two cars. I rode with Bill in his car, and Tim and Pam followed in theirs.

As people gathered at the top of the road outside the
prison, we had a chance to talk with those whom we had
helped to join The Longest Walk in Topeka. Many of them
had become so uncomfortable that they were hoping we would
be going back and they could return with us.

"These people are racist," one of them told us. "They
openly dislike non-Indian people." Others felt that it was not
racism. After all, they had encouraged the non-Indians to
join them. Perhaps long frustration and renewed anger at recent events had made them openly blameful. "Well, I agree
with them," said the first, "but they shouldn't include all of
us. Why do they think I'm here supporting them? They use
really strong language talking about 'the white man' and I'm
sitting right there with them. And they never talk to us directly, they just talk to each other so that we can hear them.
They do it on purpose, too. They do it to embarrass us." They
all agreed that the Indians wanted them to hear their criticism
and wanted them to feel ashamed. They supposed the Indians
had their reasons—perhaps to motivate them to make
changes—but it was painful to be with them, and they all
wanted to leave. We convinced them that they were making a
contribution and that, in fact, this was an opportunity to experience what the Native people had almost universally experienced over centuries. In any case, we told them, unless they
could see their way to get themselves back home, they would
have to stick it out for the duration. This was not an easy trek
for any of the walkers, we reminded them, and the Indians
were at least sharing their food and their supplies—and their
hospitality—such as it was.

The entire group lined up three and four abreast all along
the side of the road and arranged themselves to begin the
march down the hill to the prison gates. Some of the leaders
walked up and down the line to make sure that people did not
crowd into the road but left room for the prison vehicles to
pass back and forth. There were many police and prison

guards at the top of the hill and along the shoulders on either side of the road, but they only stood quietly and watched or occasionally talked or joked with the Indian organizers. Then the march began to move slowly down the hill toward the prison. It was a spectacular sight: many Indians in striking regalia and with vividly colorful banners, flags, and posters. There were singers and drummers and people with flutes and rattles. It was an impressive display, but there was no one here to see it or hear it but the police officers and the marchers themselves. Perhaps it was indeed a protest, an expression of opposition against the incarceration of Leonard Pelletier and others whom the Indians regarded as "political prisoners," but to these traditionals, this was a ceremony and they had come with great hardship to offer prayers and sacrifices for their cause.

To the surprise and disappointment of the organizers, the march never reached sight of the outer prison walls. The marchers had obtained permission, they had thought, to proceed to the outer gate of the prison, and then for one or two representatives to visit Leonard Pelletier inside the prison. But somehow, some officials had had a change of heart, and barricades had been placed far up the road out of sight of the prison. It was for security reasons, they were told, and to ease the coming and going of prison officials.

At the barricades the march stopped and everyone crowded into a circle as best they could at the side of the road. Here songs were sung and prayers led, and some of the medicine people conducted the personal sacrifices—the "offerings of flesh"—for all who volunteered to participate. "This offering symbolizes our will and determination," one of them explained. "Even those of us who think we have nothing to give, nothing to offer in prayer, can give the ultimate gift. We can give of ourselves. We can offer our very flesh." The medicine people who were adept at carrying out this tradition carefully peeled razor-thin slices of skin from the arms of those who stepped forward to make their sacrifices. We remained for what seemed like nearly the whole day, continuing the ceremonies and waiting to see whether anyone would be allowed inside. At times people came out of the prison and stood on the other side of the barricades to talk with the leaders. At last, two of the leaders were allowed to pass through the barriers and were escorted inside. Then, gradually, the group dispersed, ambling randomly up the hill to where the vehicles waited.

Later that evening, the two who had been inside the prison returned to the campsite. We watched as various groups gathered around to hear the news of Leonard Pelletier. They had spoken with him, we learned, and had talked of many issues and of The Longest Walk. There was not much they could offer him in the way of immediate hope. One of those who had been inside walked up to us and said: "All this concrete and all these walls create a false feeling of power and control. People think they can achieve control by creating something unnatural. But it's just an illusion. One day the little blades of grass will come back and claim what's theirs, and all this concrete will crumble into dust! There's no justification for keeping anybody inside those walls in such unhealthy circumstances—I don't care who they are. The Native peoples of these continents lived for thousands of years without these prisons. This notion belongs to a foreign culture—it's foreign to mankind, actually, foreign to all life. You people brought this prison system over here from over there—and look what a mess it's made of everything. It's made people all the more cruel and cold—and scared. To tell you the truth, I think you people have your prisons out of fear—though fear never solves anything. You people get yourselves so far away from nature you get weak and scared—afraid of one another, your very own people. Imagine. And yet, you go on doing just what it takes to make your society even worse! I'll make one prediction here. One day in the future you're going to have more prisons than schools and hospitals put together. And then soon after that—because of that—everything will come tumbling down and the grass will come back."

We returned to our motel that night, and the following day

as the Indians prepared to break camp, we drove out of town. We bought a local paper from the vending machine outside the restaurant where we had breakfast. There was a small item on the front page reporting that Indian militants had launched a protest outside the prison and that police had to be called out to break up a riot. We considered stopping to phone the paper, but we went on our way. There was no way to know whether this report was racist, politically motivated, or simply a case of misinformation. Perhaps it was an attempt on the part of the editors to make a more engaging story of an event whose real meaning they were not prepared to understand.

When the Indians came to the end of The Longest Walk in Washington, D.C., spring had passed and it was summer. The air was hot and sticky and it was difficult to walk along the glaring sidewalks. The District of Columbia was a domain of concrete, and everything reflected heat onto everything else. Our cars had no air-conditioning and neither, we discovered, did the humble hotel rooms that had been arranged for us through a friend. It was hard to decide whether to be in our rooms, on the street, or in the cars. Though the cherry blossoms and the beautiful weather had left, summer tourists were here in abundance. In any case, inside or out, we had to spend the time in town until The Longest Walk arrived and completed their initial meetings. We tried our best to enjoy our sight-seeing and hoped the air would be more accommodating for the walkers at their campsite in the woods.

Tim and Pam and I rode with Bill in his car out to Greenbelt Park, leaving their Honda at the hotel. It was only mid-morning and the sun had not yet reached its full potential, but as soon as we had entered the park and driven in under the shade of the trees, it was apparent that the days and nights would be at least somewhat more hospitable in this setting. Camping would be easier, especially for the little ones, and lack of warm wraps and blankets would no longer be a problem. The Indian camp, we supposed, should have grown quite large, and we should quite easily come upon it. One of the main roads seemed to be closed, so we turned on to a side road and drove past several groups of people preparing their picnic lunches; but when we came to a dead end we reversed our direction.

"This side of the park is closed," the man in the gatehouse told us as we pulled up to where the chain was stretched across the main road. "There's a special event in here this week." This was no doubt what we were looking for and we explained we were working with the Indian group on The Longest Walk. "You can drive right on in," he said. "Just pull around the other side of that post there."

We drove through the campsite wondering where to stop or where to park or whom to approach. For a long while we saw no one whom we recognized. The number of Indians, and non-Indians as well, had multiplied, it seemed, with each eastward mile of The Longest Walk. People from many tribes had been ready and waiting to take up the march as the growing caravan passed through their territories; and representatives from several Northeastern tribes had come down to rendezvous at this site. The place looked like a huge intertribal village—or, in fact, an international village. Many non-Indians, especially young students and activists, and East Coast members of the Buddhist organization had joined the movement and arranged themselves in the campsite.

We pulled off the road at a place where several other cars were parked and got out to walk. Finally, some of the Indian people recognized us, and we greeted them and told them we were looking for Mad Bear's camp. We found him in his tent, asleep. "Let him wake up," someone called to us. "We're all going down to the capital, down by the Washington Monument. Everyone's heading out pretty quick."

"Hey, there you are. I was expecting you just about now," he mumbled groggily from inside the tent. "I knew you were arriving. I wasn't asleep, I was just dreaming. Give me a moment here, and I'll be right out."

We walked down the road to find the "non-Indian camp," as it had been labeled by the others, and to see the friends we

had last seen in Marion who had indeed stuck it out and made
it all the way. We passed the camp where the Japanese Buddhist monks were staying and stopped to talk with them.
"They have us all separated out," they told us. "Some of them
did not want it like this, but other ones—some of the leaders—they think it is better so we can talk our own way each
other whatever we want. But the white camp—they call the
white camp—it's too far, way over there. You can't see from
here. Maybe they are okay with it."

Before we had a chance to find the "white camp," someone
came to tell us that Mad Bear was up and waiting for us. On
our way back, we found Grandfather David Monongye being
slowly led along the road toward Mad Bear's camp. We all
spoke to him and he responded cheerfully, but we did not
bother to identify or introduce ourselves to him. At this final
destination of The Longest Walk there were over three thousand Indians, from perhaps every tribe, and many dozens of
others, and there was no need for Grandfather David to try to
keep track of everyone.

"Well, here you all are," Mad Bear smiled, shaking our
hands. "And by golly, it's good to see you. I just needed a
minute there to crawl out of my cot and try to look halfway
charming for you people." He was dressed in his full regalia
with his buckskin vest and feathered cap. "We're heading out
just now, so your timing was right on the button. These people
are taking care of David, but I'm going to ride with you folks
if you've got room."

All five of us piled into Bill's car, with three of us in back
and Mad Bear in the front seat.

We followed the long caravan of cars, vans, and buses
through the town and then followed the directions of the officers who stood on the streets around the monuments to control traffic. Hundreds walked from the parking lot to the
Washington Monument. There was an additional congrega-
tion of Indians from many tribes at the monument, and a colorful exhibition of tents and teepees, banners, posters,
information tables, drummers, and singers stretched across

the grounds. When the entire crowd had gathered on the grounds, the group was assembled and organized for the march to Lafayette Park. The huge crowd of traditional Indians made a spectacular sight as they marched through the streets of the capital in their various colorful regalia. Of all the marches, celebrations, pageants, exhibits, and social events seen in this large park across the road behind the White House, this gathering was no doubt among the most eccentric and picturesque. There were thousands of Indians in this park and they were joined by hundreds of others. The non-Indian contingency had grown considerably since last we had seen the group. No doubt many had come from both North and South to join the campers at Greenbelt Park; but also, no doubt, many local people had come just for this event. Perhaps even some tourists and other passersby had been attracted by the crowd and the music and banners.

Nearly all the tribal leaders and spokespersons, it seemed, gave talks, and there was singing and drumming, and the event went on throughout the entire day. Grandfather David Monongye was among the first to speak. He spoke his lengthy opening prayer in the Hopi language. Then he paused and began in English.

"Well, we have just gathered here together to see that we will respect one another from now on. We are all brothers and sisters—all of us—all over the Earth and we will always be brothers and sisters. So it's time from now on to begin to respect one another all over this land and to carry this out from now on. We have no, uh, weapons of any kind. We have come here without weapons. We have come here without any purpose to harm anyone. We only want to preserve our culture. We do not want to be dissolved. We have come here from all over, many tribes, from great distances. We all know what purpose we are here for. We are here because we want freedom!"

There was loud applause from all around him and, as I had seen happen before, it appeared to me that David may have caught a faint glimpse of the view from where he stood. "Well, now is the time to share our prophesies to the world. I cannot go into it in detail here because my time here may be limited, and I have lack of English. Some of you may be aware of our prophesies because Thomas Banyaka and I, we went all around, different areas, to instruct on the prophesies. We are doing this so that we will all work together. That is why we need freedom for our people, not to be dissolved. We believe our culture must blossom forth so that we can all work together. Not only Indian people but many other people as well, all over the world, are having problems, and we all need to stand together. We are gathered here because we believe in our sacred instructions and we want to preserve our way of life."

He went on for some time until someone stepped up beside him and said something in his ear. There were many spokespersons scheduled to speak. "So, in closing, I would just like to pray for everyone, all brothers and sisters. I pray that we will not be dissolved but that we may be able to preserve our way of life. May the fragrance of love go into every human heart and soul so that we can live in peace and brotherhood and respect one another as brothers and sisters and live a good life from now on."

Russell Means followed Grandfather David, and he referred to the Hopi records and prophesies as enduring over tens of thousands of years of "near perfect" existence and as among the most profound revelations of mankind. "I also want to thank David," he said, "for asking for the support of non-Indian peoples. And now I would like to ask for the support of our non-Indian friends—because now that The Longest Walk is almost over, I would like to ask all of our white support groups to get behind our next big national project. And that project is called 'The Longest Swim'!"

Like Grandfather David, Russell Means referred again and again to the concept of respect. Speaking of the bills before the House and Senate for the abrogation of the treaties and the "termination" of Indian lands—bills that, he claimed, were intended to do away with the Indian tribes, culture, and religion, and bills in response to which The Longest Walk had been organized—he reminded his audience that since the Native peoples began to be given the rights of citizenship in the 1950s, the Indians had become subject to over two thousand more laws than other citizens of this same nation, and the bills now before Congress would only add to that number. Nazi Germany's historic genocide against Jews was initiated "through legislation," he pointed out, while the population believed that the government was taking care of them and looking after the best interests of all of its citizens.

"There is only one color of mankind that has not been allowed to participate in the international community and that's the red people of the Western Hemisphere. The white man, the black man, the yellow man, the brown man, in some form or another, have all been allowed to participate in the international community. It should be an insult to that house across the street and to its programs in foreign relations that the only color of mankind that cannot walk shoulder to shoulder in the international community is right in its own backyard." The reason for this, he contended, was fear—fear on the part of what he called the "multinational corporations," the "takers of the fat," and those who he alleged were guilty of raping their own mother.

"And the multinationals!" he said. "You know, at Geneva, we tried to explain, specifically to the imperialistic countries of the world, we tried to explain to them in their own terms the meaning of respect! We told them: 'Do not think of our natural resources any longer as income. Think if it as capital.' When the multinational corporations—if they could open up their eyes to see down the road to the next generations, if they would treat the natural resources as capital instead of as income—then they would make sure that in the future the capital would remain. Because it is basic economics that once you do away with your capital, you do away with your income. And it's beside me why the multinationals and the governments cannot grasp the fact—because this is elementary economic fact."

There was applause and a few cheers and whoops of approval from here and there around the park.

"They fear our collective way of life," he went on, "even though they took their form of government from us. Benjamin

Franklin, in seventeen forty-six, stood before delegates of ten colonies in Philadelphia, thirty years before the independence, and said, 'If the Iroquois up North can form a near perfect union that appears almost indestructible, why cannot we, a more civilized people, form an even more perfect union?' And so they drafted the Constitution of the United States after that of the Iroquois Confederacy. But yet they fear our culture. They fear the power of our spirituality. They want to legislate us out of existence because they fear a culture that never had zoos or penitentiaries or old-age homes or orphanages. They fear a culture that respects all life and respects the Earth. They call us primitive and pagan savages, and yet we can talk to a tree or a mountain or a rock—and they talk back to us. The winged things of the air, the four leggeds, we have conversation with them to this day. It is because we know the meaning of respect. I would like all people to know that if they could understand the meaning of respect, they would not fear us—because they would understand something of the psyche and the beauty of our people."

Clyde Bellecorte was introduced as a member of the Ojibwa Nation, a cofounder of AIM, and founder and director of the Heart of the Earth Survival School in Minnesota. He spoke of the several survival schools around the United States and Canada that were established and maintained by AIM. He said that Indians and non-Indians had come to realize that conditions would never change for Indian people until they themselves took charge, and direct control, of their own education, and he explained how, in spite of the erroneous image of AIM as militant and extremist, AIM had amended the education and restored the self-esteem of thousands of Indian children who had fallen behind and who had been let down by the public school system where the Native people's history and heritage was ignored or distorted.

Then I saw, for the first time, Philip Deere, the well-known Muskogee Creek medicine man and spokesman. He was advisor to the leaders and members of AIM, and they called him "uncle." He spoke slowly and clearly and, at times, with a gentle smile in his voice, but there was an awesome strength in his simple directness:

"Today I do not want to talk about the past. Today I want to talk about the issues going on now. We do have problems among our many nations of Indian people. For many years I was not acquainted with other tribes, but I was well aware of my own problems. One day I walked outside of my community and met with other tribes. Talking with them, I began to realize that they have similar problems. I began to go to their reservations and I found out that their problems are the same as mine. I knew that different tribes had different treaties, but I learned that their treatment was similar to ours.

"When the reservations began to shrink to small areas, Indian people could not continue to live on these reservations. So not out of choice, but because of the necessities of life, many of our Indian people had to move off the reservations. They had to move to large cities—Chicago, New York, Los Angeles—all over this country our people began to move off the reservations and into urban areas. Because their land and their rights were being taken over by somebody else, they had to leave their homeland and move into the cities. In the cities, they felt the pains of discrimination. Our Indian people had to walk the streets of New York City, had to walk the streets of Chicago and of Washington, D.C., with their heads hanging down in shame because they were Indians. But I tell you today, those days are over. Those days are over because our young people have the courage to stand up for their rights. These young people, I talk with them and I protect them. They draw attention to the Indian people. They have brought pride back to the Indian people.

"Over many years I heard how my grandfather and my uncles came here to Washington, D.C., year after year, trying to talk with government officials and representatives. They were always denied and they were always turned away. Today we are here. But we have walked long enough. I do not want my grandchildren to have to come up here and stand on this very ground and beg for human rights. I don't want our people to have to go over to Geneva and to other countries and talk about human rights over there. I think that in a nice kind way we should remind President Carter to look around in his backyard. We bring to this city Indian awareness. I have noticed that in these buildings people are so far removed from reality. The truth is hidden from these people. But we are proud to say that, as Indian people, we still understand the truth!"

At the conclusion of the long afternoon, everyone walked to the Washington Monument and returned to their various cars and buses for the ride back to Greenbelt Park.

"You people stick around if you can," Mad Bear suggested. "Later on there'll be some gatherings in the main area with singing and social dances and whatnot."

"This whole affair is really organized," I commented. "The way they have all the buses and the camps assigned is pretty impressive. I noticed when they were making announcements they have everything labeled—Camp A, Camp B, Camp C, and so on. But it seems like some of the non-Indian people think things are a little too segregated."

"Well, it's partly just the way everything's laid out here," he explained. "You have to realize, too, that there are thousands of people camped here, and lots of 'em have been on the road for many a long week. And a lot of the traditionals are getting acquainted with each other for the first time. Yet everything is peaceful and harmonious. It's about the opposite of what most people would think, right? Pretty contrary to the stereotype that's been given us. You won't see any drinking here or any fighting—not even arguing or raised voices. You won't hear elders yelling at the little ones. And when all these thousands of people have left, no one will be able to tell we've even been here. But these grounds will have been cared for and will be honored and graced by the ceremonies and blessings of the traditionals. It's part of the respect these people were talking about."

He was right. It was peaceful. Except for those who stayed at the Monument, everyone had returned to the camps. There were people all around us, but they walked and talked softly. Even the children, who were left to run about and play as they wished, spoke quietly, and no one shouted.

"I think some of the traditionals may have had a little bit of a segregation thing in mind," Mad Bear allowed. "I went down to the 'White Camp' before you people came today and had a talk with them down there. I think they're mostly okay with it. Well, for one, they're more comfortable in the long run. It's better for all the various people to have a chance just to be with each other so they can talk among themselves and carry on however they wish without feeling judged or criticized. Funny thing, some of these young whites told me they were thinking about getting married and asked if there was any medicine person around who could marry people. I told 'em I could do an Indian ceremony and it'd be recognized in an Indian way. So that could hold 'em for now, anyways. You know, another thing we've all got to realize—this is just a beginning. Look how all these tribes and races and cultures are gathered here and living together. This is kind of a first. And it's only a sample of what's coming—only a taste of the way it's going to be in the future. But people have to be left to their own ways, or it won't happen. Every culture and religion has to be supported for what it is. The time for any one culture or race or religion to try to do away with another is over. That time has got to be over or else everyone's time is over. That's what this whole thing is about here."

"You know," I said, "we phoned Ron Dellums's committee and some of the Senate offices before we left and again from on the road to check on the status of these so-called termination bills in both the House and the Senate. They're telling us now that these bills don't have a chance. Ron Dellums's office claims that they'll never make it to a vote on the floor. They'll never even make it out of committee."

"That's what we're hearing too," Mad Bear responded, "and that's what we believe. But if that's the case, our purpose is only furthered, because then maybe we can go on from here. Anyways, it's a constant struggle, and we have to keep going with it. Bills like this keep comin' around. When

they're extreme, like these abrogation things, well they're not
so likely to go through—but it's really dangerous for us if they
do pass. And some of these milder steps are even worse—
these laws and rules and policies that they keep adding to apply to our indigenous people only. All these new rules and
regulations keep eatin' away at the freedom and dignity of
our people, and no one but our people seems to notice or care.
So we have to keep at it—keep going forward from here—and
I'm glad, for one, that we have all these different races and
religions here. I hope this only grows. If all of us can keep this
up—can share our days and nights and ceremonies together
as close as we're doing here—without trying to Christianize
or convert each other—we might still have a chance to feel
safe and easy again like our people used to in the past."

"They're startin' to serve supper down here," someone
yelled. "Hey, Mad Bear! Ain't you gonna eat?"

"Are you kidding?"

We noticed that daylight was already beginning to wane as
we started for the main area. "I was just thinking about what
Russell Means said back there at Lafayette Park," I reflected
as we walked. "He said something like only the red people
have not been allowed to participate in the international community."

"There may be some others somewhere whose very existence and identity is denied, but I believe we're the only ones
to whom that applies as an entire race. It presents a challenge, see, because of this wish to ignore our sovereignty. It's
kind of ironic. Some folks in Congress want to do away with
all our treaties across the board, unilaterally, but they can't
even get it to a vote. So what about these treaties? Treaties, by
your government's definition, are agreements between sovereign nations. Isn't it embarrassing? They want to disregard
our sovereignty—but not actually vote on it. We are not
s'posed to be involved, though we're parties to the treaties,
because we're not s'posed to represent ourselves. How can we
participate in international affairs if we don't represent anything?"

Supper and the festivities that followed were collective af-

fairs, but, owing to the large number of people and the structure of the campsites, there were several groups spread
throughout the grounds. We sat with a large group of people,
mostly Indian elders, gathered around in a large circle of picnic tables and listened to those who offered their songs. Some
people applauded after each performance, but most of the traditionals refrained from clapping. One elder eventually explained to the group that it was not their custom to clap at the
people who offered their prayers or dances or even social songs
because it was more like a judgment than an endorsement.

"If you'll notice, those of you who aren't used to us, we just
give a 'Ho!' in appreciation and agreement," he explained.
"That way nobody has to compare who's better than the others. Besides, somebody sings a beautiful song—why, you
kinda rattle the air and disturb the feelin' if you jump right in
and make that clatter." After that, there were only 'Ho's' and
no clapping.

We sat with Mad Bear until he was ready to retire, and
walked with him back to his camp. "You know, I was thinking
again about the U.N.," he told us. "Now there was an international gathering in which we were very much represented,
our culture and our religion. I'd say that in that case we were
recognized by the international community."

"That's right," I acknowledged. "I think every race and religion was represented at that event—that was the intent."

"You remember? We were talking about that a while back.
We were talking about that Shinto priest. Did you tell these
guys about him? The one with the serpents?" He looked at
them for their reaction, but I had indeed told them about
him. "You remember? It's not just the political and corpora-
tion representatives, it's the spiritual representatives that
have got to get together now. That was his point. You could
call it international, or intercultural or whatever, but this
kind of gathering has got to be promoted. While these multinational corporations are getting together, the spiritual leaders have got to get together."

"Sort of like international summit conferences of spiritual
leaders," Tim remarked.

"Right. But not international in the sense of just representing their nations. And not spiritual in the sense of just representing their religions. It wouldn't be just to acknowledge each other's religion and religious rights—although that's important, so that's part of it. It would be to represent the people as a human race. Who represents the people of the villages and the city streets? Who is there to address their common condition whatever their race or nationality? And not only that, but all our relations. Who is there to represent the rights of the four leggeds and the finned and the winged? Who is there to speak for the trees and growing things? Who will represent the rights of the rain forests and all the precious medicines that have been helping us out? And who will there be who will speak on behalf of the Mother? The people I'd like to see come and put their minds and hearts together are those who follow the spiritual paths, know the sacred ways, and can guide the people."

It was late at night when we left him to return to our hotel in town. He and the others he had come with would be returning to their reservations in upstate New York and Canada, and we would be heading west.

"So I guess I'll crawl in here and get a little shut-eye. I wake up early, you know. Might be having a sunrise ceremony, anyways. Can you see your way up the road to your car? I'd walk up with you, but then, you'd just hafta walk me back again."

We assured him there was no problem and thanked him for spending so much of his sleep time with us.

"So come up home when you can," he called after us as we started up the road. "Think about what we've been talkin'. We couldn't really get into it here with all the goin's on, but we should talk about it. We're ready to start workin' on it."

We four discussed our conversation with Mad Bear on our way to the hotel that night, and we discussed it again on our way out of town on the following day. I told them about similar conversations with Mad Bear. I had already talked with Jon Cates about this, some time ago, I explained, and we had almost considered the idea of organizing and sponsoring a

gathering of what Mad Bear had called the spiritual leaders
and spokespersons. Jon and I had realized that it would be a
difficult undertaking and would require much money and effort, and we could hardly pull it off by ourselves without a lot
of help. I told them that Jon and I had not been sure whether
we hoped Mad Bear would push the idea or let it go. But as
Mad Bear had sat with us in the dark beside his tent in Greenbelt Park, he had come one step closer to giving us an assignment. The next step, we agreed, was up to us. He had
suggested he wanted to meet to talk about it further. We decided that we should contact Mad Bear again and find out
what he had in mind—or what, if anything, he had in mind
for us.

Our first stop on our return trip, though it was somewhat
out of our way, was to visit the Himalayan Institute of Yoga
Science and Philosophy near Honesdale, Pennsylvania. The
Himalayan Institute had purchased a property that had once
been a large Catholic monastery and had created their new
main branch in this location to be accessible to New York and
other major cities. I had never seen the place, though I had
been invited to visit, so we had planned this stop as part of
our itinerary from the beginning of our journey. We had set
aside several days to see the new biofeedback lab and research projects and to visit the staff and classes. This space of
time, we decided, could allow us our opportunity to have a focused conversation with Mad Bear, and we phoned him from
the institute to set it up. Tim and Pam remained behind to attend some classes and workshops while Bill and I made a long
one-day side trip in his car so that we could sit and talk with
Mad Bear.

"I don't really have much here good to eat," Mad Bear announced as soon as we had gone though our customary Indian
handshakes and were inside. "Or at least not enough of anything." So we turned around and went back out and drove
Mad Bear to the restaurant of his choice.

Fortunately, I had explained to Bill that one cannot simply
sit down and conduct a conversation with Mad Bear. "You

have to simply follow along and feel your way as you go," I had told him, "and first you eat."

"There's this great place I've been to a few times," Mad Bear said, "but we've never been there together. I've been wantin' to show you this place. You go through the line and order your main course and potatoes and then get your vegetables and soup as you go. Or you can pay one price and get all you can eat from the salad bar, and it's a doozie of a salad bar. I generally go through the line and do the salad bar too. You know, do the whole show."

We were not able to talk much during supper, except about supper. I knew that all the necessary conversation always happened, eventually, partly because Mad Bear was continually "picking up" my thoughts, as he put it. Our time was limited on this occasion, however—Bill was doing all the driving, and was expecting to be tired—and I knew he wanted me to take charge of the conversation. But as soon as we were seated around the little kitchen table back at the house, Mad Bear began again.

"It's up to you guys just how we do it, you know," he said, as though the conversation had already been progressing and "doing it" had already been agreed upon.

"Do what?" Bill asked.

"Well, we've been planning to call a council of sorts. We're planning on holding a gathering of spiritual spokespersons from the four directions. These'll be representing all races and colors."

It's not a question of "what," I thought to myself, it's a question of "how." But then, I wondered, would Mad Bear know the "how" part any more than we would?

"We've been working on the idea of communications and gatherings among the various traditionals," Mad Bear continued, "—thinkin' about a sorta joint communication on the records and prophesies and what can be shared. You heard what David said down there in Washington about sharing the prophesies. But we're thinkin' now about bringing in the other races and cultures. It might even help our own people come around to whatever they feel is appropriate at this time. But just how you wanna pull it off, it's up to you guys. I'll help in any way I can. This thing is meant to be, so it'll happen. Just get the ball rolling and it'll all fall out some way or another."

He got up, opened the cupboard, and brought back a large package and a bowl. "The only thing to pin down here is the date, I guess," he went on, as he tore open the package with his teeth. "We should pin that down so that it's a reality in our minds, you know? A set thing that we can focus on." He dumped the contents into the bowl and popped a piece into his mouth. They were pinkish, wormy-looking little cheese snacks that might have seemed a bit less sorry-looking to me if I were not so stuffed. "Somewhere buried under here is a calendar. It's a kind of notebooklike calendar with the moon phases on it. That's what we gotta go by. We're looking at spring or summer because wintertime's not right for it. Wintertime's a kind of withdrawal time when everything snuggles back to the Mother. It's not a reaching-out time. Oh, here it is, now looky here."

He opened the calendar and leafed through the pages. We decided on June. It would be warm, which would make things easier, because we supposed the gathering would require camping and cooking out. "Okay, then June—then we just find the new moon here. See, that's the Indian way. Indian people, we go by the moon calendar, you know that. Most people do. It works best, is the reason they do, if you want to bring into consideration any kind of conditions whatsoever. It's the moon we're influenced by. The new moon—then all the people and the traditionals will agree to it." He drew a dark circle on his calendar. "The new moon is good. The full moon—that's crazy—we avoid that and don't mess around too much with the full moon." Suddenly, he threw himself back in his chair and slapped his forehead. "Look at this, by golly! Just look at us! Here we are chompin' on these silly things, and we just had that great big supper. We're so full we're not even hungry, and yet we can't help ourselves. They're just so doggone delicious!"

Bill tried to stifle a snicker, but it was audible. Neither of us had tasted even one of the "silly things."

"Well," Mad Bear continued, "looks like we got it pretty much pinned down. Next thing's the location. So you can set that up out your way. There's places out there that'll be good, and it's kind of right in the middle there where we can all come in from the four directions." He closed the calendar and set it aside, looking as though our meeting was adjourned. "So we'll just keep in touch," he concluded, "and you guys see what you can put together. I can help out with contacting some of our people. I pretty much know who's who among our traditionals, and they know me. Oh, by the way, that Philip Deere, you remember him, we'll get him—we'll talk to him when the time is right." He looked at me pointedly. "You know, by golly, we might just go out there to his place and pay him a little visit. When do you think we might oughta do that? Can you manage it?"

I had no answer. I had enough to think about at the moment without having to plan yet another travel itinerary for Mad Bear.

He reached again for his calendar and leafed through the pages.

"Maybe we shouldn't try to pin that down exactly right now," I suggested.

"No, no, I was just realizing something," he said, finding the June date he had just circled and tapping it with his pen. "You know, by that time I should be already moved—though I doubt I'll have my new place up yet. I told you I'm moving, right?"

"That's right, you mentioned it. I'd forgotten about that."

"I got a spot up there on High Mountain road picked out. That oughta be settled any day now. I'm selling this place and getting that property up there, but there's no building on it yet. I get to put that up myself. Meantime, I've got me a good-size trailer lined up—a big two-bedroom job with a kitchen and everything. Maybe next time you get out this way, we'll be up there in that trailer."

"I hope that was okay for you," I told Bill when we were on

the road heading back to Honesdale. "It was a pretty brief
meeting for such a long drive, and there's always a lot of ex-
traneous talk and stuff."

"Yeah, but look at the result," Bill said. "We did get the
ball rolling, and I guess that's what we wanted. But it's a
pretty big ball. I hope we didn't bite off more than we can
chew—speaking of overeating. We committed to a certain
event on a certain date, so we're into it now. Now all we have
to do is come up with the place and the people and the money
and whatever else will dawn on us once we realize what we've
done."

• • •

Jon and others at the center wanted to hear all that the four
of us could relate about the last weeks of The Longest Walk
and about events in Washington, and in our rap-session gathering, we shared the details. "We learned that it was a pretty
trying experience for most of them," I told them. "But I think
that, all things considered, it was one they won't regret or
ever forget." We talked about the AIM leaders and the elders
and some of their speeches and about Greenbelt Park where
thousands of people were camped together and held their
meetings and ceremonies.

"That's one thing I wish everyone could have seen," I said.
"I wish everyone could have experienced the atmosphere
among all those Indians gathered from all different tribes—
the way they got along together and the way they walked
around on the land. Just think, thousands of Native people in
one campsite and most of the time, except when they were
singing and dancing, you could have heard a pine needle
drop. And I'll bet if we'd go back in there today, we'd never
be able to tell that they were even there—just like when they
left this campsite out here at Lake Perry."

We thought about mentioning the Cross-Cultural Spiritual
Summit Conference, as we had come to call it, but we decided
to keep it to ourselves until the plan had become more certain.

◐

"We have plenty of time," Jon said, in our evening meeting, "but we'll need it. I think we have to talk with Mad Bear more. If he's got something specific in mind, and I think he does, I want to hear it from him. I mean, where is this thing supposed to happen—and with whom? Are we talking about a few people or a few dozen? Are we talking about a day or a week or what? Why don't you get back to him? We could meet on the phone for some of it—we don't always have to meet in person. But I think some time soon he should come out here. And there are things that have to get started soon. Some of these people we're thinking of inviting—they have to set up their schedules way ahead, you know."

I agreed. Mad Bear would be coming out in the spring to speak at the Prairie View Mental Health Center in southern Kansas with Jack Schwarz and me. Arrangements for that event were already under way. That could be a chance, I told him, for all of us to meet with him at our center. In the meantime, we could speak with him on the phone. And we would need to make our lists and send out invitations soon. "You know, though, a lot of this is going to be up to us," I said, "and I want it to be because I know that we're the ones who are going to have to organize it, not him. We're going to have to locate the site and raise all the money. We'll have to communicate with most of the people ourselves. Anyway, I will call him soon and go over some of the first steps with him."

That evening, Mad Bear phoned. "I was just planning to call you," I said.

"So now I'm s'posed to say I picked up your thoughts again? Anyways, I'm calling now because I just talked with Philip Deere. I told you we'd be going out there. He wants us to visit him. Well, I mean, I figured it might be good and so he agreed. I can fly into Oklahoma and you guys could drive out. It's not too far for you—just a pretty straight shot down south. We can rendezvous there at the airport and drive out to the reservation. I've never been to his place, you know, but we kind of connected there in Washington."

Within only a few days after our return home, the four of

us were back on the road again in our same two-car caravan headed for Oklahoma—and within only a week after the first time we saw Philip Deere, we were arriving at his home. We spent a whole day sitting on an old bench and some folding chairs in the yard beside his house. We listened, mostly, as he and Mad Bear talked. For a long time, we visited with Philip's son so that Philip and Mad Bear could have a private conversation. But Philip also spoke with us. He told us about how "the bureaucrats" in the nearby town had attempted to connect these reservation homes to the town's water system and how he had prevented it. It is another way of terminating our reservation status, he explained, and bringing the traditionals and their land under local juristiction.

"We went through the same thing up North, remember?" Mad Bear said, giving me a poke.

"Our people out here, we have our wells and we raise and gather our food and stay pretty close to the land, so we don't look too modern in some people's eyes," Philip explained. "Maybe that's what they're so concerned about. Or maybe they'd like to get ahold of the rest of this land—what little's left. But our people out here, we're pretty educated and learned, and we'd like to hang on to that. Some of these modern schoolkids don't even know where their milk and eggs come from. Our kids know where their milk and eggs come from—where their vegetables come from—and just how that happens. We can understand pretty well how this life works and how to get along with it. I've been through school, and our kids go to school. Some things you can get okay from books, we know that. But some things you can't just set around and read about and call it done. Some things you gotta see for yourself and get to know directly—not secondhand."

That brief rendezvous and meeting did not provide much chance for us to confer with Mad Bear about our upcoming project; but our meeting with Philip Deere did result in our first confirmation for the traditional American-Indian delegation.

◑

CHAPTER FOURTEEN

The Cross-Cultural Conference

"We can no longer consider our various issues and hopes separately, for we are no longer separated upon this planet."

❶ During the winter months, we began to put together a list of delegates for the June Cross-Cultural Spiritual Summit and to make some initial contacts. We were able to collect a few contributions for outreach and planning. Eventually, we knew, we would have to raise more funds. We would have to rent a large site with facilities, purchase airline tickets for delegates, and buy food and supplies.

Mad Bear typed a personal petition on his own stationery and put it in the mail so that we could include it in our packets for invitations and fund-raising:

To Whom It May Concern:
As an advisor and consultant to the Cross-Cultural Studies Program, I have overseen and been directly involved in most of the American Indian research work of

that organization over the past five or six years. Now, under the sponsorship of the Cross-Cultural Studies Program, we are planning a gathering of American Indian traditional leaders. The people who are about to come together are the spiritual spokespersons of their Nation or Tribe. They are the custodians of the teachings and prophecies. We are gathering together for a "meeting of minds." Our people welcome the chance to gather to speak in concert to those who seek to learn from us—for we are a united people and we are of one tradition.

Doug Boyd of CCSP and I have long traveled and worked together, and we have long planned this cross-tribal conference. Now I have urged the Cross-Cultural Studies Program to develop this into a cross-cultural conference. It will be useful for our people and for the goals of CCSP to have this be a gathering of races and religions. We can no longer consider our various issues and hopes separately, for we are no longer separated upon this planet.

We have much to share—one tradition with the other. The day is here when my people and all people must look beyond the affairs of the Red or the White race and must consider the Human Race. Having traveled many times around this world, I can only conclude that we are truly one people who could only benefit by meeting together to work out the solutions to the benefit of all, including the many creatures, birds, animals and plantlife which were given to us by the Great Spirit—the Creator of all.

We must all share in the wisdom, teachings, instructions of our ancestors who knew and practised these secrets that kept our sacred Earth Mother clean and in balance and good health. I now propose a great Council of the Races where my own Redpeople will have a seat and voice to add to the united and ultimate understanding of all.

O-Neh,

(signed "Mad Bear")

In the spring of 1978, Mad Bear came out to Kansas. The occasion was a three-day Human-Potential Conference sponsored by the Prairie View Mental Health Center. We met in nearby Newton, Kansas, and Mad Bear and Jack Schwarz met in person for the first time. The two already knew one another, in a way. I had introduced them on the telephone months earlier as I was arranging for their participation in the Prairie View conference. Long before that, however, Jack had offered a sort of intuitive reading of Mad Bear. It had happened one evening as Masayuki and I were having supper with him in a Chinese restaurant near San Francisco. In the course of our conversation, I had mentioned Mad Bear to Jack, perhaps for the first time, and Jack had instantly volunteered an account of Mad Bear's "nurturing nature," describing his journeys, his magic, his humor, his challenges and his challengers, and the reason for his overeating. Though I knew Mad Bear and Jack did not, Jack's intuitive insights had been helpful to me.

I had been a speaker at the Prairie View conference the previous year and the directors had asked whether I would be willing to arrange the next conference and perhaps include an American Indian presenter. Both Jack Schwarz and Mad Bear had immediately come to mind. Jack had contributed to the research in psychophysiological self-regulation as both a subject and a consultant at the Voluntary Controls Program at The Menninger Foundation some years earlier, and I had met with him several times since. He had become known among various investigators for his ability to control pain and bleeding and various normally involuntary functions. When I consulted with Jack he agreed—with the condition that no concurrent talks or meetings were to be scheduled during the entire three-day seminar. "I don't believe in these three-ring circus affairs," he told me. "I don't want to have to hope that people will come to my presentation instead of going to hear Mad Bear. I'm not interested in competing with anyone. I'll do this thing if I get to be there listening whenever Mad Bear is talking, and if I get to share what I have to say with you and him both."

The conference sponsors concurred, and their announcements and programs stated: "This will be the first time these three presenters have worked together in one conference; all three will be involved in each session."

Eight of us checked into our hotel in the little town of Newton. Jack had come with Lois, his wife and associate, and I was joined by Tim and Pam, who had driven out once again from Utah, this time bringing Stu, one of their students from the university art department. Mad Bear was with Jerry, his "adopted son," also a young medicine person and a skilled singer and dancer. Jack and Mad Bear were eager to talk and get acquainted before the conference began, and they sat together in the lobby as we were checking in. Throughout the entire weekend—before, during, and after the conference— all eight of us spent every possible moment together, in the dining room or the faculty room at Prairie View, or at the hotel. It was entertaining to listen to Jack and Mad Bear. It seemed as though they were trying to outdo one another's humor, insights, and tales of personal episodes and experiences. But their conversations were fun and friendly, and they were amusing to each other as well as to us.

"You know what I have in my personal possession?" Mad Bear blurted, during one of these conversations. "Doug has seen this, but no one outside of our own people even knows about it. I have in my possession an actual skull of one of those little people who live among us up North—a real human skull only this big!" He held out his thumb and forefinger slightly apart in demonstration and moved his hand around our circle so that all could clearly see. Then he realized what he had done. As the two had led one another on to greater levels of intrigue, they had begun to talk of nature sprites, wood nymphs, water nymphs, and elementals. Mad Bear told of how the Iroquois women used to carry their infants deep into the woods and lean their cradle boards against a tree and then hide behind another tree. The little elementals and the wood and water spirits were attracted to the babies, he explained. In their excitement, they became less subtle and easier to spot—and the infants could quite readily see them. The mothers, waiting patiently in hiding and watching for some reaction from their babies, were thus sometimes able to catch a glimpse of the little creatures. "They are not exactly physical like we are—they're more etheric," he had expounded, "a kind of high frequency that we usually don't perceive." Then he had begun to speak of the human beings known to them as the "little people," who are a coexisting evolution and have physical bodies similar to ours, and he had not been able to hold back his cherished secret. "Well," he said, scratching his head, "the time might be right for some of these things to come out. Maybe people should know about it. Something has to draw us out from these walls we've put up, back to the natural world we're so alienated from."

In the conference, Jack and Mad Bear were mutually supportive and empowering. We three sat together before our audience and listened to one another's talks. Most of the time, we spoke together as a panel or invoked group discussion among the participants. Though Newton was a small town in the Kansas prairie, the Prairie View conferences had developed a wide national outreach and recognition, and a large diversity of people came from virtually all parts of the country. Mad Bear, a full-blooded American Indian medicine man, and Jack Schwarz, a Holland-born mystic and naturopath, were two very different people with somewhat complementary philosophies. The contrast was fascinating to observe.

As one of the presenters, I was able to introduce and talk about both Mad Bear and Jack Schwarz and to say things about them or in their behalf that they were not likely to say about themselves; and I was glad that we three had arranged to present in concert. Jack focused on health and healing and personal empowerment for effective living. Mad Bear spoke of the planet, of ancient records and prophesies, and of the emergence of the new world. I talked about issues and involvement and strategies for social action. Our various topics and approaches, in combination, seemed to bridge the concepts and concerns of personal development, planetary consciousness, and group endeavor—a potent mix of power-potential access and practical application—and produced what I thought were some relevant implications for our audience as well as some useful concepts and strategies for our own future projects and pursuits.

On Sunday afternoon, for the conclusion of our conference, I offered some chants and invocations and Jerry performed, in his spectacular costume of buckskin boots, bells, and bustle, some traditional songs and dances. Jack Schwarz guided a moving internal vision quest and meditation. Then the entire assembly went outside for Mad Bear's closing ceremony.

In a nearby field, the group formed the traditional circle. It was huge and Mad Bear had to shout. But his loud voice was calm and clear as he gave his thanks and his blessings and his prayer for a safe journey home for all present. In the midst of his words, he commented that he was sensing some disturbance "way out West." He felt that it was a demonstration or protest of some sort perhaps at a nuclear plant. "I feel a lot of caring and at the same time I feel a lot of conflict and contention," he said. "So may there be a soft and warm breeze from the East and may it carry power and peace to the people there that they may be helped to receive greater courage and wisdom—and may all people change their path away from danger and destruction." He closed his eyes and raised his palms slightly, and we stood quietly and watched, as though to join him in his silent prayer. But then there came an unmistakable breeze. It was warm indeed and soft, perhaps, but everyone's clothing and Mad Bear's medicine fan began to flutter, and it lasted for two or three minutes. Then Mad Bear offered his blessing, though he did not call it that. "Now as we break our circle and prepare to return to the four directions from where we came, I'm going to give my thanks and respects to each and every one of you, one by one, as you pass around and go on your way. And may you all go in peace."

"So, Mad Bear, it looks like we'll have a chance to hang out and have a pretty good meeting here tonight," I said when we were on our way, speaking to him as he often spoke to me. I wanted him to feel committed. We had said our good-byes to the Prairie View staff and seen Jack and Lois on their way— with assurances all around that we would all meet again—and we were heading north. We would soon be back in Topeka with most of the evening ahead of us. He was serious about our work, I knew. But as he felt the need to "move as the wind blows," I felt the need, sometimes, to pin him down—and there was our project group in Topeka who felt the need for his help. Mad Bear and Jerry had return tickets for late the next day, and we had booked a room for them. There was no way, this time, that they could just suddenly leave. It only remained for us to get Mad Bear cornered for the evening.

"Wait a minute, hold up!" he said, and I feared I had been too aggressive. "Hold up a minute. Stop and pull over here. I see something I can use. See those plants just off the road there? Lemme get out—I'll just make a little offering and take some of these . . ." and he was out of the car and standing over some small plants whose leaves nearly hugged the ground, making his offering. "Yeah," he said with a groan, as he wrestled to pull himself back into the car while carefully holding his leaves. "Looks like we'll have a chance for a pretty good get-together here tonight."

By the time we got them checked into their hotel and washed up and changed and fed and over to our College Avenue center, however, there was not a great deal left of the evening. Also, we listened to a number of songs because, once Jerry was asked to sing, and really got into the spirit of it, seeing how everyone enjoyed it, he went on for a long time, with one song after another—adeptly pounding on a shoe box, as he had left his drum at the hotel. We did discuss, to some extent, our Cross-Cultural Spiritual Summit—enough, at least, to arrive at a general scenario: As suggested by Mad Bear's written communication, we considered a two-phase affair with the Indians to arrive in advance of the others for an intertribal conference, and the representatives from the other

cultures or religions for the main cross-cultural conference—
the whole event to last about five days. With advance preparations, set up, and clean up, we would need for our staff and
plenty of helpers to be on site for more than a week.

Mad Bear and Jerry returned to their hotel at nearly midnight. They would sleep late in the morning, and we would
meet them and drive them to the airport. It seemed to some of
us that our plans were developing well, but to others, we had
only raised more questions—and the conference was only two
months away. We still had not selected the site or named all
the delegates, and there was the question of the remaining
budget.

"But we can't arrange these things in a meeting," I said,
"and Mad Bear can't do much more than he's done. We've got
his letter and some of his names and it's up to us to communicate with most of them and to make all the other contacts.
What we have to do now is to raise the rest of the money and
then to pick one of these camps or parks. And we'd better do
it right away—these places fill up in June."

"But we still need his approval before we settle anything,"
Jon insisted. "I don't want to firm up anything without his
approval and then have him veto it. I wish he could stay out
here and work with us."

"Let's complete all the arrangements," I suggested, "and
I'll get his approval. You know, I have to be in Des Moines,
Iowa, in a few weeks for a seminar. I guess I could, without
much difficulty or additional expense, schedule another meeting with Mad Bear at his place. If we can just get everything
pretty much wrapped up by then, I'm sure he'll be all right
with it." So during those weeks before I left, we completed
most of our remaining preparations. We got on the phone to
expedite our fund-raising and to confirm or invite the remaining conference delegates, and Jon found a four-hundred-acre
site—a Presbyterian camp near Parkville, Missouri.

The education center in Des Moines had authorized two
round-trip tickets plus expenses for me and an assistant, in
addition to my fee, and the fee would cover the cost of the trip
from there to Mad Bear's. I telephoned Stu and took him up

on his recent offer to help. I had originally met him with Tim
and Pam in Utah, and he had met Mad Bear when he came
with them to Prairie View. "You'll have to go as a volunteer,"
I told him. "You won't get paid, but you'll get an all-expense
paid trip from your place to out here and then to Iowa, on to
Mad Bear's, and to New York City and back." Stu was more
than willing, and Mad Bear promised to make himself available for our meeting.

After my seminar, we flew directly from Des Moines to Buffalo and took the bus to our hotel in Niagara Falls. Mad Bear
did not answer the phone. "I hope he comes back soon," I told
Stu. "We can't go in there on our own. Besides, he's moved
and I could never find his place. He's in a trailer on his new
property somewhere way up on High Mountain Road."

"So, are you sure that's his right number?" Stu asked.

"Well, it worked when last I called him from Topeka. He
does change it all the time, and it's always unlisted. I should
have tried reaching him while we were in Iowa to make sure
he'd be home. You just can't tell about him—he's always
'moving like the wind blows.' "

We tried calling several times from the hotel room. I began
to fear that he had either changed his number or was gone
with the wind. "We might as well walk around the falls," I
suggested. We walked across the bridge to view the falls from
the Canada side, and every time we passed a pay phone I tried
dialing Mad Bear again and waited through many rings. We
had supper in a restaurant that overlooked the falls and sat
until the sun went down and the colored spotlights came on.
When Mad Bear finally answered, I was standing at a pay
phone in the park, right near the Horseshoe Falls. It was a
strange conversation.

Mad Bear mumbled "Hullo?" in a groggy voice, and I assumed he'd been sleeping while we'd been trying to reach him.

"You should see where we are," I said. "We're across the
bridge—over here at the falls. I'm standing almost in the
mist, and the blue and silver spotlights make it look like glowing, dancing clouds!"

"I got this ant bite today," he answered.

"Stu's here with me."

"Funny-looking thing. Partly purple."

"Mad Bear, I was thinking we'd get together tonight, maybe in town?"

"I'm workin' on my new place out here, and I just stopped to grab a sandwich. The thing ran right up my arm!"

"Would you like to come out to the hotel?"

"We watched it bite me."

"Oh. Wow. So, anyway, maybe it's feeling kind of late to you now?"

"It sorta dug in like it was trying to go inside or something. John Bastine was with me. He pulled it off."

"Oh. So, would you rather not meet now? Do you want to get together in the morning . . ."

"Well, part of it stuck in my arm, I think. But we could meet tomorrow. John's comin' down with his family 'cause I told 'em you'd be here. Mike—you remember his son, Mike— he's plannin' on cookin' up a feast for us. John was looking right at it when the thing bit me."

"So I guess we'll just set it up for tomorrow?"

"You shoulda seen that thing. It was kinda silver-lookin' an' had a purple rear end."

"Wow. Listen, I'll give you a call in the morning, okay?"

"Okay, g'night. Say 'hello' to Stu, there."

I stood by the phone for a moment to think. There was nothing I could do. We had agreed on this meeting, but now we had missed both the afternoon and the evening. That left only the following day, and there was going to be company—a family and a feast.

Stu was over by the railing, looking into the falls. "You got him! Is he coming out here?"

"No, he wants to wait till tomorrow, and we'll go out there. Sometimes it's so weird talking to Mad Bear. I'm trying to get something arranged, and he's going on about this silly ant!"

"What, she's still over there now?"

"No, a bug! He got bit by an ant—hours ago, I guess, and that's all he wants to talk about."

That was nearly all he talked about the following day when

he rode in with Mike Bastine to pick us up. He sat slumped in a chair in our hotel room and redescribed the ant. "I'm a little better today, I guess. To tell the truth, I still feel pretty rugged."

I realized that the bite had made him feel sick. "So you really weren't feeling well," I said. "That's why you didn't answer the phone, I can see that now."

"Well, I guess it made me sleepy. I mighta passed out a little bit."

"I was afraid that you had gone off somewhere or maybe changed your phone number again."

"Well, I am gonna do that. Got to. My number's always gettin' out and around. You know, some people call me by mistake. Wrong number. Then they recognize my voice, and they say, 'Is this Mad Bear? Hey, I'm glad I got ahold of you, I never had your number.' And if they remember what they dialed, they pass . . ." His voice trailed off and he closed his eyes. I thought perhaps he was feeling faint.

"Mad Bear, you okay?" Mike asked.

"Here, take one of these matchbooks on the table," he told Mike. "No, don't give it to me, just take my pen here. I don't feel like writin'. I want you to jot something down for me."

"I'll need something more than this matchbook," Mike said.

"No, just hold it." Mad Bear closed his eyes again and, after a moment, slowly dictated, one by one, a series of numbers, and Mike wrote them in the matchbook. "Here, give me my pen, but you hang on to that. Keep it till we need it. See, that's another way my number gets around. Every time they change it for me, they give me someone else's recent number. Then I just have to change it again. Once they gave me the garage's old number, and people called every day. I'd say, 'Sorry, this isn't their number anymore,' and they'd say, 'Hey, Bear! Is that you?' That's what bugs me, when that happens. Speakin' of bugs, I do feel pretty lousy."

"Let's drive on in, Bear," Mike said, "and you can get some rest."

"Not sure what good that'll do. Might have to brew somethin' up here."

The Bastines and their two other sons were waiting for us at Mad Bear's place. I saw the new property and the temporary trailer home for the first time, and we sat around an old picnic table under a large tree while Mike cooked over a grill in the yard. Cinder blocks, lumber, and bags of cement were stacked up in piles nearby. "This is where it bit me," Mad Bear told us. "I was right here at this table. We stopped for a break, I was eatin' my san'wich, and this thing got on me and went right up my arm. I didn't show you this—I don't know if you wanna see this right before eating, but just take a look, anyways."

He slid up his shirtsleeve. It was startling. His upper arm was swollen and very discolored. "Good grief!" I said. "It looks bad. You'd better check into that."

"I had my medicine bag off, that's the thing. You know I never take it off, except just to wash up. Well, we'd been really workin' here, more than I should. I was so exhausted— had dust in my eyes and nose and everything. I slipped it off and splashed some water on my face. So I was out here with my san'wich, and my medicine bag was sitting in there by the sink. I can't believe I did that. John was here, he can tell you."

"That's right. The minute he spotted that ant on him, Mad Bear knew he was in trouble."

"See, these things are always bein' sent around. Usually I give it no mind—just my natural precautions. This one was waiting for its chance, and I gave it to it. When I saw it goin' up my arm, I automatically made a grab for my medicine bag. And then I realized. I told John to slip my shirt off real careful, so we could see it. I wanted it off, not to hurt it, then I'd get my medicine. But it dug right in, and when John pulled it, it came apart. It's in there, I know it. Boy, I sure got caught off guard this time!"

The food seemed to revive him, and he joked and laughed while we were eating, and even recited one of his poems. But after the meal, he began to nod off. From time to time he would catch himself and try to hold his eyes open and look at-

tentive. "You should sleep," I told him, as people began to
clear the dishes and carry the leftovers into the trailer.
"You're obviously really drowsy, I don't know why you fight
it. There's no need, you can sleep."

"I should," he said, "I really should. I think I may have a
fever. But you know how I am with company. I just don't
think it's right with company here."

But the Bastines had been thinking as I was and were
straightening up so that Mad Bear would not have to. "We're
gonna square everything away and send you to bed," John
told him. "We figured we'd do a little sight-seeing with these
guys while we're here in the area, and you've got no need to
do that."

"Well, I guess I'll get a little shut-eye," Mad Bear said, and
we left him. He called after me as we were getting in the car,
but his voice came too weak to be understood, and I walked
back to the doorway of the trailer. "This conference thing'll
go ahead one way or the other," he said. "But you do as you
see fit. However you see it, that's the way I see it, too, and
that's the way it's gonna be."

We spent the rest of the afternoon with the Bastines, driving or walking along the Niagara River. The next day, as we
were taking the bus back to the airport, Mad Bear was being
taken to the hospital. Mad Bear knew we would be at the Lexington in New York City and, though he was in great pain and
almost delirious with fever, he managed to have us notified.
The message was alarming: "Mad Bear has received an insect
bite that may be fatal, and was admitted to the hospital with a
high fever, kidney failure, and other serious complications." I
thought of going back up to his place, but it was unlikely I
would be able to see him or that I could be of any help by being there. I had no idea where he was hospitalized or how to
contact him, and I was not able to reach any of the Bastines.
By the time we were back in Topeka, however, Mad Bear had
himself telephoned our place and left a number where he
could be reached.

"Yeah, they got this phone where I can receive calls in

here," he said, "but they don't want me talking much. I'm trying to get out of here, though. I can't do what I gotta do in here, you know that. It's good I was here though, for this surgery. They cut a huge hole in my arm—you should see it— you could almost get your fist in there. John went back to my place and found the rest of that ant where he'd pulled it off. Can you believe that? That's something strange right there, 'cause we were all sitting around that table the next day after. How's come that little piece of ant was still waitin' there? Anyways, they identified the thing. They said that particular ant can even kill cattle with its bite but it's never been seen anywheres up North here. Well, I knew that—but I didn't wanna explain too much to these doctors."

"Do they think you're going to be all right?"

"They don't know. They think I'm going to be in here for a couple months at the least. But I'm not. I've got ways to deal with this if I can just get outa here. Look, call me back or I'll call you. They're trying to get me off the phone. I'm not s'posed to be sittin' up."

"Well," Jon declared, "that takes care of the Spiritual Summit. We'll have to notify everybody it's canceled."

"I don't know, I didn't talk to him about it. We'd better wait to notify people. Maybe we can set a later date."

The next time we heard from Mad Bear, he was calling from home. "Listen, I just got home here. I signed myself out and promised I'd be back in three days. It wasn't easy. I told 'em I had my new house all spread out on the ground here, and all my valuables were in this flimsy trailer, just asking to be stolen. That was true, but I claimed I was worried half to death and that this worryin' would kill me first, for sure, unless I could take care of it myself. I had to exaggerate a little. I told them I got no one I can trust, and there's many things only I can touch. So they let me out—but I had to sign for it so they can't be responsible for discharging me."

"What do you think about our June date?" I asked. "I don't think we can make that now."

"Well, I don't know. It depends what they do, they could

keep me in there when I go back. What I'm countin' on is I'll
be completely okay when I get back to these doctors. They'll
check me over and they'll be surprised, but they'll have to let
me go. Why don't you call me back tonight? Let me think this
thing over."

By that evening, he had decided to postpone. "This is
gonna be a bit of a contest I gotta deal with here—a bit more
than I realized," he said. "I got some real work to handle
here." We decided upon the new moon in September for our
conference date. "That'll be okay, it's a significant new moon.
But that's the latest in the year we can get away with. Like I
said, after that everything draws back in to renew again. But
that'll be a good date. That'll work."

"How are you feeling now? Are you feeling any better?"

"Well, we're working on it. There's a lot that's gotta happen here, but it's happening even now. Even right now, I can
feel the energy comin' in. That's what I came back here for, to
do my medicine, and it's all comin' in right now."

"I was just talking with one of the people we invited to the
conference," I related. "I was telling her about your ant bite,
the fever and everything, because I wanted her to know we
might be changing the date. You might remember her from
Council Grove. She's a healer herself—a medicine woman, I
guess you could say—and she's offered to help you. Only if
you want. She told me she wouldn't do anything, couldn't do
anything, unless you wanted it."

"What's the woman's name?" he asked.

"Ethel. Ethel Lombardi. You know, in addition to the cultural or religious delegates, we've asked several healers . . ."

"Yeah, that'd be all right. Tell her I said thank-you. If
she's willing to do that, that'd be good, all right."

Jon and I were going over my conversation with Mad Bear
and discussing the new conference date when Joel Friedman
called from Wisconsin. He was just calling to see that everyone was fine, he said, but he sounded gloomy. His medical
school curriculum had provided an opportunity for a two-
week elective study program and, through my introduction,

he had arranged to work with Norman Shealy at his clinic in La Crosse. I was afraid that perhaps things were not going well for him. "Is everything all right out there?" I asked.

He was hesitant. "Well, maybe. With me, I guess, but I was wondering about Mad Bear. How's Mad Bear?"

"Interesting you should ask. It's kind of a long story to tell you the truth, but, in a word, he's okay now, I think—or soon will be."

"Are you sure? Tell me what's going on, okay?"

Briefly, I recounted the ant-bite story. "But really, I believe he's going to be all right. It's interesting you asked about him just now."

"When did you last talk with him?"

"About an hour ago."

"Because I've been sitting here worrying about him for a couple hours at least, and wondering if I should call you or what. Well, let me tell you what happened. I have my own room here at the clinic and I was pretty wiped out when I got back here. I was just kickin' back in this rocking chair." He paused.

"Right," I said. "What happened?"

"It's pretty weird, man. I don't know why, but it's hard to say it. You know that necklace Mad Bear gave me? It popped. I had it around my neck, I've been wearing it the whole time. It didn't break, it actually exploded! I mean, I was just leaning back and the thing went 'bang!' and pieces flew all over—bouncing off all the walls and the ceiling and everything. All I could think is, 'Oh my God, it's Mad Bear.' I mean, I've been sitting here wondering if he's dead or what. Maybe you could call him back and just check one more time."

I recalled what Mad Bear had just told me about "doing his medicine" and "getting the energy," but it did not feel right to call him back. Whatever it was he was doing, I did not want to tell him what had happened with Joel. "Look," I said. "I don't want to call him just yet. This guy Marty's going to call me from up there. He lives right near Mad Bear—he's kind of an apprentice—and Mad Bear was planning on sending him

out here. You know, we were working on this conference out
here, and Marty was supposed to come out to help. We're
changing the date because of all this, but I'll be talking to
Marty tonight. I'll get him to check again on Mad Bear and
then I'll call you back."

As soon as I hung up, I called Marty and then phoned Joel
back to assure him Mad Bear was still alive. Then I talked
with Ethel Lombardi to relay that Mad Bear would be grateful for her help. Over the next several days, we made many
calls to notify the conferees and to rearrange schedules.
Luckily, there were no confirmed delegates who had to cancel
because of the change of dates, and some for whom June had
been impossible who could now be added to the list. Marty,
whose arrangements had already been made, decided not to
postpone his trip, and he arrived in Topeka to be available
for several months. In a sense the change in schedule had become an advantage.

Mad Bear recovered so quickly and so thoroughly that,
just as he had hoped, the doctors checked him over, marveled
aloud, and released him. "I still gotta go back in for checkups
and bandages and stuff," he told me on the phone. "You know
I've got this big ol' hole in my arm, and I gotta keep it ban-
daged up for a while so some bird doesn't try to build a nest in
there or something. My place is comin' together pretty decent, by the way. I've had lots of good help out here and we're
gettin' it up in a hurry. Jerry's movin' in—gonna have his
own room and everything. Wait'll you see the place, you'll get
a kick out of it."

"Sounds good," I said, "but I hope we see you out here before that."

"By the way, I'll have me a new phone number before long.
And it's the right one this time, believe it or not. I'll give it to
you out there—but don't you tell a living soul. Or did you already get it?"

"No, how would I get it?"

"We wrote it down, it was in that matchbook. They were
kinda surprised in the phone company. I went in there in per-

son—with Mike. I told him to make sure he had that matchbook on him. I told this guy I came around in person to make
sure they gave me the number that's been the longest out of
use. The guy told me that'd take a while to search out, and I
convinced him we were prepared to wait right there. So he
went and came back with it—on an actual computer paper—
you know, those long pages with the holes down the side. He
says he's found this number that's been out of use more than
a year and he's sure that it's the oldest unused one of all. So
he shows me the number, and I says, 'Mike, let's see that
matchbook. Yep, that's it, that's just the one I wanted.' I
showed him the number in the matchbook and he looked
pretty darn funny. He told me he had just then found that
number himself. 'There's no way you coulda got this,' he
says. So I told him of course there was. All I did was look it up
too, same way he did, only a little more like in a dream.' That
guy started scratchin' his head and nodding at the same time,
and Mike, he busted out laughing!"

"I remember when Mike took that number down," I told
him. "I wondered what that was all about, but I never did remember the number."

"I didn't remember it either, that's why we wrote it down. I
had a pretty good fever then, anyways. Course, that coulda
been what helped me catch the number. So looky here, lemme
put the finishing touches on my place here and on myself and
then I thought Jerry and I'd maybe come out and have a look.
You'll have to arrange the right time, I mean out there at the
site when it'll be open for us to do it. 'Cause we're going to
have to go out there and have a little ceremony for the land
and all.'"

Mad Bear appeared to have fully recovered and was in excellent high spirits when he and Jerry flew out in late summer
to look over the conference site. Marty and I and several of
our people met their plane, and we all checked into a hotel
near the Kansas City International Airport so that we could
go together to the conference site in the morning.

"The conference site is really convenient to the airport," I told them. "It's about ten minutes from there to the hotel here, and it's maybe another fifteen minutes or so on out to the Presbyterian Camp in Parkville. We already have a number of volunteer drivers set up with their own vehicles. All the delegates will be met at their gates as they arrive and chauffeured from the airport to the camp. We've got this whole place you know, all four hundred acres, buildings, grounds, and everything. So we'll show you around tomorrow."

"Yeah, but it'll be raining. At least I hope it will. How much we'll be able to look around—it depends what the land is like out there when it's wet. I'd like it to be really soaked so everything gets cleansed real good. That's part of it."

"But I don't think it's going to rain," I said. "Do you think it's going to rain?"

"If it s'posed to rain, it rains, huh Bear?" Marty laughed.

"Well, we'll see," Mad Bear responded.

"Oh," I said.

In the morning after breakfast, we started for the Presbyterian Camp in two cars. As we rode, I was thinking how Mad Bear's energy and effervescence had revived, and I remembered that Joel had wanted me to ask about his necklace. I had recently gotten back to Joel to report on Mad Bear's condition. "When you get a chance," Joel had requested, "tell him about what happened to my necklace and ask him if he has an explanation for it." I looked at Mad Bear as he joked and laughed in the front seat, and I could not bring myself to mention that necklace.

It was a beautiful day, and the sky was blue, and I had forgotten about the aforementioned rain until Mad Bear brought it up. "I got a feelin' we shouldn't hafta wait too long for the rain," he remarked. "I picked up a pretty good picture of that land out there already. I've been looking into that. It'd kinda put a snag in everything if the ground gets wet during the gathering. We'll have the sweat lodges and fires and all. That's why I'd like to have the opening rain now—and a real good one so's we can wash everything real clear."

It began with only one loud clap of thunder, just as we were

entering the camp, and then it was a strong, steady rain with
no wind or roar. But it was a hard rain and, by the time we
pulled up to the main building, rainwater was running
through the streets and the ditches. "I had no idea it'd be
raining like this," the camp director complained. "It's going
to be a hassle getting around here. Let's just hope this doesn't
happen when you're out here in September. I understand
most of you are camping out, right?"

"Maybe it won't rain then," Mad Bear said. "Maybe that's
why it's raining now."

"Well, who all needs to look around? Some of you've been
out already, and you might better wait inside here, because
you won't be able to drive—it's all hills and dirt roads farther
up. We'll take my four-wheeler up and I can fit about four of
you, I guess."

Mad Bear, Jerry, Marty, and I rode around the camp with
the director. We had to remain inside the vehicle, wiping the
windows with our hands and sleeves to see, as we pointed out
to Mad Bear the various sites and facilities. "This is where the
huge conference room is, and there are rooms on the lower
level, and this building here is the dining room and kitchen.
All the rest is way up the hill, but it is possible to walk to it."

"Of course, we can look around inside the buildings if you
want," the director suggested.

"No, that's okay," Mad Bear said, "but I'll have to get
out somewhere up here, 'cause I got a little something I have
to do."

"We can get out up there at the Indian Meadow. There's a
big pavilion up there with a roof we can stand under."

"Indian Meadow?" Mad Bear asked.

"Actually, that's what we've named it," the director explained. "That's what it's always been called. Not sure why."

We showed Mad Bear the outdoor camp areas: the one with
the Quonset-like hogan tents where the staff and volunteers
would stay, and the wooded area adjacent to the Indian
Meadow where the tents, teepees, and sweat lodges for the Indians were to be. "So we've got all the options, here," I ex-

plained. "Plenty of indoor rooms for the delegates who wanted them, even some private bathrooms, and then the tents and teepees and facilities for indoor and outdoor cooking."

We parked at the Indian Meadow and stood under the shelter of the pavilion. Mad Bear took a pipe from his pocket and slowly filled it. The rain sounded loud on the wooden roof and, though we stood for a long time, no one spoke. At last Mad Bear said, simply, "Wait," and he walked out under the downpour into the middle of the grassy meadow. He stood with his back to us, absolutely still, and his large form appeared rooted to the ground and undaunted in the pouring rain. The rain lapsed for only a moment, and Mad Bear lit his pipe; but when the billows of smoke began to rise above his head, it came down even harder. When he had completed his rite, he walked back under the roof. He was very wet, but no one mentioned it. In fact, no one spoke, not even the camp director, until we were back in the office.

"So I guess you follow your Indian ways and traditions," the director remarked. "We've gotten a little rundown from these fellows on what you people are doing here, and we respect that. So I'm sure glad you could come out. It's just too bad it had to rain like this."

"Yeah, but it's got its good side, though." Mad Bear looked satisfied. "You know, it kinda settles the dust." As we pulled out onto the highway, the sky cleared and the sun came out again.

Back in Topeka, I telephoned Joel to tell him that Mad Bear was in excellent form but that I had not yet asked him about what had happened to his necklace. "It's not necessary now," Joel told me. "I know about it now. You know, I collected all the pieces and I saved them. The other day I took the pieces to a man here at the clinic who sometimes works with Dr. Shealy. I came to know he's extremely intuitive, so I thought I'd run it by him and see what he had to say. At the time I was more concerned about Mad Bear than about the necklace, so I said, 'What can you tell me about the person who gave me this?' "

◗

"What did he say?" I inquired.

"He told me it was a gift. I said, 'I know that, but what can you tell me about the person who gave it to me?' I didn't go into any explanation about how it broke. He asked me what the person said about the necklace when he gave it to me, so I told him he said he'd doctored it for me, but I didn't mention Mad Bear's name. He repeated that it was a very extraordinary gift, and I told him I agreed but that this wasn't what I needed to know. He said, 'Maybe you don't understand what the gift was. Maybe it was intended to be that way—for you not to know.' So I pressed him and he told me that whoever had given the necklace had helpers working with him like the ones we call allies, and it wasn't just a necklace I'd been given but this helper—maybe for protection or something. So I described a little about Mad Bear, and about how the necklace had literally flown apart. I think you know what he told me."

"What?"

"He said, 'I assume that in his urgent need, the man called upon all possible available resources, and this force was torn free and drawn back.' "

•   •   •

In September 1978, staff and volunteers arrived at the site, two days ahead of the conference, with truckloads of food and supplies to begin the preparations. Tents and firewood and willows and rocks for the sweat lodges were hauled up the road into the Indian camp. The huge teepees came in on special con-tracted trucks—with the long poles with red flags attached ex-tending out over the backs of the flatbeds. Another truck carried our "stage." It was a sturdy raised platform with a high backdrop that had to be custom made and then transported and assembled on the spot; and it was set up at the bottom of a grassy horseshoe hill to create an outdoor amphitheater for the postconference festivities. The lighting and sound systems were brought in and set up by another contractor.

Our staff and volunteers called ourselves the "support

group," for we were there to chauffeur, chop, cook, clean, and carry—neither to spectate nor to participate. We were nearly one hundred—more volunteer helpers than the number of delegates and invitees. We held our final briefing in the large conference room in the main building.

"As everyone knows, we have a sort of four-act scenario to be played out over the five conference days," Jon told them. "This sort of thing has not been done before, so we'll have to wing it as we go along. In any case, we seem to be pretty well organized. We just have to keep in mind that we're here as a silent serving support group and not as students, seekers, or spectators. We don't want any of the spokespersons or representatives to feel they have to perform for us or satisfy us in any way. None of them have followers here for whom they have to maintain any kind of a front. Most of us will not be attending their meetings, and we'll only see them in passing or when we're driving or serving them or whatever. Except for the specially arranged social times, there will be no cameras, recorders, or note taking. And we should approach or engage the delegates only as hosts and helpers or if they approach us. Because if we can feel right about missing some precious contact and learning opportunities ourselves, we'll be most helpful as a support group. This is a closed and confidential conference, and we want all the delegates to feel comfortable and totally free, perhaps for the first time, to be entirely themselves and completely open among themselves."

"We're thinking of this event as an important prototype," I told them, "a small-scale sampling or model of what we hope will become an ongoing intercultural, interracial, interreligious process of contact and communication. It's our hope that in the future others with greater capacity and capital than what we've had available here will carry forward this model on an ever-greater scale. I think it's important to keep these points in mind, for the sake of supporting them here and for whatever we may be able to do with this in the future. We believe that the special and nearly unique considerations we've attended to here are what will make this sort of dialogue

or interlogue process work. For one thing, the support-group
situation we're just talking about is unusual. We're apprecia-
tive of the fact that so many dozens of us here are willing to
chop wood or chop carrots, sight unseen, so that these delegates can be together comfortably and without distraction.
Almost always when well-known spokespersons or religious
leaders or holy persons are found in the same place, they're
put in a competitive situation where they're concurrently
scheduled. They talk to audiences who buy tickets, or whatever, and rarely talk with one another. Or else they're before
their devoted followers and they have to think of their image
and behave as they're expected to behave. I can't think of
anything more distracting to really meaningful dialogue than
an audience. In addition, there's the unusual consideration
that has to be given to supporting and honoring the diversity
of all the various cultures."

There was a large team of cooks and cooks' helpers, all
overseen by Bo Sheafor, who was an associate of our program
in Topeka and was a culinary artist in her own right. She had
planned diverse menus for the feasts and buffets as well as for
outdoor cooking in the camps. They all talked about the special consideration given the menus and food preparation as
being a major part of the support process. There were dairy,
nondairy, vegetarian, fruitarian, and kosher foods. Also,
since many Native medicine people require massive supplies
of meat to maintain their medicine power, or so they proclaimed to us, we saw to its provision. Furthermore, there
were living potted plants for those who could not easily abide
by the abundant bouquets and garlands of cut flowers that
had been ordered for those for whom these had important
meaning.

"I think this will be one of the most conducive characteris-
tics of this event," I said. "We need diversity and not unifor-
mity in a situation like this. If we can honor and attend to
each and every individual's cultural customs and comforts, I
think they'll all be much more empowered to contact and
communicate with people of differing colors and customs.

They'll all sense that it's their event, and they'll feel safe, with
nothing to defend or demand. It's really crucial that this sort
of event be facilitated by a neutral force—not under the wing
of the Buddhists or Catholics or any temple or guru or whatever. So everybody's equal here. We've asked for the guidance and participation of traditional American Indians—but
it's not organized or controlled by them, and that makes it
even stronger for them."

"Over the five days of the conference, these four phases
will unfold in order," Jon continued. "The intertribal traditional American Indian Conference will take place before
other delegates arrive. And that's a completely closed council—just them. We'll all be here, but in our own staff house
and in the hogan camp, and the Indian camp will be off-limits
to everyone else, so that they can get used to each other, and
it'll be completely roped off so that none of us inadvertently
walk in on a sweat lodge or something. Then, after they've
concluded, we'll have our team meeting with the Indian delegation. That'll be mainly to work out appropriate access and
communication policies for future cooperation. For that one,
we will all participate, and we'll try to get everyone free for
that. Then comes the two-day cross-cultural summit conference with all the delegates. That's right here in this room. As
hosts, we'll open that conference and get the ball rolling, and
then we'll step aside. We changed the name of the closing
event from Festival of Brotherhood, to Festival of Humanity.
Some people suggested it's a better choice of words, and we
agreed. As you know, that part's open to the public—for the
delegates themselves to present or share whatever they want.
That program will come together as the conference unfolds.
The first step now is to get set up."

• • •

Traditional Native American delegates representing many
major tribes—Tuscarora, Seneca, Mohawk, Chippewa,
Apache, Hopi, Navaho, Yaqui, Muskogee-Creek, K'san, and

others—arrived with their friends and families throughout the evening and night before the first day of the conference. Through the night they had their sweats and ceremonies, and all through the following day they held their councils. Except for a few drivers and hosts, no one saw them, and there was no contact or communication between the Indian camp and the support camp. Among the nondelegate invitees were Cosme, a Philippine healer and physical therapist and his wife, Clara, and Gabriel, therapists from the Bay Area in California, and they drove out to Parkville in a large motor home. As the Indians were holding their council, volunteers worked to prepare the rooms for the main conference and the food for the upcoming opening banquet, and cooked in the camp for the support group. Some of the invited guests talked among themselves, and Cosme, Clara, and Gabriel were soon busy offering treatments and energy therapy to the workers. One by one, they attended to nearly half our group, and there was a steady flow of clients in and out of their mobile clinic.

All the staff, volunteers, and invited guests had supper together in the hogan camp that night and sat around a large open fire after dark. We could hear faint sounds of drumming coming from over the hill. "What do you suppose they're doing?" someone asked, and someone else responded, "Well, it's none of our business. We could have our own ceremony, if we want."

"I thought we were supposed to be invited to join them by now," said another, "since they've finished their own conference with each other. Most of us haven't even seen them. We're not allowed to go in there, and I don't think they'll ever come out."

"No, we were intentionally planning to have no contact with them until tomorrow," Jon explained. "And then we'll visit them up there. They're not supposed to have to come out—they don't even know where we are."

Just then there was a tall figure wrapped in a blanket standing beside us. He had approached so quietly in the dark that no one had heard him. It was Philip Deere. Everyone fell silent. For a while he only watched us, perhaps waiting for someone to say something, and then he spoke: "Well, I just thought I'd walk over here and check. I was hopin' maybe somebody here knew something about giving a massage. I'd sure appreciate it. Our Indian people, we don't do that no more. At least nowadays nobody seems to know about it. There's nobody up there can do it." After a moment of awkward hesitation, several people volunteered at once. One of our people was a certified masseur, and he led Philip away to find an appropriate setting.

Later, I sent a message requesting to meet with the Indian delegates to arrange for the conference with our group. It was agreed, and I and a volunteer drove up over the hill, past the barricades and the Indian guards, and into their camp. I had watched the tents and teepees arrive from the main area down below, but it was my first view of the Indian village since Mad Bear had stood under the rain in the Indian Meadow weeks earlier. It was an enchanting sight. There were sacred fires near the sweat lodges in the woods, little ceremonial fires flickering among the trees, and fires inside the tall, graceful teepees that made them glow in the dark. Sacred ceremonial objects were in the trees and near the fires at the sweat lodges. Because I was expected, there were no sweats or ceremonies as I arrived and, except for the guards and the ever-watchful fire tenders, everyone had gathered around the tables under the large pavilion.

They greeted me nonchalantly, and sat with obvious detachment, only watching me and waiting. I was supposed to make some sort of presentation. I wanted to welcome them on behalf of our sponsoring group and thank them for coming— but thoughtfully—because I did not want them to think that we considered this our event or that they were here for us. I decided to simply say that and to tell them that we wished, as facilitators, to support them in their future involvement and influence in national and international affairs. But I also told them that we had gathered here and had sought to meet with them to petition for their help. We hoped for more outreach on their part and greater and more meaningful contact. "Our people want to correct our misinformation and misunderstanding," I told them. "But we can hardly do that properly without your help. Many of us want to learn from you—even to learn the appropriate way to learn from you. I think we agree that we are all here to expand, or begin to expand, our communication with each other. But we request your guidance as to how this should best be done."

They sipped their coffee and tended to their little ones who had become restless and had begun to run around outside the pavilion, and they continued to appear detached. But they talked quietly among themselves. "So we're s'posed to set down with you folks and talk?" one asked.

"Well, if you'd be willing to do that," I said, though that was what had already been agreed.

There was no further comment or suggestion. No one said anything until Mad Bear, who had been sitting quietly in deference to the others, spoke up in his diplomatic way and initiated an arrangement without seeming to steer or advise his people. "I think since you've approached us," he said to me, "they may be waiting for you to extend the offer. Maybe it would be appropriate if you, on behalf of your bunch there, would invite our Indian delegation down to your place."

In the hogan camp, early in the morning, our people gathered to confer, even as dozens of hotcakes were being grilled, round after round, above the open fire. The Indians had been invited, the hour had been set, and we decided to prepare for them. Perhaps they would arrive, those who were willing to come, sauntering up, a few at a time, with their earthy walk and their stern expressions, and say, "Well, what did you want?" But we would be prepared, we decided, and we would receive them in a ceremonial way, all in a circle with our arms around each other, standing strong as a group. And we would invite them as they came to join our circle. There was some question whether it all might appear a bit staged and overdramatic. If that was the case, we agreed, so be it: We needed it for ourselves. We needed to be calm, clear, and centered, and

to establish, in unity, an atmosphere of receptivity and respect so strong that they would sense it and respond.

We hurried through breakfast and cleanup and the few
chores that could not be put off so that we would have time to
undertake our ritual and create a strong and balanced circle.
With all our staff and volunteers and all our associate members and advisors who had been invited as guests, we made a
gigantic circle. We considered that it would be nice to honor
the Indian delegates in the center of our circle, but decided we
could not expect them to go along with our preconceived scenario.

One who had been a martial arts teacher led the circle
through some preparatory steps. We grounded ourselves and
rooted our feet strongly to the Earth, cleared our minds, and
let go of our physical and emotional distractions—as best we
could—and then we worked to purify and energize our circle
and the space in the center. That was our ritual, and when it
was done and we were able to stand in balance, we clasped
our arms around the backs and shoulders on our left and
right, closed our eyes, and stood together in silent meditation.

We heard drumming in the distance. It was the sound of
many drums, and it grew louder as it came near. Then there
was singing—a chorus of Indian voices. We all opened our
eyes to look. Over the top of the hill appeared heads and
shoulders and finally a long line of Indians, marching single
file, drumming and singing down the path. The entire Indian
camp had come, more than fifty of them, dressed up in fine
regalia. No one could have expected or even imagined this
phenomenon. Without a sign of direction or suggestion, they
walked right up to and through our ring and circled around
the center. They had joined our ritual—or we theirs—as
beautifully and easily as if it had been collectively conceived
and orchestrated. Then there arrived clouds of birds—black-
birds—perhaps thousands of them, and they settled in the
branches of the trees all around us and remained nearly
silent, with only an occasional flutter or peep. One gigantic
eagle had flown in above this cloud of birds and, for a mo-

ment, all eyes were on him as he sat, stone still, at the very top
of the tallest tree.

From that beginning, our "meeting of minds," as Mad Bear
had envisioned it, was easy and enjoyable. Everyone spoke
freely, asking questions and sharing thoughts. People asked
for advice from the elders and listened attentively as they
spoke. But they also asked questions and listened to our people, even to the young people.

"We know some of you people have respect for our ways,
and you're interested in our culture," said one delegate. "But
you people must have your own sacred path and your own
natural traditions somewhere in your cultural roots. Maybe
you could get that back. Maybe, though, there is some things
we could help you learn about the land, since you're interested, because your people are spoilin' it for everyone."

"We don't want you to sit at our feet," said another. "And
we're not about to sit at yours. We want you to stand up with
us and walk with us."

"But there is some things they maybe don't know about
that we could help with," contended the first. "Like these
bees here."

"The bees?" someone asked.

"We know, 'cause we just now heard from one of your people that the bees are stingin' everybody around here. He
called it a problem. He says, 'We're having a big problem
with the bees in our camp.' "

It was true. Bees had been buzzing around the camp, especially around the food, ever since we had arrived, and many
of our people had been stung, some more than once.

"This here's supposed to be a meetin' for gettin' together
and gettin' along right?" posed one of the elders. "Everybody
lookin' at gettin' along with one another, right?"

"Right."

"Well, I ain't passin' judgment or bein' critical of you folks
here, but some of you might still got a habit of forgettin' who
was here first. You can't just come into some territory and
take over. First place, ever' territory belongs to Nature and

the Great Spirit and whoever they had in there in the first place. Those bees live here. Where they s'posed to go? Then they see all the food, but they don't understand. They musta picked up from somebody that you folks don't appreciate 'em and you folks want 'em outa here. That kinda thing shakes people up—even the bee people."

"So we oughta help 'em out here," Mad Bear said. "We know how to do that, and we should make that offering. They can't do it, because they don't know, and it takes time to get that back. I'll tell you one thing, none of these people are try- ing to hurt the bees or anything else here. They're here with respect and we're all here to help each other."

"Yeah, Mad Bear, that should be done, and in the right way. That's our place to do that here. So, you people, just like you're promotin' dialogue all around, we'll open up the dia- logue with the bees in your behalf."

"But we'll have to do it after lunch," Mad Bear advised us. "We'll set it up and some of us will come back down here this afternoon."

At the close of our meeting, we shared lunch and friendly conversation, and the Indians left, walking single file back up the path, with only the soft "thump, thump, thump" of their drums. As soon as they were out of sight, the many birds, who had been waiting in the trees, chirped noisily and then swiftly swooped up over the hill. Only the eagle remained, still perched on the top of the tree, and many of our people pointed at it and marveled at its presence.

Later that day, Mad Bear and several others came back to have their conference with the bees. There was fire and sage and drumming and song and, with the offering of tobacco and various sacraments, Mad Bear and the others spoke in their own languages; but as it was with the Indians themselves in my initial meeting with them in their camp, the bees appeared to remain indifferent. At the close of their ceremony, they an- nounced that they had been requested, on behalf of the In- dian Village, to extend an invitation to all of us to share the evening meal with them. Just as they were taking their leave,

the eagle spread his wings and lifted himself majestically into
the air, and our heads turned at the sound. It flew high and
went out of sight beyond the hill toward the Indian village.

Again we gathered our group, as many as could, to plan for
our evening visit. We discussed whether it would be appropriate to contribute something to the meal. Those who were veg-
etarians favored the idea, because the Indians, they knew,
would have mostly meat and meat dishes, and this would give
them an additional option. "Right now, I don't care," one of
them said. "Whatever they offer, I'm going to accept it." We
decided to go with soup. We had a gigantic cauldron—big
enough to hold more than one hundred servings—and the
cooks made a thick, hearty porridge. The only challenge was
to carry the huge vessel of steaming liquid up the steep path
and over the hill. At dusk, we were ready to start. Two large
poles were slipped under the handle of the pot, crossed to
form an "X," and tied in the middle so that the whole precar-
ious arrangement could be carried like a palanquin by the
strongest volunteers. We had to go the long way around the
hill, rather than over, because the hot soup was likely to spill
on the steep path. We walked in the sunset along the dirt road
that rounded the hill. We moved in a slow procession, singing
in harmony as we went, the song that we had chosen and re-
hearsed.

As we walked around the last bend and the Indian camp
came into view, our vigorous and buoyant caroling fell almost
to a whisper, and some stopped in their tracks, bringing our
group and our heavy pot to a halt. Right ahead of us, in the
fading sunset, was the Indian Meadow with the ceremonial
fires and the lantern-lit pavilion; and just beyond, tall
teepees, standing majestically against the soft, gray sky and
deep purple clouds, were glowing in the twilight. Among the
trees were circles of tents, and bright fires blazed near the
domed sweat lodges in the distance. For a moment, we only
stood and looked, but we regained our sense of purpose, and
resumed our procession and our song—for our arrival had
been observed and some of the delegates had started out to

meet us. Graciously they welcomed us and our soup as well.
The soup was cooling off, and some of the women showed us to
a fire pit on which to place the pot to heat.

There was an abundance of things to eat, every sort of
food, and plenty for everyone. No one spoke of plans or procedures or of anything pertinent, and our official agenda was
forgotten for a time. It was simply a sociable evening, with
easy conversation and laughter, as though we were longtime
neighbors from a nearby village. There was some rotation
during the meal among those who were guarding the outer
roads, minding the perpetual fires, or tending the fires that
heated the rocks for the sweats.

"And, by the way, I might mention we'll be havin' our
sweats again later tonight," one of the elders announced. "So
if you people, any of you who would like, why, you'd be welcome—and you could just see me and I'll talk to you about
it." Immediately, two dozen or more from our camp gathered
around him.

"Well, he offered it," Mad Bear said to me. "That's several
sweats there, 'cause they can only go a few at a time. I guess
he knows what he's got himself in for, but I'm not sure if some
of those people do. Oh, yeah, I was going to tell you—and you
might mention it to the others when you're back there at your
camp. If these people like to have an eagle around, they can
have an eagle if they want. It's a good thing, because Eagle
sees and knows a lot, but it should be respected, and, by the
way, it's not necessary to point at it."

The next day, the other delegates began to arrive. Those
who came early had the day to settle in, to rest, or to get acquainted with the site and with the others. The rabbis were
the last to appear, as it was Rosh Hashanah and they would
travel only after starsight on that day. Rabbi Herbert Weiner
had to fly from Boston and thus had to arrive in the night.
Rabbi David Zeller had flown in days ahead from California
to spend the holidays with friends in Kansas City, and it had
been arranged that he would appear after starsight, in time to
blow the shofar to start off the opening ceremony. All through

the day, the cooks worked to prepare the banquet to culmi-
nate the opening ceremony.

By nightfall everything was ready. Chairs, place cards,
notebooks and pens, mikes and speakers had been arranged
in the main conference room in preparation for the following
day. The banquet was prepared and the tables were set in the
main dining room. The entire group, nearly two hundred people, were gathered on the grounds below the main building.
The timing was perfect. Just as everyone had gathered, David
Zeller arrived, and the first sound that the assembly heard—
the blowing of the ram's horn—marked the close of Rosh
Hashanah and the opening of the Cross-Cultural Conference.
There were greetings and opening remarks, and prayers and
blessings in various tongues were offered to initiate the event
in a manner appropriate to everyone present. The banquet
was a feast fit for all. The variety of dishes were spread out
buffet style and there was an abundance for every taste and
custom. Even the one delegate who was required to have his
food prepared by his private cook joined the others at the
table.

The Indian delegation extended an invitation to these holy
persons to join them in the Indian Village in the night to pray
with them in the sweat lodges. Nearly all of them accepted and
even Rabbi Weiner, who arrived at midnight, went directly up
to join them. In the dark of night they removed their robes
and garments, stooped through the small sweat lodge door,
and shared the sacred ritual with the Indians. So by the opening of the conference on the following morning, monk, lama,
priest, pastor, swami, rabbi, and medicine person had already prayed together.

In the morning, as all the delegates gathered for an early
breakfast, fresh flowers and water and other final touches
made ready the conference room. Twenty-one mikes were
placed and tested at twenty-one seats around the conference
table, and all the chairs that could fit—nearly one hundred of
them—were arranged around the four walls and through the
doorway into the adjoining room. As there were many Ameri-

can Indian delegates, seven representative spokespersons
were selected among them to sit at the mikes, and chairs for
the remaining delegates were placed just behind the table.
When the twenty-one conference delegates were seated at the
table, all the invitees, staff, and volunteers made their entrance and filled the waiting chairs. The invitees would remain through the conference as associate-delegate observers,
but the support group would be present only for the introduction. They had come to witness the opening—and to be themselves witnessed by the delegates.

A standing microphone had been placed near one end of
the table, and I stepped to that mike to initiate the meeting.
That step was our official role as the sponsoring support
group, and our only role, in the conference dialogue. I told
the conferees that though they might pursue their own
agenda, we had collectively prepared some questions that we
should like to present, only that they might know that these
questions exist and that they might respond to them if they
wished. "I should be honored to introduce each and every one
of you," I told them, "but I will ask you to introduce yourselves so that you may present yourselves to the others as you
wish."

Every delegate spoke English, to some extent, and in the interest of time and for the sake of directness, there were no in-
terpreters. Every delegate had a microphone so that he or
she, in spite of mannerism or accent, could at least be clearly
heard by the others. They introduced themselves in the order
of their seating around the conference table:

Donald Keys, of Planetary Citizens (as chairperson and
moderator); Geshe Sopa, Tibetan Lama, personal representative to the Dalai Lama; Abdul Khalifah, of the Muhsin
Vahir Salahadeen Masjid; Sonja Margulies, ordained Zen
priest; Buraq Gruber, Sufi teacher, personal representative
of Pir Vilayat Khan; Dr. David Zeller, rabbi and Jewish mystic; Viento Stan-Padilla, Yaqui medicine man; David Paladin,
Navajo artist and medicine man; Oh Shinnah, Apache guide
and lecturer; Lame Buffalo, K'san spiritual spokesman and

teacher; Mad Bear, Tuscarora medicine man and spokesman;
Philip Deere, Muskogee-Creek medicine man and spokesman;
Sun Bear, Chippewa medicine man and Bear Tribe leader;
Pandit Usharbudh Arya, Sanskrit scholar and Hindu spiri-
tual teacher; Joel Levey, Sufi and holistic practitioner and
teacher; Dr. Herbert Weiner, rabbi and Jewish mystic;
Kobun Chino, Zen Roshe and founding director of Tassajara
Zen Monastery; Father Thomas Hennigan, Augustinian
teacher and associate of Brother David Stendl-Rast; Swami
Sri Ramanathan, teacher and world traveler; Father Paul
Clemens of the Catholic Church of Antioch; and Dudley
Weeks, planetary mediator, founding director of The World
We Share (as cochair and comoderator).

   After all the principal delegates at the table had given their
names and described themselves briefly, I asked them to turn
around in their chairs and try to see all the other faces in the
room. "We will introduce ourselves collectively as a group," I
told them. "There is no way to introduce each individual. We
have agreed to introduce ourselves as representatives of your
students and followers everywhere. We are here because you
are here and we want to see what you will do. We represent
the population of this planet who are looking to you and others in your positions as our only hope for safety and survival.
There are many reasons why this is so. The spiritual leaders
are the only representatives with whom the population has direct contact, and the only representatives who are certain to
put their welfare first. You are the ones to whom all peoples
look for guidance. You are the guardians of the principles of
ethics and health. Furthermore, you are the leaders most
likely to work in concert and cooperation and are therefore
the most powerful and influential of all the world's leaders.
We believe that for years to come, political leaders and business leaders must continue competitively, as in the game of
monopoly, to best serve their principal responsibilities. But
we also believe that our safety depends much more upon the
safety of our planet—the air, the water, the land, and the
forests—than it does upon the safety of corporations or na-

tions. Therefore, we introduce ourselves to you as the ones
who depend upon you for our safety and survival. But as we
depend on you, you may also depend on us. Therefore, we
will be awaiting your guidance and your assignments."

At that time, nearly all the people who were crowded into
the room stood and quietly left, and nearly all the chairs were
empty. The conferees were now able to feel somewhat alone
together, free to speak as they wished, and they sat facing one
another. Most of them found themselves in a situation unlike
anything they had experienced before. "Before I sit down, I'd
like to articulate what we've expressed to you in terms of the
questions we've prepared. We would like to ask you whether
you can conceive and consider working together, today and to
an even greater degree into the future, not as an ecumenical
group of theological scholars, but as a mind bank addressing
urgent planetary issues. Can you agree to do this even if it
means changing your schedules and being away from your
people and your own congregations? And can you then arrive
at solutions and resolutions—guidance and instruction for
your people who, all together, represent virtually all of humankind? Also, as most of you find yourselves for the first
time in conference with American Indians, can you acknowledge that this race, religion, and culture is as ancient, valid,
and valuable as any other, and that these people must be recognized, embraced, and involved as a people in their own
right? If so, could you so concur and so state?"

When I sat down, the conference delegates were in each
other's hands. As a first step, they did collectively and "officially" recognize the Native peoples of North and South America as a race, religion, and culture in their own right and
acknowledge that they had a rightful role in future international and planetary affairs. Throughout the long day, they
considered issues—planetary and humanitarian issues, and
environmental issues. They agreed that any harm done to any
place or people anywhere affects and endangers all land and
life everywhere, and they considered issues facing many places
and people. Toward the end of the conference, they deter-

mined to execute a resolution. It would advance, identify, and respond to at least one example, one issue. Since the American Indian presence and participation had made a strong impression and impact upon all the other delegates, they decided upon a contemporary American Indian "issue." It was to be considered simply a beginning, and they called it "The First Resolution of the Cross-Cultural Summit Conference":

> As cross-cultural leaders from around the world, we support in spirit and action the right of Native Americans to protect and maintain their traditional spiritual lands. Threats to these lands are threats to the survival and development of the Native American people. As a priority example, we demand the cessation of the mining of coal, uranium, oil, and gas in the Four Corners Territory, where Utah, Arizona, Nevada, and Colorado touch. We further demand an increase in the scientific research that has shown the severe ecological dangers that will result from mining efforts in this unique geophysical area. And finally, we demand that the U.S. Government uphold the spirit and letter of the Native American Religious Act, an act that protects Native American sacred lands, and that other governments, especially those of the Americas, support our demands.
>
> We understand that the sacred traditions of all peoples are threatened when the traditions of one culture are threatened. Thus our attention to this specific Native American cause is a beginning of our efforts on behalf of all cultures whose spiritual roots hold certain lands and/or traditions to be sacred.

Local members of the press arrived for the press conference at the end of the day. The resolution was read, questions were asked, and interviews were given. The principal conferees and associate delegates gathered outside for a brief closing service, and then the delegates dispersed to eat or rest or be alone as they wished. When nearly everyone had left, someone noticed that Marty had collapsed. He was discovered lying on the ground near one of the buildings. He was conscious but totally disoriented, and he was weak and partially paralyzed. We carried him into the staff house and lay him on one of the cots. Cosme, Clara, and Gabriel were notified, and they came at once. David Paladin, the Navajo medicine man, was still in the main area, and he also was called in. He held Marty's head and shoulders while the three healers stood over him, trying to pick up what was happening to him. Together, they seemed to bring him around. He regained his balance and his presence, but he remained too weak to stand or even to move.

"We know what is happening here," Gabriel said. "It is an attack of sorts. It has been a potential all the while, but we have all been all right—until now."

Several of our group had come in to see. Those who were attending to Marty asked to clear the room, as it was getting crowded. So people left and we locked the door. "But you should get Mad Bear," someone told me. "He's Mad Bear's apprentice and this is a case for Mad Bear."

"I'll have to have a vehicle," I said. "He's back at the Indian camp, but I'll try to find a driver and go get him." I unlocked and opened the door to see Mad Bear standing just outside as though he were trying to stare through the wall. Instantly when he saw me, he looked down at the ground. "How did you get all the way down here?" I asked him.

"Why not? I just came back to get something."

"I mean, something's wrong with Marty inside there. Did you know about it?"

"I'm just looking for a little feather. Do you see one?"

"Why don't you come inside? Something's wrong with Marty."

"I know, but I think I may have dropped a feather off my ceremonial hat." He continued to stare at the ground. "Do you see a little feather anywheres here?"

"I don't, but we can look later. Don't you want to see Marty?"

"Well, I do see him. He'll be okay, if I can do my work. I have my own work to do. They're takin' care of him okay in there. Long as someone's with him—and I feel good about those people in there."

He went on looking at the ground. I opened the door to check inside, and when I turned around he was gone.

"I talked to Mad Bear," I said. "He was right here, but now he's gone." I wondered how to explain it.

"It's all right," Cosme said. "We'll take care of him. Gabriel's said he'll bring his sleeping bag in here and stay right by his side all night."

I went out again and many people were standing by the door, waiting to see what was happening. People insisted that Mad Bear ought to be there and I explained that he had been and gone. But no one had seen him. "I talked to him," I said, "and I told him about Marty. He said he was trying to find this feather that dropped off his hat."

"He wasn't here, so that doesn't make sense," people told me. "He hasn't even been over here where he could have dropped anything."

I went back inside to consult with Gabriel. "They don't think Mad Bear knows," I said. "They think I should go up there and make sure. It's good that you're going to stay here with Marty, and I think Mad Bear knows it. But maybe we should check and see if Mad Bear wants him up there with him."

"You could go check if you want—or if they want—just so it's confirmed. But only you go. It's really important that Mad Bear not be disturbed."

I located the driver who had driven me into the Indian camp days earlier, and we went to look for Mad Bear. It was quiet in the Indian village. Perhaps they were resting or having sweats or other ceremonies. "I think Mad Bear's way up there in that campin' trailer," one of them told me. "He stays in that trailer sometimes." When Mad Bear had first noticed the little trailer by the road in the main area, he had asked whether it could be arranged that he might use it to get away when he needed to or to protect his paraphernalia. I had not

seen or thought about the trailer since or been aware that
Mad Bear had managed to have it hauled up to his camp.

We found the trailer among the trees at the very edge of the
camp. "Wait here," I said and, with some hesitation, I tapped
softly on the metal door. I waited. There was no response. I
was trying to decide whether to knock again, a little louder,
when I thought I heard his muffled voice inside. But I could
not make it out, so I tapped again, softly.

"Doug, is that you?" He sounded half asleep. "See if the
door's open. Just a minute. Okay . . . Uh, just open the
door." It was pitch black inside and I could see nothing of him
or the inside of the trailer. "Just step up here—up the step.
Can you see?" I could see nothing. Except for the sound, I
didn't know where he was or where to stand or face. I put out
my hands trying to feel whether there was anything around
me. He said something, but I could not hear him clearly and I
thought perhaps he was dropping off to sleep again. Then he
cleared his throat and tried to speak up, but his voice was still
faint as though he were trying not to become fully conscious.
"He doesn't have to be here. It's best not—best for the others. He'll be . . . you know . . ." I waited to hear if he had
anything else to say. For a moment I had the feeling that there
was nothing of him in this space but his faint voice. I stood
motionless. "Lemme be, just lemme work with . . ." His voice
trailed off, and I felt that I was standing alone in a dark container. I felt for the handle and stepped outside, closing the
door behind me.

The volunteer who had brought me had been waiting near
the trailer. "It's okay," I said. "He knows. Let's go back."
There was nothing else to explain, and we drove back down
the hill to the main area in silence. I went back to the staff
house to talk with Gabriel and saw him walking toward the
door with his sleeping bag.

"What did you tell Mad Bear?" Gabriel asked.

"Nothing," I said, without thinking. Then I realized I had not
spoken a single word to Mad Bear. I had a fleeting fear that I
might have imagined I had heard him speak to me. But I knew
that he had conveyed what he had wished. "He thinks it's best

that Marty not go back up there. It seems he'll be all right."

"You mean Marty or Mad Bear?"

"I meant Marty. But you were right. Mad Bear wants to be left alone."

"He's busy, and we can only let him be busy in his own way. He knows what he's doing and he's busy doing it. This is Mad Bear's challenge really. Well, it's our challenge in that we're all here. It's everyone's challenge and we're accepting it in a way. But I have a feeling this sort of thing is Mad Bear's constant work. We're doing more here than appears, I guess you know that. I guess you know Mad Bear is mostly doing what cannot be seen from here."

"I know," I said.

"He happens to have his physical presence," Gabriel continued, "but he works on another level."

"And on this level too," I said. "He's traveled all around the world, you know, he's met with so many . . ."

"He's a mediator—just like the professional mediators you've had as moderators in this conference. They know, like we do, that there are opponents to dialogue itself. You may already be aware of this, but there are other forces on other realms that oppose what we're doing here—that cannot stand that this is happening. I don't think you should discuss it with the others, not until later, anyway. There's no need for anyone to hold such an image, but we have our counterforce, and it's very present. It's around and yet it's not very potent in the presence of all this prayer and goodwill. Marty unwittingly became the weak link. I think he was a little overanxious about something, I'm not sure what. Anyway, he was overtired, that's for sure."

"Yeah, he must have been tired," I agreed. "He's been working up here from the beginning, and he set up a lot of the Indian camp by himself."

"Well, anyway," Gabriel concluded, "he'll be taken care of. So I should go back inside. Like I said, Mad Bear knows what he's doing—and, frankly, so do we."

I walked alone along the road toward the camp, considering what Gabriel had said. He was right about the counter-force, I thought, because that's always there—even in physics. And he was right about not bringing it up with the group. There was no need for this to become an issue now. I would talk about it at some point, I decided. It was a fascinating subject—at least when considered from Mad Bear's perspective. I thought again about the nature of Mad Bear's medicine. In all the time I had known him, I had rarely seen him work with infirmity or physical ills or injuries. His work, I knew, whether on the road or on the reservation or in some unseen realm, was conflict resolution. He had often spoken of a place or perception beyond conflict—beyond the perspective of "other" or "outsider" or "opponent." I supposed that was where he was, and where he often was—as a mediator, basically.

In the morning, one of our people noticed a small turkey feather in the middle of the mat right in front of the door of the staff house.

CHAPTER FIFTEEN
Focus and Move Energy

"A day like today—it's a good day for untroubling."

◑ Weeks after our Cross-Cultural Conference in Parkville, I talked with Ethel Lombardi on the telephone. We had missed her at our conference: She was the only one of the special guests who had accepted our invitation and not attended. I was aware of her absence but, in my preoccupation with all the other delegates and staff, I had not been able to give her much thought, and I had not heard from her since the summer when we had talked about Mad Bear.

I was at a gathering in a private home following a seminar in Minneapolis when I discovered that our host was a friend of Ethel's. "In fact, I'm expecting to be in touch with her soon," he told me. "When I talk to her, I'll mention that I've met you and that you send your regards, if that's all right with you."

"That would be good," I told him. "I haven't spoken with her for quite a while."

Later, while everyone was having coffee and dessert, he beckoned to me from the hallway. "I've got Ethel on the phone now," he said. "I thought I'd give her a try while you were here, and she does want to talk with you. Take the phone in the bedroom there." He closed the door after me and went back to join the others.

I picked up the phone. "Hello, Ethel?"

"I think it's about time I let you know why I did not show up at the conference," she said directly.

"Well, we missed you," I responded, "but I understand. I know you have a really busy . . ."

"No, that wasn't it," she said. "First, let me ask you, how's Mad Bear, and how did everything go?"

"Fine," I told her, "and wonderfully." She listened while I gave a brief but positive report.

"Good," she said. "I had a good feeling about it, but I knew I shouldn't go. Well, let me tell you what happened. We arranged I would do a healing for Mad Bear, right? When I sat down to do my work—you know what I do, I think, the healing is directed and sent to him."

"Right," I said.

"As soon as I focused my attention on Mad Bear—well, I have, or had, a squash-blossom necklace, an American Indian piece. It was a gift to me and it hung on the wall behind me where I sat. As soon as I focused my attention on him, the squash-blossom necklace blew apart. I knew what it was, in a sense. I knew something was going on beyond what I wanted to become involved with."

I told her about Joel and the necklace Mad Bear had given him.

"This is Mad Bear's work," she said, "so it was Mad Bear's contest. And I know he's up to it—has to be—it's his capacity. But it's not my contest, not my challenge. I realized that I had better not show up there and get pulled into something that doesn't belong to me."

"But what you did helped," I told her. "And what happened must have helped. Mad Bear did make an amazing re-

covery, and a pretty fast and complete recovery, as far as I
could see. In fact, I was talking with him right around that
time, and he told me on the phone—he said, 'I can feel the energy. I can feel it coming in now.' "

"Since I'd already engaged myself to some extent," she continued, "I decided to disengage and pull out—not get caught in
it. So that's the reason I didn't show up or even get in touch. I
thought it best to stay completely disconnected. But it's good
to talk to you. And it's good to hear everything went well."

"And it really did. Like I said, everything unfolded beautifully. There was the contest, though, I know, but I think
hardly anyone was aware of that. The delegates knew they
were working with their challenge—the planetary challenge—
but in the background there was a challenge as well."

"In the background," she said, "there is always a challenge
as well."

●   ●   ●

Jison returned to the United States one day while I was at
Mad Bear's new home on the Tuscarora Reservation, and Tim
and Pam telephoned to tell me that he had arrived in San
Francisco with his party and was hoping to meet with me and
Mad Bear.

"I knew he'd be back," Mad Bear said. "What's he doing,
is he coming up here? Sounded like you were talking about
New York."

"I don't know, I was only talking with Tim and Pam. He's
already arrived with whomever he's brought with him, but
they haven't actually seen him yet. Maybe Jison could call
here. You don't mind if he has your number, do you?"

"Well, that'd be okay, far as Jison goes—or it'd have to be
Hiro, I guess. But it's not a good time for him to be comin' up
here though, with us going back out to Arizona. Maybe that's
what we should all do—go out to Arizona. I bet we could talk
him into that."

Tim and Pam met the group in San Francisco and, during

the several days they were out there together, they did all the communicating. Once they had their tickets and their schedules, I spoke briefly with Hiro to assure him that I would meet them at the airport in New York at the right time and place and would arrange accommodations in the city. Lightly, I suggested the possibility of Tucson, and Hiro said something like, "You know Sen Sei is anytime okay for anything. If Mr. Mad Bear will want, he will satisfy for anything."

Occasionally, I had corresponded with Hiro and Yoko in Japan and, occasionally, they had mentioned Jison was thinking of another visit. Nothing, however, had been planned. As was often the case with Mad Bear, Jison had apparently felt the time was right one morning and had gotten his people together and had started for the airport. So I myself was to set out for the airport.

"But it'll all work out good," Mad Bear assured me. "You and Mike and I gotta fly outa New York anyways. We'll get together down there, see if Jison wants to go to Tucson—which I'm willing to bet he'll go—and if not, we at least got our chance to see him in New York. You think we could get another room or two for Mike Bastine and me?" Mad Bear only wanted a couple days "to secure the place and throw a few things together," and he and Mike would join us in the city.

When I arrived in New York City, I went first to the Lexington Hotel. I was assured that rooms were available and that our group could be accommodated however they should wish as soon as they arrived. So I brought them all by taxi from the airport to the Lexington Hotel. Jison seemed elated when we met, and excited, in his quiet way, to be back in the United States and at the prospect of seeing Mad Bear once again.

Hiro introduced me to the others. They were an artist and his son and a young woman about the son's age—perhaps twenty-five or so. Yoko and her mother had remained in Japan, but Hiro was once again at Jison's service, and the three who had come along were new friends of Jison's—or actually, I learned, they were his followers. Hiro explained that the man was a well-known and respected classical traditional artist in Japan whose son had been helped by Jison. The son had fallen face first into the propellor of an outboard motor and had his face ripped to shreds. Someone at the scene of the accident knew about Jison and persuaded them that they should go at once to this healer-monk and avoid stitches and plastic surgery, which would result in permanent disfiguration. The son had been taken instantly to Jison with the flesh hanging down from his face. Right before the father's eyes, Jison had repaired the young man's face with his hands so that not a scar or a single sign of injury remained, and both father and son had been with him ever since. The young woman was also a follower who had met Jison only months earlier. Owing to some disease that Hiro could not identify in English, she had been so thin, frail, and shapeless that the others had thought she was a weak little boy. I told Hiro that she looked fragile but quite healthy.

"If we have photographs from before, nobody will believe it," he said.

I was afraid, at first, that Hiro was the only one among the group who spoke English at all, and that he would surely tire as the days went by; but the young woman and the son, I soon discovered, could understand me fairly well and, in time, they began to speak. Jison assured me, as soon as we were settled in the hotel, and before I had a chance to mention it to him, that they would be interested in going to Tucson, if it would not be a disturbance to Mi-su-ta Bear. Their schedules were open, he told me, and they were willing to do whatever we advised.

"He has money now," Hiro told me. "So much his own money, he is getting. Because now he became a kind of famous—maybe because of Yoko's mother, someway. Many people, rich people, know he helped so much for their life, and they gave him lots of money even he never requests. So he will use it for travel and for his temple."

"Well, I don't know what you have in mind for now," I told them. "But Mad Bear won't be here for a couple of days. We have time to do New York City, if you're interested. We could be tourists for a while, if you want."

"You can be our guide," he said.

We walked along Broadway, ate in the Waldorf-Astoria, visited the Empire State Building and the United Nations, and rode on the Staten Island Ferry. Jison had designed and made himself some clothing for just this sort of occasion so that, without totally relinquishing his monk's bearing, he could appear a bit more like a natural person to the Western public. I wanted, in the limited time that Jison had to spend in New York, to accomplish something more meaningful than simply sight-seeing. I knew someone in the city who was pursuing shamanic studies with Michael Harner, and I was friends with the International Center for Integrative Studies. Through these friends, I arranged some visits and mini-conferences with Jison.

"He is willing and able to give some pretty fascinating demonstrations that are not healing demonstrations," I explained. "Healers can't usually give demonstrations because healing demonstrations don't usually work. I think what Jison does is more closely related to martial arts—which is a common practice of Buddhist monks, actually—but it does have implications for healing."

For our first meeting in Michael Harner's office, Jison and Hiro wanted to arrange an additional interpreter. "Sen Sei doesn't want to make a speech," Hiro told me. "But, anyway, you know people ask questions and it's hard for me because maybe I cannot understand American way to think this kind of subject." But I did not know of anyone in New York City whom we could get to fill the role. "There is," Hiro reminded me. "You remember the lady that guided for us at United Nations? She was so good in Japanese, and she's American."

We met with her at the United Nations building. She agreed, and she came along with our group when we met with Michael Harner and his colleagues in his office. But our American interpreter found it even more of a challenge than Hiro did to speak for Jison. She was perhaps fluent in con-

versation and she had trained and practiced for her United
Nations tours, but she explained that Jison was difficult to
understand even in his everyday conversation and especially
in his esoteric explanations. His demonstrations stimulated
questions and the questions stimulated him to offer elaboration in Japanese that she found impossible to translate completely.

I had no idea what Jison would do until I watched him
along with the others. I had already seen him produce heat on
whatever part of his subject's body the observers pointed to.
Whatever specific area on the legs, back, neck, or shoulders
was selected, the heat was very evident to both the subject
and the observers. This demonstration Jison repeated many
times so that the group could experience it subjectively as well
as see it. He then introduced the young woman in their party
and told something of how he had been working with her. We
moved two of the tables in the room and he placed her on the
tables with the back of her head on the edge of one table and
her heels on the other, so that she stretched between them like
a human bridge. Then he had someone sit on her stomach.
She was not stiff or tense, but would bend with the weight and
still not slip off the tables.

Jison had to prepare her for this by sweeping his hands
over her body—a process similar to the one he used to produce heat—but he explained that the essence of the procedure
was probably not visible to us. Without this preparatory assis-
tance on Jison's part, neither she nor any of the others who
tried it could do it. They could not maintain their position on
the table, even when there was no added weight. But with his
help, all who tried could stay stretched between the tables,
comfortably relaxed, while others sat upon them or walked
across them from one table to the other. As I had seen happen
before with Jison, people assumed hypnosis was involved.
Hiro had come to know the word for hypnosis and both he and
the interpreter could only repeat: "He says it isn't. He knows
what you mean, but he said that it isn't related."

People wanted to question me, but I could not interpret his

language and did not want to try to interpret his philosophy or his methodology.

Very shortly after Mad Bear and Mike arrived at the Lexington Hotel, we all left for the International Center for Integrative Studies. A different group had gathered in the conference room at the center to meet with Jison. This time, Jison and Mad Bear would be together—which made both of them happy—and our little misadventure as we went only added to their amusement. Since there were eight of us, we needed two taxis. The doorman blew his whistle, and two taxis pulled up. But, as Hiro was talking to Mad Bear and me, I was temporarily distracted, and the doorman herded four of our group into one of the cabs, and waved it on, and put a different party in the other cab. I, who was supposed to be constantly attentive, started to run down the street, but it was useless, and I gave up.

"Those four don't know where to go," I told the doorman, as I walked back, "and none of them speak English. This is terrible!"

"Not really," the doorman responded. "The driver probably don't speak English neither."

Mad Bear, Hiro, Mike, and I finally got another cab and set out to look for them. We drove around a while and then back to the hotel in case the driver had returned them. "As soon as the driver saw they were foreigners," I said, "he probably headed for the airport." Hiro became quite concerned, but Mad Bear only laughed.

"We'll find 'em," Mad Bear insisted, and he directed our driver along one of the midtown cross streets until we saw their cab stopped at the side of the road. Their driver appeared to be trying to talk to them. We waved and they followed, and they pulled up behind us outside of the building. Jison had not been concerned at all—he had simply been waiting for Mad Bear to catch up.

Jison went through the same demonstrations as before and this time Mad Bear watched and shared thoughts and comments of his own. Those who had gathered in the conference room experienced Jison in the same way the other group had, and they asked similar questions. For this event, there was a Japanese professor from Columbia University who was known to the International Center for Integrative Studies. He translated nearly instantaneously—and directly, speaking as Jison rather than referring to him in the third person. Still, the two had to spend much time conferring with each other in Japanese.

"Jison makes up his own terminology," the professor explained, "and he speaks metaphorically, which takes getting used to. In his way of saying, he is working with the blood, so I translate 'blood,' but I think he means a sort of energy or energy field. Perhaps he conceives an energy structure or function similar to the bloodstream. As he claims he enters the bloodstream, I think perhaps he may mean he can influence the energy system of the individual with his own energy system. I've suggested this to him, and he seems to concur."

When the fragile young woman had demonstrated holding a heavy weight while stretched between the tables, with not more than an inch of her head or an inch of her heels resting on either table, several others were eager to try. Even the professor experienced it, and he laughed compulsively as we piled heavy books from the conference room shelves in several high stacks upon his chest and stomach; but he remained safely in place, though his body shook with laughter.

Again the question of hypnosis was brought up, and the professor relayed the question to Jison. Jison replied, and this time, there was instant and direct translation: "Hypnosis is for tricking another person to circumvent conscious volition. Hypnosis is in every case an attack upon an individual's integrity and dignity."

"What is it, then, that you are doing?" came the question.

"Something is added, not taken away. When there is a clear desire in mind, I only contribute to the cost."

"Great!" Mad Bear exclaimed.

Jison did want to be with us in Arizona, but he had already scheduled a visit to the Midwest. Jon and our group in Kansas had arranged a busy three-day itinerary for him in Kansas City and at the Psychophysiology Lab at The Menninger Research Department. While Jison and party were busy in the Midwest, Mad Bear, Mike, and I were guests in a private home in Tucson. Our host was a doctor who had met Mad Bear through my introduction. He had visited the Tuscarora Reservation weeks earlier and had offered to help Mad Bear with his Southwest travels to pursue his contacts with traditional tribes—and Mad Bear had agreed to conduct a traditional ceremony and blessing for their land in Flagstaff where they planned to build a medical research facility.

"I've been telling the doctor here about Jison," Mad Bear said to me, "and I even suggested that he might be willing to do a little demonstration when he gets here. Seems like I'm keeping him busy—volunteering him for one thing after another."

"Well, if he wants to keep coming back," I said, "I guess it's a good start for him. At least he's making a lot of contacts, and he's getting used to people."

When Jison and party arrived in Tucson, I took them to the Arizona Inn and stayed there with them for several days while Mad Bear and Mike met with their people on the Hopi, Navajo, and Zuni reservations. Mad Bear's "American Indian Unity Movement," as he called it, was delicate work and, had all the rest of us tagged along for these meetings, it may have created a distraction for many of the traditionals.

Jison quite willingly performed some demonstrations and even offered some treatments to the guests who gathered at the home of our host. Mad Bear suggested that Jison and his party might be invited to come along on the trip to Flagstaff for the ceremony on the land. So nearly two dozen of us drove up from Tucson: our hosts and some friends; Jison and his people; Mad Bear, Mike, and I; and a couple of young Navajos whom Mad Bear had brought from the reservation. One of our vehicles was a used car that had been contributed to Mad Bear to facilitate his travels and contacts. We spent the night in town and the next day drove out to the land. As we walked among the evergreen trees, Jison was impressed by the contrast between the forest of northern Arizona and the desert of the south.

"And tell Jison that not one of these trees will be destroyed when they put up their buildings," Mad Bear instructed Hiro. "They've told me they are not going to destroy a single living thing of any kind, and any tree that stands where the buildings are gonna go will be carefully uprooted and transplanted. This way, see, the land will give permission, and it all works out—everything cooperates. Nowadays that's pretty much lost. Modern people make a big mistake, even in your country, I think, manipulating everything, destroying whatever gets in the way. The invaders over here, they thought they had the right to mutilate whatever they wanted and they called this 'dominion.' Well, there's sure plenty of proof now that this 'dominion' business is a losing game. Can you translate all that? I want Jison to know, and I bet he agrees with it too."

"That permission from the land and all the living things is the traditional Indian way," I told Hiro when he had translated what Mad Bear had said. "The Indian people know how to do it, and the rest of us have to learn. When we had our conference in Parkville, the non-Indian people in our area got a lot of beestings the first couple days, and Mad Bear and some other Indians offered a ceremony to help—either to help us or to help the bees. During all the days after their ceremony, not one person ever got stung, even though hundreds of bees were all over us."

The young Navajo Indians built the ceremonial fire in the center of a clearing, and we all made a circle around it. Mad Bear in his hat and feathers and Jison in his robes and clogs stepped up to the flames, and Mad Bear made his offerings. "I'm going to speak in my own language," he told us, "and I'm going to make known what you've stated to me—that you will not harm anything here, not even a single living tree. So I'll say we come here in respect and ask permission and cooperation, and I'll say that what is going to be built here is something to help others." Mad Bear spoke for a long time in Tuscarora, sprinkling tobacco into the flames. It may have been partly because I could not understand the words that his language sounded enchanting to me, but it always seemed very beautifully suited to his invocations and proclamations.

When he finished, Mad Bear turned to ask Jison if he would be willing to offer a prayer or to say anything at all. Jison needed no explanation or translation. He stepped to the fire, looked directly into the flames, and spoke in Japanese. Mad Bear made a final offering and turned to our hosts. "Now you brought that little jar, right? Does somebody have that jar? All right, what we'll do, we have to wait until this has cooled down enough and we'll fill the jar with these ashes here. And you should have a little ceremony for that and do it in the right way, but you can do it yourself. Then you just put these ashes right into the foundation."

We left our ceremonial circle to walk around on the land until the fire was out and the coals cooled enough that we could scoop up some ashes. As we started out, Jison stopped and looked back. One young Navajo was sitting on the ground beside the fire. He said something to Hiro and he sounded concerned. "Sen Sei is asking why one man is stayed behind for sitting alone," Hiro translated. Then he explained to Jison that Mad Bear had asked him to be fire guard and to watch the fire and the hot coals. "We will come back here later to get the ashes," Hiro interpreted. Jison wanted to know whether Mad Bear would prefer to get the ashes now, upon the close of the ceremony, and let the young man come along with us. Mad Bear explained that they had simply to wait for the coals to cool because water would wet the ashes.

"All right, I can get the ashes for you," Jison said, as he walked back toward the fire. He stepped out of his clogs and, stooping over, pulled off his gloved white socks and lay them over his clogs. Barefoot, he stepped into the fire, holding his robes away from the flames. The fire was burning low and almost out, but the coals were glowing bright red. The coals crunched under his bare feet as he stomped on them. Sparks

flew. This was not ordinary "fire walking": Jison stayed long
in the fire, pulverizing the coals into small pieces, grinding
them to ashes by twisting his feet, and then standing on them
until they were smothered and cool enough for him to scoop
up into his hands. He held out his cupped hands and said
something in Japanese.

"May we put the ashes in the jar?" Hiro translated.

Jison and Mad Bear filled the jar with ashes and put the lid
on. With the palms of his hands, Mad Bear smoothed what remained of the ashes into a large circle on the ground and
wiped his hands with his handkerchief. Jison brushed the
ashes from his feet and put on his socks and his clogs, and we
walked away. One of our hosts, wondering what had become
of Jison's feet, continually questioned him through Hiro as we
walked. "Did his feet not even blister?" he wondered. "Can
he be sure? Did he examine them? Doesn't it hurt him now to
walk? Didn't he feel any pain at all?" Finally Hiro said, "Sen
Sei wants you not to look on him as crazy man. Maybe you
can know there is not anything strange in him." Hiro and I
discussed Jison's words and decided Jison had said he was not
a martyr.

"Jison says that he's not hurt and that he's neither crazy
nor a martyr," I explained.

Again we spent the night in Flagstaff, and in the morning
after breakfast, we drove south. "We might as well stay in
Phoenix," I had suggested to Hiro during breakfast. "When
you fly out of Tucson, you have to change planes in Phoenix
anyway, so there's no need to go back to Tucson. I'll stay with
you and see you off at the airport tomorrow. This will give us
our last chance to talk." So Jison and his party and I were
dropped off in Phoenix, and Mad Bear and Mike went on to
Tucson with our hosts and the others. Again, Mad Bear and
Jison agreed that they would meet "on down the road," as
Mad Bear had put it.

We let Jison have the afternoon to himself and in the
evening after supper we all gathered in his room. "It seems
like this was a really short trip this time," I told Hiro. "I won-

der if Jison feels that he has accomplished what he wanted."

"I think he feels okay," Hiro replied. "We had many meetings in San Francisco, New York, Kansas, and Arizona, and when we get back to San Francisco, it is two weeks completely. It looks like more short time to you because you were not with us sometimes. Anyway, you know, Sen Sei wants to do something together with more people. Now he is very much thinking about the society in this world. I told you it before. We are getting so strong for technology, but every year the society is becoming weak. So human ability is getting more and more weak and now people only believe machines and they don't develop their body. But Sen Sei is also asking what should we do now. He wants to meet doctors and people like Mad Bear's style and also do training like he was doing in his temple."

"Jison's abilities will be apparent to whomever he meets," I said. "He's done a lot of amazing things with others, but he's also demonstrated his capacity to control himself."

"But Jison is always telling that it is not so unusual, whatever he is doing. So he wants to do training. Whoever will be interesting enough, they can develop such ability, he said so. Maybe I think it takes a long time."

"But for what Jison wants to do with others, the challenge is going to be communication," I asserted. "Somehow, we have to deal with the language problem."

"It's so difficult to translate the speaking of Jison," Hiro agreed. "When Sen Sei talked in Mad Bear's ceremony at Flagstaff, almost we could not understand him, but you told us we don't need translation for that part, so I was glad. I think I could not be able to say it in English."

"And don't forget, none of us understood what Mad Bear was saying when he spoke in Tuscarora," I reminded him. "Mad Bear was the only one there who knew what he said. He explained it a little before he began, but there was no translation, and we didn't need it, because he wasn't talking to us. When Jison said his prayer, or whatever, he wasn't talking to us either."

"Maybe they were talking to the God, or what?"

"Or maybe they were talking to the animals or the trees or the land. I was thinking about that when we were walking back. I would say it's the communication behind the language. They say God or the Great Spirit can understand any language—or any thought, right? So when you pray—or when you meditate or do a ceremony or a healing—you don't need any language. What you need is the thought or the mental picture. Remember the rain at Council Grove last time you were here? And think of all Jison's demonstrations—how, for example, he affects the temperature in his own body or in others? When we or any of the patients or trainees learn to raise our skin temperature or lower our heart rate or our blood pressure, what we actually have to learn is to make mental pictures. And we use our own language for that. We actually make phrases. Our body parts don't need the language, but they respond to the mental pictures. It's what Jison does when he works with other people, or controls his own body, right? It's what the medicine people do when they prepare the land or plant seeds or make rain. Like he said himself, he has to concentrate on the result and contribute something of himself to that. It's all the same thing—the ceremony for the land in Flagstaff, or rainmaking, or Jison's demonstrations and healings, or whatever. It's just the larger body that extends outside the skin."

"What is he saying?" Jison asked, and Hiro undertook to translate.

"I don't know if I understood exactly," Hiro said, "but I think Sen Sei is also having the same idea. It is why really healers can make the same technique to the society or to any place."

"But still, for Jison's contacts with others," I maintained, "and for his explanations, we'll have to work on the interpretation, we'll have to find the right words. For example, you and everyone else who translated for him used the words 'blood' and 'bloodstream.' I guess those are the words he used in Japanese, right?"

"He says always blood. How do you say? 'Bloodstream?'

He said what we control is inside bloodstream. So we have to make a change in the blood."

"But when he says 'blood,' perhaps he means something besides the red blood you can put in a test tube. I think that the 'blood' he's referring to, or the changes in the 'blood,' could not be seen under a microscope, right?"

Hiro translated my proposition. "Now you are understanding exactly, Sen Sei says. This kind of bloodstream most of people cannot see it. It is exactly energy, like electricity, but he thinks it like bloodstream. Now he is saying that he explained already that kind of information. It is difficult for him because he cannot understand the translation and he cannot know it's communicating or not."

"You know what 'chi' is, don't you?" I asked. "Maybe Jison is referring to 'chi.' "

Jison heard the word as I said it, and commented directly. "It is relation to 'chi,' Sen Sei is saying. But it has to be understood the same as it is blood or bloodstream. To enter that, he has to know the system. The word he said, I don't know in English. Maybe I can say it is something like map, but more than, because if you know the map, you can move around in it. Anyway, Sen Sei is really understanding that we are needing the communication most. Always he is repeating that such people like Sen Sei have to make a team. Long time ago such kind of healers always did it alone or maybe just with their helpers. Now they cannot. They have to find each other among many cultures and do it like a team."

"Mad Bear and I have talked a lot about this," I said, "about teams of healers from many cultures working together." I told them about the Shinto priest that Mad Bear and I had met at the United Nations and how he had spoken for such gathering and teamwork on a planetary scale. "Tell Jison that this is Mad Bear's work."

"No," Hiro said, "he knows."

The next day, I waited with them at the airport until they boarded their plane for San Francisco and home.

• • •

◗

Back in Tucson, Mad Bear had been busy making plans. "I'm workin' on gettin' me a little place out here in Tucson," he told me. "I mighta mentioned to you a while back that it would sure be good for me to winter out here, anyways. With me havin' to chop wood and my back gettin' kinda weak . . . You know, I can picture you out here too."

I had no such picture—not until he put it there. After that I could not get that picture out of my mind.

"Anyways, we've been checking around down in South Tucson. There's some pretty cute little places over that way, and pretty cheap, too. You know me, I don't need much." He found one such "cute little place," which, he insisted, was just meant for him, and we went directly to the broker's office to start the necessary arrangements. Then he and Mike drove back to New York in their new used car.

By the time Mad Bear had boarded up and "protected" his Tuscarora home and returned to Tucson with his suitcases and boxes, I also had found a place in Tucson—and this, too, was rather suddenly arranged: We were driving through a residential area and we passed a small sign on a corner with the words OPEN HOUSE and an arrow pointing down the street, and we simply went to have a look. So, with the help and encouragement of our Tucson hosts, it took only a few weeks to move from the suggestion to the thought to the actual move. Tim and Pam had been talking for some time of their interest in the Southwest, and I phoned them after having looked at only this one place. "We're ready," they said, so we moved in. Before long, Jon and others of our group came down from Topeka, Kansas City, and Minneapolis and moved in with us, and we then had a community household and a new "national headquarters" for the Cross-Cultural Studies Program. Thus we began our next round.

Joel flew out from Florida to spend a few days with us in Tucson. On his first evening, we went to Mad Bear's place and talked until late. When Mad Bear suggested it might be time to "hit the hay," it was nearly midnight. "So, we can carry on to-

◖

morrow," he said. "Tomorrow's a whole new day. I'll give you guys a call in the morning."

He did—before sunrise. It was around five o'clock and there was only a hint of daylight in the air. "Mad Bear's on the phone already," Tim told me. "I don't know what he's got in mind, but we're going back to sleep."

"What's up?" Mad Bear inquired in a loud, cheerful voice.

"Up? Nobody. Nobody in Tucson except you, Mad Bear."

"No, no," he said. "That's what you think. Lemme tell you what's poppin'. You want to know what's poppin'? This is a good one—listen to this. Something woke me up, and I turned on the news—the local news on the radio—and they were talking about the rodeo."

"The rodeo on the radio?" I repeated sleepily. And to myself I thought, Now what does this have to do with me?

"Listen, it's a big thing, a major event around here! Now, you know me, I'm not too much for these rodeos—well, not at all, really. But guess what? The whole thing's gonna be kicked off with a big parade. I mean, this is gonna be a big one with music and dancers—everything. What do you call those Mexican bands? Something like maraschinos?"

"Mariachis."

"I mean, this is gonna be the whole works. If we go now, we can get a good spot, right up by the road. I know just where they're gonna go. Why don't I come pick you guys up? We could throw some foldin' chairs in the trunk. Now who all up there wants to go to the parade?"

"Well, I'm not really sure," I said, trying to sound somewhat engaged. I was not even sure about myself. Maybe if it were in the afternoon or evening—or next week.

"Look, why don't you grab a cuppa coffee and check it out. Call me back and lemme know what's the consensus up there. Or should I just come on up?"

"No, let me call you back."

"Well, don't be too long. You know what they say. 'The early bird . . .' "

"Yeah, I know," I said.

No one really wanted to go, or even to wake up enough to sincerely discuss it. "Who wants to get up and go to the parade?" I felt embarrassed even to pose such a proposition at five o'clock in the morning. "Well, somehow this has really struck him," I said. "I don't want to call him back and tell him that no one is interested. I guess I'll go along with him myself."

"I'll go with you," Joel offered.

So Mad Bear pulled into the driveway somewhere around six o'clock and we put two folding chairs in the trunk of his car because he had brought one of his own.

"But maybe we oughta throw a few more in there," he suggested. "I betcha we could prob'ly rent some out."

We decided not to rent chairs that day, but Mad Bear seemed in the mood to rent something. We appeared to be among the first to arrive anywhere along the parade route, and we saw that local charitable groups had roped off sections of side streets for parking and were charging five dollars per car. "That's what we'll do!" Mad Bear said. "Let's get us a piece of street before they're all gone!"

"I think we can find a spot a little ways away and won't have to pay," Joel proposed.

"No, no," Mad Bear replied. "Lemme show you what I got in mind. Let's go straight through here and hang a right." We turned onto a nearly deserted street where no cars were parked and no signs had been put up. "Pull into that alley," Mad Bear said, suddenly twisting himself in his seat and looking down the street. A woman with a carload of kids was just turning the corner. Mad Bear stuck an old cigar in his mouth and jumped out and waved to her. "You parking?" he asked with a friendly grin. "We're only charging two bucks out here. That's for all day, too!"

"Great," she said. "Where do you want me?"

"Just anywheres right along here."

With all the kids and all the things to carry, she struggled to get into her purse. "Here, hold this," she called to one of the older ones.

"That's all right," Mad Bear said. "Tell you what I'm

gonna do. Since you got all these kids, and you're the first one here anyways, I'm gonna let it go, and let's just say you're covered."

"Well, I don't really mind," she responded. "What fund does this go to?"

"It was supposed to go to my cigar fund," he answered. "But since I don't have any matches, this one seems to be lasting pretty good."

The woman gave him a puzzled look, and then she giggled happily. "I may have some matches here somewhere," she offered.

Mad Bear laughed out loud. "No, no, we're just kidding," he admitted. "We came to see the parade."

We took our chairs under our arms and started down toward the main road. "I was sure tryin' to keep a straight face," he said, "but I just got so tickled . . . Wait a minute, here comes another car . . ." Again he thrust his cigar into his mouth. "Just pull right in here!" he bellowed, trying to sound official. "Only two bucks here all day!"

They stopped in the middle of the road and glared at him. There were three macho-looking middle-aged men inside. First they frowned and then they smiled. "Yeah, sure," one of them said. "But that's before tax right? Well, we're not even parking, we're just driving through here."

"Oh, well, then. Never mind the whole thing!"

"Mad Bear, you're going to get yourself in trouble one of these days."

"Trouble? No, actually, it's the other way around. Untrouble, guess you could say. A day like today—it's a good day for untroubling."

We placed our chairs right at the road alongside the edge of a park. "Well, we'll have to sit here and wait a while. But with these front-row seats, I'd say it's worth it. And we're down low, not blockin' anybody else. And then some'll be up on that embankment behind here." He turned in his chair to look behind him and noticed that people were beginning to gather in the park, and he got up to go talk to them. "Don't let anybody grab my chair," he called back to us. "And if they do, well, see how much you can get for it!"

Joel looked at me. "What in the world is he up to today? Wonder what's got into him! Have you ever seen him like this?"

"Every once in a while, actually," I told him. "I think it has something to do with his work."

"You mean, this is part of his work—acting like this?"

"Well, I think it has more to do with his other work—or his work elsewhere, if you know what I mean. I've found that his behavior has a lot to do with whatever he's been doing somewhere else. I remember one time out in Utah when this fairly young Indian guy started talking to me. He may have been a college student, but he somehow knew Mad Bear. Mad Bear had been out with the Ute people about a year earlier, I know, working as a mediator on some intertribal issue of some sort. Anyway, this guy said to me, 'Do you understand where Mad Bear is doing his medicine?' I answered, 'Yes, I guess all over.' And he said, 'In the spirit world. You may not know,' he said, 'that only a few, maybe some medicine people, have seen him like a bear. Don't know if you've ever witnessed that yourself, but I'll tell you one thing for sure. For one of the most friendly people you'd ever hope to meet, he can be one of the most ferocious whenever he needs to be.' I still remember that guy standing in the bookstore on the campus and telling me that. That was fairly early in my acquaintance with Mad Bear. But a lot of times since then, I've seen him at work—at least from the perspective from this side—and you know what I think? I think that Mad Bear often serves himself as his own comic relief."

"But," said Joel, "you have to wonder what some of these people think. We know him, they don't. He comes on to strangers like everyone knows everyone."

"I think he really dislikes the notion of strangers," I said. "In the traditional tribes and villages, there were no strangers. The idea is actually unthinkable. Still, he's about the most forward and outgoing Indian I've ever seen. Maybe that's how he works his medicine on this level. Like we were saying before up at his place, he's always trying to break down barriers—to connect people someway, or help them feel connected. So I guess this is part of his work too—here on this level."

"Well, they do seem to get some kind of a lift out of him."

"I remember one time," I related, "when he pulled up to an intersection right alongside this old guy on a bicycle waiting for the light to change. The man was really old and feeble, and he looked pretty depressed—I mean, really down in the face. He was skinny too, really weak. He had a scruffy beard and a little backpack hanging over his dirty, torn tee-shirt. A pretty sad-looking sight, I thought. Mad Bear noticed it too. He said, 'Roll down the window real quick,' and he leaned way over from behind the wheel—almost got his head out the passenger-side window. He hollered, 'Hey!' and the old man gave a jump and spun his head around. He kind of stooped and squinted, trying to see inside the car. Well, he got one look at Mad Bear's broad face with that huge barn-door grin, and he started to smile. And Mad Bear shouted, 'My God! Are you running away from home again?' Somehow, that got to him, and the guy really cracked up. The light changed and he peddled on his way, and his whole posture was changed. Then at the next stoplight, he pulled up beside the window and waved. He was literally twinkling! I've seen that sort of thing again and again with Mad Bear. Whatever he does, I think it's very much on purpose."

"Except maybe for some of the things he eats," Joel remarked.

"Maybe that too," I replied.

Mad Bear came back and sat in his chair, and soon we could hear the sounds of the parade in the distance. Mad Bear leaned over to look down the street. "Oh, the anticipation," he joked. "We can hardly contain ourselves. I better watch I don't lean right outa this chair, though. If I hit the deck, it's hard gettin' up again. One reason I didn't want to sit on the ground. Everybody'd go home, and I'd still be sittin' here."

◑

Bands and drummers and marchers went by, and there were floats and people on horseback all dressed up in fancy hats and spurs, sitting stiff and straight and waving to the crowds.

"What'd I tell ya?" Mad Bear beamed. "Ring-side seats! Why, you can see the whites of their eyes. Do you know any of these VIP cowboys?"

"No," I said.

"Me neither, and we oughta be ashamed. These may be the so-called town fathers, spurs and all. And I told you they'd be having lots of Mexican maraschinos, didn't I? Tucson's famous for it!"

A group of teenage girls passed by in skirts and moccasins with painted faces and headbands with bright blue feathers sticking up. Mad Bear covered his grin with both hands. "Hope they don't spot me laughing," he said.

"That must seem a pretty ludicrous sight to you," Joel commented.

"Not only that," Mad Bear responded, "but it looks kinda funny too! I just hope they don't start flapping their hands over their lips and goin' 'woo, woo, woo,' or I may have to step out there. Too bad they couldn't get any of the real people, with all these Indians around here. But then others, when they do, look on them as tokens or uncle tomahawks or something. It's a shame too—we've got some out-of-sight dancers and performers. This is just our sort of thing. Our people are a social, festive people—s'posed to be, anyways." As the costumed group passed right in front of us, he called out rather loudly, "Some of Woolworth's finest regalia!" He looked at us for our reaction. "Sorry, I couldn't help that."

When the last of the parade had passed, he suggested we spend a few more moments sitting in our chairs. "I don't want to go packin' our foldin' chairs through all these crowds of people. Besides, they're all going to the rodeo except for us. We'll have to cook up somethin' else, though. It's sure too early to go home on a big day like this."

"Oh, I don't know," Joel said.

◑

"Speaking of somethin' cookin', it just hit me. We'll head on out to the mission. Wait'll you sink your teeth into some of that delicious Navajo fry bread!"

We pulled up onto the grounds of the San Xavier Mission and walked through the gate into the adjacent courtyard where the local people had their shops and concessions. "This'll be just the ticket," Mad Bear exclaimed. "A good heap of delicious fry bread and we'll look in on some of our friends. I've got some little Navajo buddies sellin' stuff in here. Well, Navajo to you folks—we say 'Dine.' This place is always buzzin' with tourists. They come to see the famous mission and then they come in here for their tax-free cigarettes."

"Mad Bear talks to these people like old friends," Joel repeated, as we stood at the booth eating our fry bread. "This bread's not bad, by the way, but I hope I can get away with only one piece of it."

"I like it," I told him, "so I can eat some of yours. And these people, I suppose, really are old friends."

But the place was rather dead, and Mad Bear seemed concerned. There were people in and out of the cigarette shop, and some did pause to look over the several tables around the courtyard with their beautiful displays of turquoise chokers and other Native jewelry—but from a distance.

"C'mon, let's say hello to my friends over here," Mad Bear suggested, gulping down one last big piece of fry bread and rubbing his hands together. "This young friend here is Joe. And this man right here is Joel. Pretty near the same name, right? Just that 'L'—so yous two might be related—just sorta distant like. And this is Doug here, we've been traveling together."

"I think I may have seen you before," I offered.

"No, you didn't," Mad Bear responded. "So how's it going? Anything moving today?"

"Nope," the young man said simply.

"You mean nothin'? You sold nothin' yet?"

The young Navajo sat behind a long table with a black velvet cloth covered with beautiful bracelets, chokers, and neck-laces. It looked spectacular. "Nope," he repeated. "Nothin'."

"And who's that young couple over there?" he asked point-ing. The young man and woman were sitting across the court-yard behind a table with a similar display of jewelry, and no one was going near it. They were sitting on the edge of a brick wall that formed a small enclosure that perhaps once served as a barbecue pit or was the remains of some sort of chimney, and inside the enclosure was a baby goat. "I haven't seen them before. Are they from the reservation?"

"Nope," Joe replied. "They been comin' up every day from Mexico with their stuff. But they ain't sold nothin'—nothin' ever since they been here."

Mad Bear glanced around the grounds. There were a few people around, but only a few—mostly out-of-state tourists, by appearances. "You know, Joe," he said. "I had a dream about you the other night. I've been meanin' to tell you. You know my dreams can be significant, prophetic, even, most of the time. I dreamed you got married."

"Oh, yeah?"

"Yeah. But the thing was—this woman. I mean she was a real shocker. Older than you, and about three times your weight—maybe four. And in my dream, she came walking right up to you in a public place and proposed, right on the spot. She had on this bright green jacket and a hat. I mean, that hat! It had huge feathers, ostrich, maybe, dyed bright orange and stretchin' way out a couple feet in the air. An' you accepted right off the bat, that's what got me. You were trying to explain, maybe for your own sake. You said, 'Well, I can't help myself. She reminds me of someone I used to love in high school.'"

Joe was staring across the courtyard and Mad Bear looked at him. "What?" he said. "What's the matter with you? What're you starin' at? You look like you've seen a ghost." Then he followed Joe's gaze to the main gate and he gaped at the entrance with feigned surprise. "Oh, my God! That's her! That's the very one. It's my dream comin' true, right here on the spot!"

"Oh, c'mon, Bear . . ."

"No, really. It's her and you're gonna flip out when she proposes. Look, look, she's comin' over this way. I think she spotted you, Joe. What's gonna happen next, that's the big question. Speakin' of the big question, I know she's gonna pop it." The woman noticed us looking at her, and she and the man she was with walked right toward us, with their eyes on Joe's table. "Now, don't you dare crack a smile," he warned Joe, "or I'm sure to bust out laughin'!"

We must have all looked considerably cheerful to the couple, for they both greeted us with big smiles. Actually, we were trying to keep from laughing. "Do you have anything you'd like to say to this young man?" Mad Bear asked her.

"Well, maybe," she answered, "I'm not sure yet."

"My God!" he said to Joe. "She's standing here trying to make up her mind! And here you are, tryin' to make up yours." In spite of his efforts, Joe could not keep from laughing. "He kinda got a good feelin' when he saw you coming," Mad Bear explained to the woman. "It seems you remind him of someone he once thought a great deal of. We're just hopin' he doesn't start to get a crush on you or something." She laughed. Both Mad Bear and the woman were holding cans of soda, and both were equally stout. I could see that to her, Mad Bear seemed jolly, warm, and friendly. "She seems to kinda like you too," he said to Joe. "But she doesn't want to embarrass you."

"Oh, no," the woman asserted. "I won't embarrass him."

"Joe? Joe? Are you okay? Are you . . ."

"Mad Bear, don't bother him now," Joel interrupted. "He's busy right now." Her husband, or whoever he was, was holding a necklace and handing Joe some money. Joe was making a sale.

"What did you pick?" the woman asked. She stepped up to make her own selection and another woman stepped up beside her.

"Maybe they'll pick the same thing," Mad Bear observed,

loudly enough to be heard. "But maybe they won't. Different people like different things." Within moments, there was a small crowd around the table, and those who were ready to pay began to form a line. "We better step aside," Mad Bear said to us. "Let's go meet that Mexican couple."

As we started in their direction, Mad Bear noticed another tourist couple with a boy of perhaps twelve years who was watching a bee flying around him and looking somewhat apprehensive. "Look out!" Mad Bear shouted. "It's a bee! It's a bee!" The boy was startled and he jumped back. Just then, the bee landed on the boy's leg. "Oh my God!" Mad Bear went on. "It's on your jeans! It's on your jeans! Right there on your jeans—now what're you going to do?" The boy looked at his parents. "It's all right," Mad Bear said. "I'm going to take care of it for you." He was drawing a crowd with his loud voice. People who had just come through the entrance were gathering around to see what was happening, and everyone stood watching the bee crawl up the boy's pantleg. "Looks like this is where I come in," Mad Bear said. "Lemme handle this." At that moment, the bee flew right toward Mad Bear. Mad Bear made a quick snatch in the air and held his clenched fist to his ear. "Got him!" he exclaimed, putting his hand to his mouth and opening his fist between his lips. He stuck out his chin and his belly as well, and he began to chew contemplatively. He made a big exaggerated gulp and announced, "Well, that takes care of that!" People stared with their mouths open. "Oh, it's okay," he said, reassuringly. "We eat 'em raw. They're too small to cook."

Joel and I had no idea whether the bee had flown away unseen or whether it had literally disappeared. It might have been in Mad Bear's pocket, but we were almost certain it was not in his stomach—and we supposed it didn't matter what the others thought. The courtyard was crowded with tourists, and it felt like a fair or a festival.

"I just came to say greetings and hello," Mad Bear announced to the couple from Mexico. Now there were people listening to his every word. "But most of all, I came to give my respects to your fine-looking goat. My friends over there were telling me how they've been admiring your goat. It's about the most handsome thing they've seen in a long time."

"Much thanks you," said the young man, looking in Joe's direction.

"Yeah," Mad Bear declared, "they admire it so much, they gave it a name—a Navajo name."

"Oh, that's right?"

"That's right, a Navajo name! It means 'supper'!" Several looked at him in surprise and, seeing his wide grin, began to laugh. He looked back at them and laughed with them and proclaimed loudly, still laughing, "These people have some beautiful items here, while they last. They've brought them in all the way from south of the border—and at the same astounding prices. But it's first come first serve on the choicest items." For the first time, if what Joe had said was true, the couple got busy. "I believe they'll sell out pretty quick," Mad Bear told us." I hope we didn't overdo it."

"We?" Joel said to me.

"So what we'll do, see that other Navajo over there? That's Joe's cousin—or so he told me the other day. I don't know him too well, but I'll introduce you anyways." Mad Bear made the introductions, but several people were following him around, and they now began to look over the items on the cousin's table. Mad Bear stepped back, cupped his hand to the side of his mouth and confided to us in the loudest possible whisper, "There's one piece here I got my eye on and, by golly, I hope no one notices it. It's so precious that if anyone looks too closely, they'll snap it right up! I'd like to point it out to you, but that'd sure as heck give it away."

Some looked at Mad Bear to see where his eyes were focused, but others simply examined the items to find their own choices. "I believe they may all sell out today," Mad Bear declared. "Anyways, these guys are too preoccupied, so we might as well be on our way—unless you got some appetite for a little more of that fry bread." We did not need more fry bread and, in any case, there was now a long line at that

◐

booth. We walked to the side gate, and Mad Bear turned around and looked over the crowd. "Good-bye!" he bellowed in a roaring voice, raising his arm high in the air, and many waved back. It was as though this was his village. "Take good care of Supper, there! And all you people, thanks for coming, and have a great day!"

"You too!" came many cheery voices, and we went out the gate and back to the car.

"That's a medicine man at work!" Joel remarked to me as Mad Bear stopped to talk with one of the local Indians. "That's medicine in the classical sense, if I've ever seen it. A sort of questionable application, maybe, but there's no doubt what he was doing there. And people were happy with it. He wasn't twisting any arms at all, just breaking the ice, I guess you could say."

"Breaking the ice, that's what it is," I agreed. "Whatever level he's working on that's a major part of it."

"He energizes people, is what he does," Joel deliberated. "In this physical realm, anyway, it's kind of like putting energy into the atmosphere. We had like, what? Four, five hours sleep? And here he is, moving all this energy around."

"That's it," I concurred. "That's the medicine person in a nutshell. That's the medicine person, the shaman, the rainmaker, the martial arts adept, the healer—whatever. They may look different on the outside, and they may have a different focus or objective—but they're all adept at the same powerful technique, whoever they are, and they all claim it's part of the natural human potential. They focus and they move energy!"

A visit to Mad Bear's had for so long required a cross-country flight, a change of planes, a shuttle bus out of Buffalo, and a rendezvous in Niagara Falls; but now he was a short drive away. As I look back, it occurs to me that the whole Arizona arrangement may have been an intentional strategy on his part. In any case, as it turned out, he made use of his proximity and he made his presence felt. There were times when I would think of his old place on the reservation and the elaborate setup that allowed him his evasion when it was convenient, and I would consider how we might arrange for ourselves such an option. With his talent for finding something "popping" or, if necessary, ordering it, and with his many contacts and connections and his constant suggestions and encouragement, Mad Bear induced us into his ongoing journey of many destinations and no end.

Epilogue

◑ Mad Bear's physical body yielded to his challengers long before he actually left the Earth. It was a slow and painful process and, for those who knew and worked with him, it was sad to see.

"He's going to leave us," lamented the woman from the Indian Center in Niagara Falls, "and when that happens, that's it. We will never have another like him ever again."

"I wish he'd take better care of himself," people would say as his health worsened. "He thinks about everyone except himself."

"He knows what he's doing," others would say. "He's mainly active on another level, out of sight of most of us. The opposing forces may be able to get to his body, but they can't get the best of his medicine."

The "opposing forces" notwithstanding, it seemed to me, as I watched him weaken, his own inattentiveness to his physical health was destroying the only aspect of Mad Bear that I could consciously see and relate to. "What are you trying to do?" I confronted him one day, speaking to him, in my dis-

◑

may, as I had never spoken to him before. "Are you trying to die or what?" In April 1979, I and a friend had left a conference in Toronto, and had driven to Mad Bear's home on the reservation because Mad Bear was to have joined us and we had not heard from him or been able to reach him. We found him at home sitting in the dark, barely able to stand or to speak. His back was badly bruised.

"I've been banging myself against this post here," he explained, "until my back's all black and blue. It brings me back. Sometimes my body starts to quit on me, or I start to give it up. It takes some pretty darn good whacks sometimes to crank it up again and keep myself in here."

"Why don't you tell us straightforward what's going on with you?" I said. "I can't understand if you want to die or not. It's up to you, but if you don't want to die, you've got to let us help you."

"I'd be happy to go, to tell you the truth. Sometimes I'm mighty tempted to just give up the ghost and turn away from the whole thing. Somehow I've got to hang around till I get some of these things taken care of."

Mad Bear did "hang around" for more than six years. In the winter of 1984 we flew him back out to Tucson and arranged for him to stay on the Papago Reservation near the San Xavier Mission where he could be cared for by his old Indian friends. He needed care: He was often confused and disoriented as well as weak and in pain. During those last months in Tucson—his last months on Earth—I was away on travel most of the time, and I saw little of him. Tim and Jon and several of our staff tried to spend time with him and to help with his affairs as much as they could. Various healers and medicine people came to see him or to look in on him in their own way. "Don't worry about what is going on with his person," they would tell us. "Most of Mad Bear is out of sight of you now. He keeps only enough presence to sustain the body."

I did not know Mad Bear's age, but I knew he was not old—somewhere in his early sixties, I supposed—and I kept hoping he would recover. I thought about him sitting at his table back home on the reservation, happily making notes on his travel plans and projects or on his book, *Earth Mother Crying*, and wondered what would become of his important work. But when I consulted with the medicine people and with his closest colleagues, I was assured that he would not return in this particular body. Though his body had succumbed sooner than he would have wished, he was carrying on, nevertheless, and not retreating from the contest. It was all part of being his sort of warrior. The plans and projects he had pursued in his lifetime would be carried on by others just as he had served a vision that had been initiated long before his time.

He was involved in a great contest, I was told by those who claimed they knew, serving as a mediator in a struggle over the Earth. So long as his heart was beating, his body served as an anchor to hold his presence and his focus to the Earthly realm. "He's working with others who need him. He volunteered for it, and he knows what he's doing. But it won't be long and we'll bury him and he'll go on."

Mad Bear left his body in November 1985.

I like to imagine that he was with—or working with—the ones we had come to call "Those Who Care" and I often recall his response when I related to him the "message" he had urged me to listen for: *"Those Who Care care deeply and strongly, and blame is beside the point with us . . . and for those who fear . . . jump up . . . unto the level of the Heart."*

"Maybe that's the important part," he had said, " . . . that part about no blame and about the heart level. . . . That's the Fourth World."

Mad Bear had committed to memory and had often recited—in public presentations, or even as we sat in the quiet of his own home—the well-known speech of Chief Seattle. I hear Mad Bear's voice when I recall it, and the closing lines remain strong in my memory: *"At night when the streets of your cities and villages will be silent, and you think them deserted, they will throng with the returning hosts that once filled and still love this beautiful land. The white man will never be alone. Let him be just and deal kindly with my people, for the dead are not powerless. 'Dead' did I say? There is no death, only a change of worlds."*

Index

◑